THE FAILED ENTREPRENEUR

DUNCAN RIDLER

Copyright © 2012 Duncan Ridler

All rights reserved.

ISBN: 1477457925

ISBN 13: 9781477457924

DEDICATION

A big thank you to David Wardale and Rupert Waddington whose wisdom and determination helped see this book through to completion. And special thanks must go to Bill and my big pal Drew Munro – without the two of you my life would definitely have been beige!

PREFACE

Entrepreneur: the owner or manager of a business enterprise who, by risk and initiative, attempts to make profit (from the French entreprendre, meaning 'to undertake'

COLLINS ENGLISH DICTIONARY

My name is Duncan. I'm an entrepreneur. But I'm also a failure and I always thought that made me a failed entrepreneur - until now.

In everyday life, failures are quite hard to spot. We don't walk with the aid of a crutch nor can you see any visible wounds. What we do carry is the stigma, the embarrassment, the blame. But if you look a little closer, you may see us sitting quietly in the corner of a pub or café. We don't attract attention because that would mean having to explain our loss of confidence and belief, sometimes even our self-respect.

We used to be the same as you, trusted, respected and confident; but we woke up one day to the guilt of failure; to the people we'd let down whose lives had changed because of our action. You see, we made a choice; we crossed a line without guaranteeing what the effect would be. And if the outcome is bad, no one wants to know. Forget about friendships built up over years; forget about all the favours we once did, and the colleagues we did business with. Failure means the door is firmly shut.

When you fall, you do at least reach the bottom eventually, but on the way down you sustain many invisible injuries; you watch as everything that could have been slips through your fingers - the business, maybe the family, the house, even watching your children grow up. And the thud when you land is a lot worse than any physical pain you have ever felt. So, when you've fallen as far as you can go, and everyone's pointing out what a failure you are, do you just give up? Not in my case.

You see, people identify very easily with failure as long as it isn't their own. But they can remain blind to why you were doing what you were doing before it all went wrong. And at last, writing this book, I've discovered that even if you're a failure, you can still be an entrepreneur - just not at the same time.

> *"Courage is going from failure to*
> *failure without losing enthusiasm."*
>
> WINSTON CHURCHILL

CHAPTER ONE

I was born on 5th April 1971, which makes me an Aries - 'Hot-headed and quick decision-maker, can be generous and is loyal to friends.'

The youngest of two, I arrived six years after my sister. My earliest years were played out in a desirable, new, suburban (detached) house built for the upwardly-mobile branch of the West Midlands' working classes. It was a house with aspirations; but in truth, qualifying for it meant my father owned a newsagent's and drove a Ford Cortina with a plastic roof, while Mum stayed at home to look after us. Of the two, she was always the more ambitious for us, insisting we had the best start in life. This meant my sister and I were educated at local private schools, though heaven knows how they afforded it.

Once I'd settled at primary school, I made associations quite quickly. I couldn't call them friendships as I soon realised school was made up of two very different groups of people, and I fitted in with neither. On the one hand there were the Gifted - children whose parents split the atom for a living. The Gifted kept themselves separate and you could see the school courted them for the academic kudos they brought with them. Then there were the Moneyed - kids of self-made parents who'd got rich through business or dubious means, or both, and the school loved them as well. I can remember an awards evening where "winners" were presented with a shield or cup for being top in a subject. Serious competition to stimulate the Gifted, and a serious trophy to reward the winner. A great idea, but with one flaw: the awards were sponsored by the Moneyed's parents... 'And the winner of the Roberts Trophy for Maths this year is.... Rachel Roberts.'

I never won anything. Subjects just bored me, unless disguised as something exciting like a school outing or going to the park. And then there was the issue of my reading and writing. Mum was called in one day to be told I had a problem. 'Don't worry, Mrs Ridler,' they said, 'We can help you,' and they sold her a very expensive and completely useless quill-like pen. We had beans on toast for the rest of the week.

Home life was much more fun. I honestly don't remember my dad being there at all. He was working six and a half days a week to keep us at private school; but with Mum at home, it wasn't a problem. Mum had everything under control.

Then one day I was playing outside when a car pulled up in front of the house. It was my uncle. He got out and started loading up boxes from the garage. While he did this, Dad came over and told me he was going away for a while. He said I was to be good and to help Mum. A few weeks later, I learned that the house had been sold and we were relocating to my grandparents a few miles down the road. Only then did it dawn on me that my parents had split up.

The new house was a pre-war semi on a busy main road. We soon settled into a routine and I loved it. My grandparents were fantastic and completely mad. Grandad worked most of his life at the Austin car factory in Longbridge, but also had stints as a cobbler and a fire engine driver. He didn't exactly cover himself in glory and was forced to take early retirement from this after running out of petrol on the way to a factory blaze. As it turned out, this wasn't an isolated incident; other highlights included losing the hoses and reversing over a workmate.

They had clear roles, my grandparents. He was constantly drinking tea while she fried bacon and smoked. They were both very bad insomniacs. I think that in all the time I was there, I never once saw them in bed. Even if I woke in the middle of the night and came downstairs they would still be up, kettle on and rashers in the pan, and all in the usual haze of blue smoke.

In a way they were my heroes, always coming up with grand projects. I would sit listening, intrigued, as they discussed the next big idea and was thrilled when they included me in the plans. The house was in a permanent state of refurbishment, always a wall being knocked down or a room being decorated. Grandad would sit at the table drawing plans on paper, but always without a ruler, and allocating tasks like mixing the wallpaper paste or filling the wheelbarrow with rubble. Grandma, myself and usually a couple of their friends formed the workforce and although they had all the time in the world, for some reason they always had to work through the night. To me it was an intoxicating adventure; spending the early hours of the morning blinded by cigarette smoke and covered in dust and debris, drinking tea and eating bacon sandwiches, listening to conversations and laughter. I was part of the team.

ﭢ

With Dad gone, money was tight and Mum had to get work, becoming a barmaid at the local golf club. My sister just seemed to disappear. I had no recollection of her being there much, except at night when she came into the bedroom we shared. The room was filled with Grandad's used Oxo tins, all labelled up with spare parts for everything he didn't have. There were hundreds of them and she was always tripping over them.

With Mum working day and night, it was Grandad's job to get me to school. He had a Datsun; original colour red, new colour beige due to rust and a terrible filler and paint job. And if I'd had any social standing at school, I lost it the moment Grandad parked up outside the gates to pick me up. If he was early, he'd amuse himself by putting his false teeth between his index finger and thumb and doing Jaws impressions for my schoolmates.

Moving up through my primary school, I became even less interested in what they had to offer academically. I also noticed how hard it was to fit in with my peers. Hours were spent discussing who had what and where everyone had been. I must admit some of the places did sound nice, but then I only had holidays in Weston-super-Mare to compare them with. I remember an autumn day when we had to take turns telling the class where we'd been for our summer holidays. The Gifted had been digging up fossils or visiting cathedrals; the Moneyed had been to Hawaii, Disneyland, Australia - everywhere but Weston-super-Mud.

And then it was my turn to stand up. So I told them.

Grandad had a caravan in a bay just behind Weston-super-Mare. It was a pretty empty kind of bay, with a few other caravans dotted here and there. It was to be a family holiday, with me and Grandad going ahead and Mum and Grandma following a few days later. And Grandad had a plan - he was going to double the size of the caravan. I was so excited, I couldn't sleep. We loaded up the Datsun and off we went.

We were greeted on arrival by one of his fellow caravanners, Andy, an ex-workmate, who helped us unload. Andy was going to be chief engineer on our project. Most of the other site residents then came up and greeted us. It was a friendly place, but clearly the preferred destination for retired Austin car workers. Most of the men spent their time lying underneath their cars preparing them for the journey back, while the women made tea and chain smoked.

I'd gone off to explore but ran back when I heard a really loud grinding noise. They were cutting and peeling back the side of the caravan like a sardine tin. I was immediately despatched to get some water as the friction heat was setting fire to it. Disaster averted, I was wondering what Grandad planned to stick on to the new hole when an old, wheezing tractor pulled up. It was towing what looked like a wooden summerhouse, and within an hour we'd bolted it to the side of the caravan.

Over the next couple of days, Grandad and I installed a kitchen with cupboards, a sink and a table. It was a real team effort and we were both really pleased with the result. Grandma turned up and was overwhelmed, praising me to the skies. But what startled me was my Mum. Her hands covered her face and she was in tears when she realised our amazing extension, and her home for the next week, was in fact an old potting shed.

The class and the teacher looked at me in complete silence.

We'd been staying with my grandparents for nearly two years when one day everything changed, heralded by the arrival of a large red Mercedes. I was waiting to be collected from school, looking out for the beige magnificence of Grandad's car. Instead, an executive saloon drew up and out stepped Mum. As she opened the back door for me, I was greeted through the driver's window by the smartest man I'd ever seen; his dazzling white shirt was offset by a large gold watch so shiny that it blinded you. With all this and his tanned complexion as well, I thought he was a film star. He seemed friendly, smiling and introducing himself as 'a friend of your Mum's.' Pah! Parents must think children are daft. By the age of four, we have a pretty good idea of what's going on.

Anyway, instead of going home we went straight to this big, empty house; detached, set back from a busy main road, in a small residential close. It was clean and smelled fresh, and had these beautiful, leaded bay windows and a massive garden. I was told we'd be moving in in a few weeks and Mum's 'friend' was getting excited, talking about how it would all be done out. But he also showed an interest in me and what made me tick. I liked him for that.

So, the day came to pack up and leave my grandparents. We didn't have any furniture to speak of, just three double mattresses which we deposited in the bedrooms. Another thing that changed was my sister. She seemed to be around much more, and most nights the house was full of her friends holding gymnastic competitions. I enjoyed it because they let me sit up on the stepladder and be the ref. My mum was always in the large kitchen, either cooking or cleaning. Occasionally her 'friend' would stop by and bring us new pieces of furniture, and bits and bobs for Mum. Or one day, the ultimate - a big, colour TV and Betamax video recorder.

I missed the chaotic routines of the grandparents, but life was certainly good.

Once again, change was afoot; this time the last big one before I finally had to grow up. I was now eleven and, out of the blue, secondary school crept up on me unannounced. I didn't even know what the place was called or where it was until Mum dropped me at the gate on my first day and I went inside.

I was greeted by a nun who welcomed me in, placing a cold hand on my cheek. She must have been a labourer in a previous life as she had the hands of a hod carrier. Her name was Sister Mary and she explained that 'these hands will bless you and encourage you. But if you do wrong, they will be used to beat you.' Charming.

I was led into the school hall, a huge room full of kids lined up in rows, but was told to sit in a separate area. Not one to follow instructions without knowing why, I wandered over to sit with the main group but was instantly hauled back by Sister Brutal to my allocated spot. Another boy was pushed towards me, a strange-looking kid who stared at a ruler that he was rotating round and round right in front of his face. No one had told me where my class was, so me and Rain Man wandered off. We saw a door, went in and sat down.

Crack!!! A big stick hit the blackboard.

'My name's Mr Bosworth!' he bellowed. 'Two rules: don't ever be caught sinning in the eyes of the Lord, and never raise your hand to ask for anything. You wait until it's your turn.'

But how are we supposed to know? I thought. I've got to raise my hand because I need to clear up so many issues, starting with, is this a school or a correction centre? And my new best mate - does he require additional support?

Up went my hand. Down came the stick, smashing onto my desk. Even Rain Man stopped twiddling his ruler for a split second before resuming, round and round.

'See me after registration!' he boomed. So we did.

'Name?'

I told him, then reeled off my questions.

He quietly explained that although I was non-Catholic, I'd been accepted to the school to show a balance. Yep - I was the one and only piece of balance. And seeing as we'd sat down in his class, this would now be our class. One last question - my new friend clearly had a problem. The teacher explained he was autistic and, as he'd come into class with me, I was being assigned to look after him. His name was Charles.

Well, that seemed to clear up most things. But later I got talking to a classmate who gave me the real low-down. Official version, he said, I'd landed at a Roman Catholic school that took teaching very seriously and was very strict. However, in practice, apparently, the teachers were fine really - they didn't mind what you did as long as you didn't get caught.

Making friends was easy. Most of them lived nearby and I got to know people walking to school. It was a welcome relief to find there was little interest or competition in material matters. And

I continued to look after Charles, which was easy. Outside the classroom he was in a world of his own, just sitting and reading whatever the teachers gave him. No one else seemed interested and although I could hardly call him a friend, I felt strangely proud of him and of my role as his unofficial guardian. For me, though, I didn't see school as a way of gaining an education. It was more of a social thing - a place to meet up and plan what we'd be doing at nights and weekends. I was getting to know a very wide circle of people, even from the years above, and I was fascinated by the depth of people's knowledge on any given subject, apart from the curriculum.

Mum, I think, was going through a period of change and it was all very positive. The house was coming together, we were both well settled at school, and the man she had met was proving to be a good influence on all of our lives. Nothing seemed a problem. I didn't know until a lot later that the divorce had cleared Dad out financially and he was paying a fortune in maintenance. But he still kept himself busy, and I was beginning to realise that people fall into two groups: those who worry and fret, and never actually do anything (I found myself avoiding them), and those who just kept going, whatever happened. I'd grasped the half-full *vs.* half-empty concept and I was determined to keep my glass at least half-full. Meanwhile, Mum's 'friend' (who we were now calling Osc) used to visit and tell us about all the adventures he was up to. He'd been popping in and out of our lives now for a few years. He looked after Mum, was always smartly dressed and drove cars that just overwhelmed an impressionable young lad. It was hard not to compare this with what I saw when visiting my Dad. Living in a bedsit and upgrading from a Cortina to a Cortina Estate just didn't cut it for a young lad. Then one morning Mum told me that Osc was going to move in. For me that was just great, meaning another male around the house.

Through all this, school just carried on as normal. The one time I felt sad and utterly powerless was in relation to Charles. Coming from a children's home run by the Church, he'd been my responsibility every day at school for three years or so. It didn't involve that much really - things like making sure he went to lunch - and at break he'd just read in a corner, his eyes no more than a centimetre away from the book. The whole time I knew him he didn't write a single word. Conversation was just repeating whatever I said, so I taught him loads of swear words that he'd then repeat loudly on cue, usually in RE with the Sister. The class would fall about and Charles, with no idea what he'd done, would just get back to his book, a centimetre away from his face. I'd raise my eyebrows as if to say, 'I've tried, Sister, I really have.'

Then one day I was told he was leaving, having been offered a place at a special school. The day he left our school, I said goodbye. I was almost in tears. Charles didn't reply until he got to the gate. He turned, looked at me and shouted, 'Fuck off!'

I smiled. I'd taught him well.

CHAPTER TWO

As I prepared to exchange adolescence for adulthood, things began to change rapidly. First Mum and Osc moved us into a huge, damp, old house in the countryside (a 'renovation project'). Then Dad made me an offer. Every Sunday Dad and I would meet up, and on one of these Sundays he turned up with a Transit van and a big idea.

'We're going into the overnight parcel business,' he announced.

'We? What's it got to do with me?'

'We're going to cover the West Midlands, collecting parcels and taking them back to the depot ready to be collected by a larger lorry and sent on to a sorting hub. Simple.'

'You have a depot?'

'Yes… your Uncle Ted's betting shop.' Dad went on. 'As long as I empty it of parcels before the shop opens and drop off all the parcels I've collected after it closes, then everyone's happy.'

I was impressed. I loved the idea and was proud of the way my dad had quietly re-built his life. Father and son in business together; it sounded good. All I had to do was wait till I was old enough to drive and any worries about my future would be over.

At school I had a big decision to make - sixth form or work? It felt like a life-changing choice and I could feel a net closing in around me. I also had exams to get through first. My plan was not to leave but to stay on, just long enough to take my driving test, and then I'd be free to start my new career. And if I failed the test the first time, I could stay on until I took it again. I approached the head of the sixth form for my interview, hoping and praying I'd be allowed to stay on.

'Sit down,' he said. 'Now, young man, what have you achieved here so far which, in theory, enables you to go further in your chosen subjects?'

This was it, my one chance at the promised land of the sixth form. I took a deep breath and was about to talk my way in.

'I'll tell you,' he carried on. 'Precisely nothing. Your best option? Go out, get a job and don't look up for fifty years. Life is not about fun and laughing and joking, it's about bettering your-self. Good luck.'

I thought for a moment and looked him in the eye. 'If I take your advice,' I asked politely, 'Will I end up like you?'

'GET OUT!'

So that was that. My exams came and went without my doing any serious revision. But now I didn't need any exam passes. I was going to work for my dad, in our own business, and this made me feel safer and more excited than any of my friends seemed to be. I just had to reach my next birthday and get that driving licence.

Meanwhile, we had now settled in the country, so I decided to check out what was happening locally. There was a bus stop a couple of minutes' walk from the house which would take me to the village. I could walk it in half an hour but, coming from a town where buses and lifts were available at the end of the driveway, walking was alien to me. So I stood at the bus stop and waited. And waited. Nothing. Eventually I gave up and was heading back home when a passing car suddenly stopped and someone shouted my name. I vaguely recognised the person in the car, but what really caught my attention was his navy and white uniform.

'You're Duncan, from my junior school. Don't you recognise me? I'm Richard.'

'Oh, yes,' I replied, not really having a clue.

'Jump in, we'll give you a lift.'

Now that sounded better. As she drove, Richard's mum kept turning to stare at me. Richard and I exchanged polite conversation about our recent move and the non-existent bus, until curiosity got the better of me and I asked about the uniform.

'Are you going to a party?'

'No, I'm in the Sea Scouts.'

'But we're nowhere near the sea.'

His mother then joined in, asking if my mum would be interested in joining the local WI. I told her she'd love to, again not having a clue.

We soon reached the village and they dropped me off in the square. I had a quick look around and felt totally deflated. Everyone had the same hairstyle. The two shops sold exactly the same items (jam and cheese), although one of them also sold alcohol and stayed open later. I bought some supplies and enquired about bus times. The next bus was due at half past never, so I walked back. Along the way, most of the houses sold eggs and jam. No wonder the shops looked so bleak. Too much competition.

When I got back home, I was in a hurry to share my discontent.

'Mum, we can't stay round here. There's nothing but jam and bad hairstyles.'

I told her about my meeting with Richard, about him being in the Sea Scouts, and about how out of place I felt.

'It's just all so dull!' I added. 'There's nothing to do.'

'Well, if you don't want to become a Sea Scout, then it's time you got a job,' she told me, practical as ever. I had to play my trump card.

'Oh, I nearly forgot, I gave Richard's mum our number. I told her you'd be interested in joining the WI, whatever it is.'

She choked on her tea and I didn't like the look on her face.

'Have I done wrong?'

She banged her cup down on the table and exploded.

'You know all those houses you passed? The ones selling jam? That's what you do in the WI - make jam.'

So I got a job, helping to run the Ford Capri Car Club HQ. It was based locally and I thought it would be OK, for now. I had a desk and various duties including opening the post, answering the phone, dealing with membership and other enquires, being in charge of dispatch and trying not to get bitten by Jake, the car club dog. It was a funny old organisation. To be a member, you had to shell out twenty quid, love your Capri more than your wife, have a beard and live in Essex. What I didn't know at the time was that even just to work there, you had to have your own Capri. Apparently I qualified because Mum drove one. But I just needed to earn some money for driving lessons, so how I got the job didn't bother me.

By now I was beginning to make a few acquaintances in the village. But this just meant that evenings and weekends were spent being bored with them rather than by myself. Village life seemed to produce sixteen year olds already firmly stuck inside their comfort zone. They had their whole life ahead of them but seemed content just to drift along.

The night would start late and end early because of the distances everyone had to come to meet up. The idea of getting some cans of lager was considered devil worship. Lighting a cigarette in full view made you the Dark Lord himself. And any mention of doing something exciting or different, like catching the bus to where I used to live or going into the city for the day, would be met by a sharp intake of breath and a look of horror. Risk-taking was clearly something other people did. It started to dawn on me that I was that other person.

While marking time at the Capri Club, I started learning to drive. This involved going up and down the drive, and practising my parallel parking. The plan was to have two weeks' worth of lessons, which I'd been saving hard for. And money for my seventeenth birthday would pay for the test. Then I'd be free to join my father's business, which had been expanding at quite a fast pace.

The plan worked. I passed my test within three weeks of turning seventeen. It was the only exam I ever worked hard for, being the only one that seemed relevant to what I wanted to do - work hard and enjoy financial independence, and all on my own terms.

Ridler and Son! OK, my father hadn't mentioned the name, but it was still my first day working in the 'family business' and it gave me an overwhelming sense of excitement. It didn't last long. My father's new premises were in a large industrial unit near Winson Green where I was greeted with undisguised contempt by a member of staff. The noise was deafening and there were vans everywhere. I was handed a uniform, told to get changed and shown my vehicle. When I asked if my dad was around, my mentor just burst out laughing and wandered off.

My uniform was a bit on the large side, making me look as though I'd been seriously ill. Laughing Boy greeted my request for a smaller uniform with more derision and then pointed at my van. It was at the far end of the depot, just visible behind a mountain of boxes. Off I went, narrowly avoiding getting run over during the long trek. Every van seemed to be on the move and the smell of exhaust fumes filled the place. Engines revved and horns blasted. I just stared at this wall of boxes, hoping they weren't all mine.

Laughing Boy popped up again, ready with his version of an induction. His own uniform was as unusually tailored as mine. With his trousers at half-mast and his jumper not quite covering his belly, we looked like a modern day Laurel and Hardy.

'Now, you're the boss's son and let me tell you right now that I don't give a fuck. See this fucking lot? I've already put it in delivery order so you can load it on the back of the fucking van. Make a mistake and the day's fucked. We're already late, so we're fucked already. Under-fucking-stand?'

Yes, I thought, he'd made it all pretty clear, and I started loading. Half an hour later I was half dead and suggested a quick breather.

'You some sort of fucking poofta? Wait 'til this lot has to be offloaded. We've got eighty deliveries and then after that, all our fucking collections.'

So, no breather then. I got behind the wheel and started the van. Putting it into reverse, I explained that I'd just passed my test and needed to get used to the vehicle by checking my mirrors. He went ballistic. Mirrors, he told me, were for Nancy boys. And when I started cautiously driving out of the depot, he stopped me and took over. I was going too slowly, apparently.

My mouth was dry and I was physically exhausted already - perfect preparation for a day spent running in and out of buildings with arms full of boxes. It didn't help that I had to use one hand to keep my trousers up. But we soon fell into a routine. The technique was to set off with a wheel spin and stop with a screech. Other drivers or pedestrians in the way? Just sound the horn, lean out of the window and give a mouthful of abuse. If the person taking delivery queried anything, the reply was, 'You have thirty seconds to decide if you want it, or I am fucking off. And remember - it will just get sent back to the sender so it's on your head.' That always seemed to work.

The afternoon arrived and the pace got more intense, as did the swearing. The radio would burst into life to tell us where our next collection point was. At one point, my silver-tongued mentor managed to eat a sandwich while simultaneously smoking, talking on the radio and reaching across to get his drink, all while driving at breakneck speed. Eventually, we got back to the depot. I was completely done in but still had to unload the van while my mentor sorted the paperwork. His was a ten minute job. Over an hour later I finished mine, caught the bus home and passed out on my bed still in my uniform.

My time at the depot was not exactly fun, but I stuck it out hoping things would change. Any idea that I would get preferential treatment because of Dad soon went out of the window. If anything, I was treated worse than the rest in a bid to toughen me up. So I toughened up and took everything they threw at me, and more. But I wasn't so tough that I couldn't see what was going on. I'd entered the world of grown men who worked to live. I listened to their problems, saw the looks of despair on their faces, and heard about the angst of their home lives. Their only joy seemed to be pay day. Still in my teens, I had little else to compare it with, but I was already terrified this would be me in years to come. Loading up my van each day gave me time to think and I knew my future had to be different. I just wasn't quite sure how.

෨෧

Home was my sanctuary. I could rely on a hot, cooked dinner waiting for me, and my uniform was always cleaned and ironed. Mum asked once or twice what had happened to the smart, young man who was always smiling. And she had a point. Coming home, the only parts of my face visible after a day of dirt and diesel fumes were the whites of my eyes. And my uniform, with string now holding up my trousers, looked even bigger because I was losing weight. Mum knew that there were problems at work, but what could she do?

My social life was zero. Most nights, including Saturdays, I'd fall asleep in my dinner. Very occasionally, I'd meet up with a few people from the village and we'd drive for bloody miles to a pub where we'd be unknown. To be seen drinking would bring shame on their families, leading to enforced resignations from the WI and all the village committees.

One night, however, I agreed to accompany Mum to the evening party of a relative's wedding. I was quite looking forward to it as it was being held at a private club in the centre of town. Walking into the place, I felt a rush of excitement at the loud music, the smiling people and the rich, alluring smell of prosperity. Leaving Mum to mingle, I headed over to get some cigarettes from the vending machine by the toilets. A guy came up and, checking no one was looking, swapped the ladies and gents signs over. He then leaned on the vending machine to chat, smiling at the screams and shouts from within the loos. He introduced himself as Jon and offered to buy me a drink. Although he was about ten years older than me, we seemed to share a sense of humour.

He started to tell me all about his new venture, something called leasing. I was intrigued. He was already some big shot sales manager for a national finance company with about twenty staff below him. But he was about to branch out on his own, and when he explained how much you could earn, I was impressed.

For the rest of the night I learned more and more about the leasing business. It was simple: first find a customer who wants a car, a van or any other piece of business equipment, then fill out the proposal form and place it with a finance house; finally, walk away with ten per cent commission on the amount that needs to be loaned, using the equipment as security. Jon then went on to explain that, this being the late eighties, we were in a boom time with no shortage of punters. Property prices were rocketing and image was everything. I blushed, thinking of my works uniform.

At the end of the evening we shook hands and he gave me his business card. I left on a high of excitement. I'd glimpsed a different world, one not filled with packing boxes and gloomy faces. And I liked it.

Back at work, news was filtering through that the Royal Mail was going on strike. It was still the dominant force in the overnight parcel industry, but companies were panicking and started to use our services. Overtime and bonuses were being introduced! With an ambition to buy my own car, I decided I quite liked boxes after all and ended up working fifteen hours a day. However, my new enthusiasm wasn't universally popular. Quite legitimately, I sometimes slipped out to the toilet or to get some water. While I was gone, someone would find an excuse to radio in saying I'd taken a lunch break or just gone AWOL. All hell would break loose until, referring my supervisor to the signing in and out book, I would prove my innocence.

Pay day! I had now saved up almost enough to buy my first car outright - a lovely, sky blue Ford Orion - and I'd earmarked my bonus to pay for the insurance. I ripped open my wage slip and looked straight down to the net amount. It was the same amount as last month. Clearly it was an admin blunder, so I went to the office to get it sorted. Everyone else had received a bonus, they said, but no, they didn't know why I hadn't. So I approached my supervisor. He looked uncomfortable and told me my father wanted to see me. I didn't think for one minute that it was going to be bad news. I knew I couldn't work any harder and my delivery and collection rate was excellent.

'I'm told your work rate isn't up to standard, Son. And you've been confrontational to the floor managers.'

'What? I was only sticking up for myself. I've done the work and earned my bonus fair and square. And I need it for the car insurance.'

'There's blokes queuing round the block for your job,' my dad replied, shrugging his shoulders. 'If your attitude and work rate improves over the next month or two, then you can have your bonus.'

I was in shock. I felt completely swindled. No bonus and a sub-standard work rate? These unfair words needed a response, but what could I say?

Not a lot, apart from 'I quit.'

But with those two little words I bought my freedom, not just from Dad, but to define my own life and create my own success story. Trouble was, apart from a driving licence, what did I have to offer the world?

Then I remembered Jon's business card.

CHAPTER THREE

To be honest, it was Mum who remembered Jon. When I told her I'd quit, she seemed relieved. Guess she hated me in that terrible uniform. But now the inevitable question hung in the air - my future. She kind of touched on it and then changed the subject, expecting I'd just shrug my shoulders and look vacant. But instead, I did the right thing, applied for jobs and got some interviews. And at each one they all talked about the same thing: the future. Which kind of made sense, except it wasn't a future I could relate to. No exciting plans and ambitions to reach for; just retirement, health insurance and pension plans. And I reckoned only half of them would actually get there, the other half dying of boredom en route. But then I got this job offer, so I tried to think positively. It was a telecoms company, fast track management programme. And the best bit? A free vending card for the drinks machine. I decided to visit Grandad on the way home to tell him the good news.

'You'll last a day, my lad, and that's only if there's a fire drill followed by a power cut.' And the wind went right out of my sails, but then he said something that really drove home. 'Look,

Duncan, don't end up like me, don't just follow the crowd. You should work for yourself, do something different. Look at all the opportunities out there. Think of all the people you'd meet.'

That night, I churned over what he said and remembered the anonymous grey faces at the interviews. 'Til now, my life'd been full of confidence and fun, and I wasn't sure I wanted it any different. So I bought myself time by making out I was just waiting for the job confirmation letter. Mum saw straight through this, although it took me a few moments to catch up.

'So you've turned Jon down then?' she asked casually.

'Who's Jon?'

'You know, the guy you were talking to at the wedding party.'

Oh, him. The nice guy with cheeky toilet humour. Ambitious, too. But what does she mean, turning him down?

'Well, you know your auntie's sister-in-law?'

Now she really was going off track.

'Please, Mum, just tell me.'

'That's how Jon got our number. He wants you to phone him about some job.'

Thank God! Whatever he had to offer, I'd take it. No time to finish dinner; I went upstairs to find his business card and give him a call.

What a dive! I walked into the pub lounge, nervous and convinced it would come to nothing. I scanned the room, looking for Jon and then - wow - my eyes hit this gorgeous girl; a blond in a white jump suit. And the man next to her in the pin-striped... yep, it was Jon. It had to be; everyone else was in overalls. Things were looking good. He jumped up, we shook hands and then he introduced his girlfriend and poured me some champagne. I don't know what went to my head first, the champagne or her cleavage.

'Mixed grill?' he asked.

'No thanks, I had shepherd's pie before I left.'

God, I wish I hadn't said that.

'Are you sure? I'm just about to eat.'

'Go on then,' I replied, just to be polite.

He shouted to the bar for an extra mixed grill and another bottle of fizz, and we exchanged small talk. Then the food arrived and the girlfriend got up to leave. She gave him a peck on the cheek but he didn't even look up. She winked at me and then she was off. The food, the champagne, the girl… if this was Jon's world, I hoped he was about to invite me in.

We worked our way through the mountain of food while Jon took me back over his big idea. It was coming back to me now; leasing, commissions, loans. Not that it made much sense, but so what? I looked around. A pub full of people eating crisps and drinking beer, and us enjoying steak and champers.

'I'll be honest,' Jon told me, 'I did ask several others before you but no one wanted to lose their job security and all the perks.'

He was checking me out but I wasn't worried. This was my kind of work and the deal seemed OK too. We'd both go out selling the finance deals and split the profits equally. We'd go fifty/fifty on set-up costs, office, furniture, fax and so on. Jon had to give a month's notice at his current job, so I'd be sorting out a bank account and forming the company. It couldn't be that hard, could it?

'Any money you need, just shout and I'll advance the cash.'

Apparently he'd already got some backing from a large multinational that wanted to dip its toe in the water.

'So, are you in?' Of course I was in, and we shook hands. I still didn't understand the small details, but he clearly did and I was happy to learn along the way. Then, on the way out, he nodded towards my Ford Orion in the car park. 'One more thing: if you're going to get anywhere in this business, image matters, so ditch that.'

And that was it, interview over. Not a mention of life insurance or a pension plan. Only trouble was, the champagne had gone to my head and there was no way I wanted to start my business life without a driving licence. I couldn't admit I was going back home to my mum's, so I made out I was heading off into town and asked for a lift to the bus stop.

'No problem,' he said, 'but if you don't mind, I need to pick up my girlfriend on the way.'

Five minutes later I did a double take when a brunette climbed in the car. How many girlfriends did this man have?

༄

I found a city centre office straight away; fully serviced and furnished, with free rubber plants and a café in the basement. It wasn't the cheapest but if Jon was right, the rent would be a drop in the ocean compared to what we were going to rake in. Then I traded in my Orion for a sporty Vauxhall Astra on just £99 deposit, bought two new suits, got my hair cut and collected the stationery. I'd also deciphered the mysteries of forming a company and getting a consumer credit licence, and was feeling quite proud of myself - not bad for someone who could only just legally buy a pint of lager.

Then, my first day in the office, bright and early, opening the post, which was all the invoices for all the set up costs. Bloody hell, it wasn't cheap to become self-employed, and I was now flat broke. But it was exciting. This was my chance to prove I could make it in the real world.

Jon walked in and, cool as a cucumber, he picked up the phone and ordered a delivery of tea and bacon sandwiches from the café. Then we discussed our game plan. I would accompany him for the day to learn his sales techniques. We'd be targeting dealers and distributors who would sell our financing and leasing products onto their own customers. Their commission would cut into our earnings, but in return, they'd be doing all the leg work. Jon would look after the dealers and distributors and I'd sell to individual businesses by going door-to-door, cold calling.

The moment arrived and we visited our first lead, a large photocopier showroom. The manager called us into his office and Jon launched into his full-on sales mode. The guy didn't stand a chance. It was so mesmerising and slick, I'd have signed up for leasing from my own company. Outside, Jon checked that I'd seen how it was all done.

'It was just a blur,' I replied.

'We'll have another go, and make sure you listen this time.'

A few hours later, we were waiting to see the general manager of a very large and very posh office furniture company. The secretary called us through and I went in first and sat down. Looking round, I then realised that Jon had vanished. Shit. He'd done it on purpose. It was just me and a guy who clearly had time issues. So I took a deep breath and went for it. I calmly introduced myself and gave him the pitch. And it worked. What I reckon clinched the deal was my last minute offer to visit his clients personally. This meant I'd be responsible for processing from start to finish. Also, he didn't have to sign any contracts so if at any time he felt our service wasn't up to scratch, he could just stop using us. He agreed and signed up. As I was leaving, he revealed something which would prove to be one of my most reliable assets.

'I can tell you're new at this job, but I like your technique. We know all the tricks salesmen use, but with you it was different. You just sat down and spoke honestly. And you offered to look after our customers, which makes our life so much easier.'

Outside, Jon magically re-appeared, laughing and waiting for me to explain exactly how I'd blown it. I just told him he was shit at his job and lucky I was here to hold his hand. I wasn't expecting every call to be that easy, but it felt great to have closed my first deal. So we returned to the office to put some sort of admin plan into effect, ready for the flood of clients' proposals. We'd need to keep on top of it all. Jon phoned down to the café for dinner to be sent up while I looked out of the window, the city spread out below me, feeling on top of the world.

I soon slipped into a routine, getting in early and planning out my day. The only problem was parking. It didn't matter how early I arrived, I always ended up on double yellow lines. It was a good day if I got just the one parking ticket. Scouting around the day before, I'd noticed some semi-derelict buildings round the back of our office with room to park. Fed up with tickets, this morning I decided to risk it. Pulling up outside a disused unit, I got out of the car. Suddenly the unit's doors opened and two people stood looking at me.

'Can't park there,' they told me, 'that's our driveway.'

'Oh, OK.'

'And that,' they added, pointing at another small disused unit, 'that there's our home. Imagine if we just turned up and parked on your driveway?'

I was sympathetic but had an idea, and decided to tell them about my parking problem.

'A fiver a day and we'll personally look after it for you.'

I agreed and told them where my office was if they had a problem.

Back at my desk, I ordered tea and bacon sandwiches. There was a knock on the door and in walked my two homeless car park attendants.

'Is there a problem?'

'No, we just forgot to ask if you wanted your car cleaned. We only charge a fiver and it'll be like new.'

They knew they were chancing it, but I caved in and agreed to pay them when they'd finished. Deal done, they were just leaving when breakfast arrived. I unwrapped my bacon sandwich and bit into it… and they stared at me like starved dogs. I didn't comment but just picked up the phone and ordered two full breakfasts and two teas on my account to be collected. Their grimy faces beamed back at me.

And that evening, the car was gleaming so I gave them their fiver. They then offered to do the inside as well next time, pointing to an old vacuum cleaner and some cloths, and we got chatting. It turned out they'd been living in the disused unit for about six months and they showed me inside. They'd got it really well organised; two settees, a table with chairs, an old fridge and electric heaters, and all acquired for free. We agreed that I could use their 'driveway' and they'd keep my car clean inside and out, all for £10 a day.

Direct selling was one of the hardest jobs I'd ever done, with twelve hour days pounding the streets, and then following up with paperwork. I was now in the office seven days a week and I couldn't remember the last time I'd gone anywhere except on business. Jon continued with his hard-sell technique while I developed my own more relaxed approach. We'd soon know if they were working. Our first full month's commission payments were now due. It was a tense morning when the cheques arrived. We first deducted all our running costs and then kept some back for emergencies. Jon went through our statement to the last penny before looking up and asking me how much I thought I'd earned. I didn't really care, I was having such a great time that it didn't seem like work. I'd be happy with enough to pay my bills. He then announced that we'd cleared ten thousand.

'Not bad for two months,' I said, beaming.

'No, that's just one month's worth. We work a month in arrears.'

Jon passed me a cheque for £4,000.

'You know, we should go out and celebrate before too long,' he suggested. With visions of champagne and beautiful woman, I didn't need my arm twisting. But then he added a cautionary note. 'Just remember, we're both of us only as good as our last deal.' I knew what he meant, but was just grateful for being given the chance in the first place. He left, and I quietly pledged to myself to beat my target twice over next month.

Walking to my car, gleaming as usual, I saw my two friends and shared my good news. I was heading off into town to renew my wardrobe and told them to have anything they wanted from the café. I think I made their day. And for my own reward, I treated myself to the latest designer clothes and bought a CD player - which had only just come onto the market - for my car.

Arriving at the office a few days later, I walked in on fax paper everywhere and the empty fax machine beeping loudly, begging for a refill. I quickly put another roll in and it started up again, spewing out proposal forms. Three rolls later it stopped. I pressed play on the answer phone and listened to Jon explaining that he'd secured some sort of deal with a large insurance company. He said they'd be sending through a few proposals and would I deal them ASAP? A few? There must have been at least sixty proposals there, more than we'd done altogether since we started. I decided I needed some sustenance first and went down to the café to get something to eat. I'd got an arrangement with the owner that I'd settle up at the end of every week. He handed me the bill. I stared at it. We'd consumed more than two hundred cups of tea, a stack of sandwiches and more than a few dinners. The total bill was well over £100 but I was flush so I handed him my debit card and settled up.

Billy, the older of my two car minders, was also at the café. He'd been waiting for me and wanted to talk. We sat down and he started to thank me for helping them. Then he went on to explain why he was in this position. It turned out he'd been a chauffeur with several luxury cars, a couple of drivers and his wife running the office. Life had been good and the work plentiful until one day he caught his wife with one of the drivers. They'd split up and he had started drinking heavily. He'd carried on the best he could, but couldn't drive and run the office at the same time. The final straw came when he was caught drinking and driving. His life fell apart and he lost his home, ending up on the streets where he met the younger lad and took him under his wing. His name was Spike and he had some sort of disability, probably from a stroke as it affected him on one side and made him mumble. But he did seem to be smiling all the time.

Billy still drank apparently, but only at night. He apologised for drinking so much tea but they'd been coming into the café to keep warm. I didn't mind but told him to keep it under one hundred and fifty cups of tea a week in future. He then asked if he could drive me - it would save me time and money in car parking and fines, and repay me for all the tea and sandwiches. I said I'd think about it. As I got up to leave, I heard Billy ordering more tea.

Back at the office, Jon had now arrived. There was another thirty feet of fax paper all over my desk, the result of his meetings with more insurance companies. Laptops were just starting to come into fashion, the new executive 'must have', but they cost several thousand pounds. Despite this, insurance salesmen wanted them because they could upload all their latest data onto them and transport it effortlessly. We were offering them laptop deals for just a small monthly payment. They were so impressed that when we also offered them vehicle leasing, they were more than happy to give us a trial. I quickly added up the proposals. If we got the majority passed, we'd looking at thousands of pounds in commission.

By now work had become non-stop, and I was often in the office until midnight sorting out the paperwork. I didn't mind - we'd earmarked a weekend celebration very soon and this would give me the chance to socialise. It would also let me get to know Jon a bit better as, apart from an hour or two sorting out the day's work, we barely saw each other. At least I knew my car was safe while I worked the late shift. I gave the keys to Spike who sat in the car while Billy retired to the settee and belted out his repertoire of tunes, his voice lubricated by a can or three of super-strength lager.

The moment I realised I'd arrived came on mine and Jon's big night out. I met up with Jon and a couple of his friends in the pub before going on to a club. He handed me a pint and explained that we'd be going into the VIP section, which would have a sprinkling of minor celebrities and the odd footballer.

'Whatever you do,' he added, 'be careful. The women are knockout, but they'll eat you alive and for God's sake, don't buy them any champagne.'

I nodded, necked my pint and off we went. As far as I was concerned, I could have done with being eaten alive.

Jon was right - the women were stunning. And they were definitely circling their prey. I didn't stand a chance. I'd been living in the countryside surrounded by jam and bad hairstyles. The gamble I'd taken on my career was paying dividends so a bottle of champagne was a small price to pay, especially if it meant keeping the attention of a woman with less stubble than me.

Unfortunately it wasn't such a small price. I immediately got separated from Jon and his two friends and got talking to two girls. All Jon's warnings signs were immediately forgotten and, being a polite chap, I offered to buy them a drink. It was, of course, champagne they wanted. The barman wondered whether I wanted to leave my debit card behind the bar. I was acting all flash by then, so that's exactly what I did. He handed me the champagne menu and I passed it over to my two number one fans. The first bottle went within minutes and another was ordered while we went to find a table. Jon appeared from nowhere to see how I was getting on and gave me a nudge and an 'I did warn you' raised eyebrow. But I was in control. Or at least, I thought I was. I shouted across the room to order another bottle and sat at the table thinking the world was my oyster. Two attractive women, good music, no money worries, and all of it being played out in a night club that I wasn't even old enough to be in.

The next thing I remembered was the cold air hitting me as the taxi door opened. I staggered out and fumbled around trying to get the key to fit in the front door. I'd gone against all Jon's advice and paid the price financially. I even had to return to the club to reunite myself with my bank card. Looking at the bar bill, I realised I'd spent everything I'd just earned. The only consolation prize was the VIP entry pass the club gave me.

That was enough for me.

Business was going crazy and we were now getting five to ten proposals a day from the large insurance companies. This meant my working day was now eighteen hours and any undone admin had to be sorted at the weekends. We had at least invested in the very latest technology - mobile phones. As well as improving communication, they also gave us extra credibility with our clients. Who wouldn't be impressed by a flash suit turning up at their office and banging a large breeze block on the receptionist's desk to show how serious they were?

With commission payments accelerating, my monthly wage had doubled. And at last, I'd got a social life, somewhat more hectic than my work life. Most nights were spent uptown, usually with clients. They were generally a lot older than me, but we all had money to burn. I always felt really confident and important, wearing the latest designer clothes and buying champagne all round. And I'd look for the most attractive girls and steam in, lying about my age but not my income. Often, I ended up going my own way, heading off to the VIP section of a nightclub, where my status was confirmed as I walked up to the front of the queue and was waved straight through. This attention almost guaranteed me an attractive woman and my night would typically end back at her flat or at a hotel.

And if we got fed up with the clubs and bars of Birmingham, simple; we'd head down to London. The women there were even more stunning, although more expensive; but it was worth every penny, and I was more than happy to work through the week so I could do it all again the next weekend. I'd even traded in my Astra for the latest BMW 7 Series. The café was doing well out of me, too, the four of us having breakfast, lunch and dinner each day and now consuming two hundred and fifty cups of tea a week. I made sure Billy and Spike were on my 'expense account' and I'd invested in car valeting equipment for them, even though they only worked on our two cars.

Some weekends, for a change, I'd pay a visit to the local pub. Most of the people my age were now either in their first jobs or had gone on to college. What they all shared in common was a shortage of money or a tight budget and without thinking, I just bought rounds of drinks. I wasn't 'flashing the cash,' just helping out. And it was such a relief to enjoy trivial conversation unrelated to work. What I didn't see coming was the resentment this caused, something which would later blow up in my face.

One morning, Jon bounced in and informed me that we were sponsoring a hole at a ProAm tournament being held at his golf club. So, I was about to experience one of the benchmarks of successful business - the round of golf. He'd recently become a full member, so no expense was to be spared. I knew nothing at all about golf. I'd never even played crazy golf, but Jon went on to inform me of my debut in a different tournament; one for golfers with a bigger handicap. Knowing the golf club was a good place for making business contacts, I was happy to go along with the idea.

I had one month in which to learn the rules of the game but, of course, no time to practise. However, talking to Billy one evening, it turned out that he'd played golf in the past. Phew, he could be my mentor. He also knew it would be a big day for the public face of the company, so offered to act as my chauffeur. All he needed was a suit and a haircut. And Spike would be my caddy, lumping round both my clubs and my breeze block mobile phone.

As the tournament grew closer, I took Billy and Spike to a golfing shop. I'm not sure if Billy knew what he was talking about or whether the salesman sensed a major commission. Either way, I was relieved of a large part of my income. I did challenge the need for player and caddy to be dressed like rainbows, but was outnumbered. I was then presented with a golf bag that was as large as I was. And when the clubs were thrown in, Spike could barely lift the thing. My concern, however, was resolved by the final purchase, an electric golfing trolley - you pressed a button on the handle and off it went. So I was now ready. Inevitably, I only found time for one brief session at the golf range but at least

I found I could actually hit the ball. And anyway, it was more about networking and taking part than actually winning.

The big day arrived. I felt contented, ready to socialise with the owners and managers of local companies, and confident I could match them in the car park, on the golf course and socially. First stop was the office to pick up my team. Spike came out in his bright caddying colours and was followed by Billy in a suit. I wasn't sure if morning suit and spats were de rigueur at the club, but he certainly looked smart and so off we went. Billy drove with Spike beside him in the passenger seat, while I lorded it in the back.

We parked in the sponsors' car park and Billy opened my door so I could make my grand entrance. Jon stood there, open-mouthed, but couldn't say anything as he was about to tee off. Spike unloaded the trolley and golf bag, and then Billy asked him to wait by the car while we went off to the clubhouse for refreshments.

I offered to buy a round of drinks, asking the barmen if I could have an account. No account, but I could leave my card behind the bar. I told Billy to help himself, but please only a couple as he'd be driving back. I planned on doing a bit of business before teeing off a couple of hours later. The drinks were soon flowing and I wondered how anyone was ever going to see the ball, let alone hit it. I was several drinks behind, but couldn't be seen not to keep up. Then an official with a clipboard approached and said I should be making my way to the first tee. I told everyone to drink up, only to be informed they'd already been round. I went outside to find Spike and the fresh air hit me. I took a few deep breaths. I'd be fine.

Spike was leaning on the car, minding his own business and my enormous phone. When he saw me, he fired up the golf trolley and off we went. I approached the first tee and met up with my partner. We made our introductions and I suggested he go first, thinking he didn't look much good as he only had a few clubs. His shot went straight and true. My turn. Spike handed me a club. A small entourage had formed by now to admire our matching outfits and the electric golf buggy. Well, at least I hit it, but the ball took a sharp left turn. Blaming the club, I handed it back to Spike and off we went to find my wayward ball. As we started down a slope, the trolley took off, its motor whining furiously. Spike was forced from a walk to a trot to a jog. He got the buggy back under control and we found the ball. I had another go. I hit it straight this time, straight and about six feet forwards. Spike looked at me and shrugged his shoulders. But I felt encouraged and had a third try. And then a fourth, a fifth and several more until eventually I got it on the green. A couple of putts and I was literally a centimetre away from the hole, but the ball decided not to go in just yet.

A club official then materialised and told us, politely enough, to give up the hole. He clearly saw through the charade of our equipment, and a large queue was forming behind us. Five more holes but things got no better. We'd been out for hours and had reached the farthest point from the clubhouse. The crescendo of muttering from the massed ranks behind us wasn't helping my concentration, and my confidence was flagging as I failed to hit a single shot in the right direction. At least I was able to enjoy the scenery as I zigzagged my way from fairway to rough to trees to bunkers. And then the battery went flat on the trolley. By this time, both Spike and I were totally worn out and dehydrated. We decided to head back to the clubhouse, pushing the broken down trolley as we went. And to think people do this for relaxation!

After our long march, I told Spike to take the kit back to the car and entered the clubhouse, where I was met with piercing stares. Someone approached, clearly a person of significant importance at the club as he was dressed as Rupert the Bear. Taking me to one side, Rupert informed me that I'd broken pretty much every single club rule during my aborted round. Worse, I'd not observed full club etiquette either, whatever that was. Even being a sponsor didn't appease Rupert, who suggested it would be best if I left. Well, if I'd felt bad out on the course, it was nothing to how I felt now. I was utterly defeated and deflated, and hoped my performance hadn't affected Jon's standing at the club.

With my last shred of dignity, I managed to walk through the members' lounge. That shred slipped from my grasp the moment I noticed Billy, fast asleep at the bar. I went to wake him, casually smiling to the members and explaining that Billy had been on nights and, what with his tablets, it was inevitable he'd end up out cold. But Billy was not ready to wake up, so I went out to get Spike to help me drag Billy from the bar.

We managed to sit him up and, with both of us nearly on our knees, half drag, half walk him to the door. The bar was now completely silent as all eyes watched each intricate moment of the pantomime. The barman broke the silence to suggest that I settle my bar bill. I let go of Billy and Spike immediately ended up in a heap on the floor. I'd bought, so I thought, a couple of rounds of drinks. The bill said otherwise. It was for hundreds of pounds. The barman explained that the man going to a wedding had been buying the drinks for himself and anyone who'd cared to join him. That bloody morning suit…

I finally escaped and, with Billy slumped across the back seat, I drove my own chauffeur back home.

It was a relief to get back to work the next day. Arriving early, I was greeted by the beeping sound of the fax machine requesting a new roll. I studied the spewed out ream of paper in amazement. This wasn't just for a car or laptop. This was a company wanting to finance a large contract for making hotel furniture, securing the loan against the machinery that made the furniture. The cost of replacing the machinery ran into millions of pounds and they wanted to borrow nearly a million secured against it.

My mobile rang. It was Jon explaining the intricate details of the proposal, most of which went straight over my head. The only thing I fully understood was that we'd be getting close on £200,000 commission and, if we pulled this deal off, we'd branch into this sector on a more permanent basis. My job was to process the proposal and this would take up all of my time, but that was fine by me. I could do with being in one place for a week or two. My days were soon filled with chasing up paperwork from the company so that it could be passed onto the underwriters. I got the operation running so smoothly I was soon ahead of myself, waiting for the next fax and the next set of questions. So, to fill in time, I'd end up in the office café with Spike and Billy.

I told them that I'd decided to buy myself a place in town, assuming the big deal went through. I wanted to get them thinking about something more permanent, too, as they were bound to be evicted sooner or later. I didn't know what their future held, I just knew that Billy had a serious drink problem and Spike definitely had mental health issues. I told them I'd help with costs and furniture. They may not be the most reliable team, but they were intensely loyal and I liked them. At times, I even envied their simple lifestyle. They were also the only people I'd told about the big deal. Mum was preoccupied by putting the finishing touches to our new home. I was impressed by how quickly things were progressing and had even agreed to stay in a hotel - taking all my suits and belongings with me - while the stairs were being painted and the carpenter was installing fitted wardrobes in my bedroom.

Jon and I were now only a couple of days from completing the deal. I'd worked my fingers to the bone dealing with all the administration, and all the while the usual business kept coming in. But the commission we were expecting would be eye-watering. It seemed only yesterday that I'd been earning a basic monthly wage. These days, I'd spend that sort of money on just a single suit.

And so to work and my usual morning routine: park my car, chat to Billy and Spike and then head up to the office. But the routine was broken when I noticed the office door already open. It couldn't be Jon, his car wasn't outside. Entering the office, I saw three men in suits going through the filing cabinets and drawers.

They saw me, stopped and asked me to confirm my name. My instincts were immediately on high alert. I knew this was trouble.

The trio comprised an auditor, an accountant and a lawyer, all from the company who were supplying the funding for our massive deal. They told me not to be alarmed and even apologised for entering without permission. They'd managed to get a spare key from the reception desk.

'Is this about the big refinancing deal?' I asked, already knowing the answer. 'Because if it is, my partner, Jon, can explain everything.'

'He doesn't need to,' I was told, 'everything we need is here.'

'Can someone tell me what's going on?' I wasn't sure I really wanted to know.

'The deal your partner has put through involves borrowing nearly a million pounds, secured against machinery, on behalf of a client that doesn't exist.'

'What?' A sick feeling spread through my stomach.

I was used to deals with people who weren't whiter than white, but they usually involved fiddling the figures to upgrade from a Ford Sierra to a Mercedes. This was in a completely different league.

'It's all a con. The client's fake and so is all the paperwork you've been processing. But the alarm bells only started ringing our end when you mentioned you hadn't even seen the company, or met anyone who worked there. Since then, we've been following you every step of the way.'

I was in shock. I'd admired Jon and had the utmost respect for him. I wasn't a close friend, but I loved working with him. I was informed that I had two choices. They needed to follow the paper trail, and I could either help them or, if I refused, the case would be handed over to the police once they were finished. They preferred not to involve the police as in their industry, confidence was everything and a scam like this would do serious damage. They went on to explain that the company would cease trading as all funding had been withdrawn, and with every financial institution in the UK made aware of our conduct within hours, new finance wasn't an option. We then sat there all day going through each piece of paperwork. Thank god something had made me keep everything, every record, just in case.

Towards the end of that long, dark day, we were interrupted by an official with a clipboard who asked me for my car keys. My vehicle was leased via our funder and belonged to them now. That was the moment all the energy finally drained out of me.

Of course, it was no surprise I couldn't reach Jon on any number all day. And when the suits finally got up to leave, they said it was Jon they were after, not me. They saw me just as the gofer who was good at filing. I watched them leave, and before following them I threw a few personal mementos into a blue holdall. I felt exhausted and empty. I went off to find a taxi and suddenly it hit me. I couldn't pay for a hotel any more, and needed a bed for the night. I decided to seek safety and familiarity back home, even if that meant sleeping on the settee. Tomorrow, I told myself, I'd find Jon. If this really was over, we'd split the money and tie up any loose ends.

On the way out, I realised I had to do one last thing: speak to Billy. I don't think he understood because his last comment to me was, 'Never mind, business as usual tomorrow.' But, selfishly, talking to him put things in to some kind of perspective for me. After all, it's not like I'd ever have to live rough in a disused industrial unit. During the taxi ride, I thought about Jon. I didn't really blame him. After all, without him I'd have been dying a slow death in telesales. We'd done what any good entrepreneur does: spotted an opportunity, grabbed it and made something of it. It had been a solid business idea and he just got greedy, and I was too green to notice. To give myself credit, I'd got some of those contracts all by myself, fair and square, and I'd certainly shown I wasn't afraid of hard work.

Back home, I paid the taxi and walked up the drive. And then I froze. All my suits, my jackets… they were all in the boot of my car, my ex-car. Everything I owned, I was wearing.

The weeks that followed were pretty lonely ones. My friends - the ones I'd bought drinks for - found my failure amusing, told me I had it coming. I knew this stemmed from a cocktail of envy and resentment of my brief success, but was surprised by just how quickly people turned away. So I reminded myself that it had indeed been a success, to a point. What I needed now was to find a new opportunity, my own venture. I wanted a second chance, and as long I make the effort and put in the hours, surely people would see I was just a normal bloke making a living?

Trouble was, I didn't have Jon's experience and connections. I had all the enthusiasm but knew very little, least of all, where to go looking for big ideas.

CHAPTER FOUR

I was sitting on Mum's driveway, smoking a cigarette, searching my brain for 'an idea' when an engine backfired round the corner. Locating the source - an oil-burning Transit piled high with pallets - I caught the eye of the driver. Just as he started shouting across to me, his sliding door closed, leaving him mouthing inaudibly through the window. It was the first time in weeks that I'd laughed out loud. I strolled over, presuming he was after some directions, and waited for the door to slide back open again.

'All right, mate. Twenty five pallets, all paid for. You wouldn't mind helping me offload 'em?'

'Did Mr Taylor order these?' I asked, suspecting it was something to do with Osc.

'Couldn't tell ya. I'm just the driver, mate.'

Various goods were dropped off all the time on the drive, so a few pallets were nothing out of the ordinary.

'Where are these from?' I asked as we set about unloading his van.

'Longbridge, Rover Number Two works.'

'Oh, right,' I said, none the wiser. 'How come we can get hold of them, then?'

'I haven't got a clue. I had a phone call, got the details and here I am.'

Then my mind started working. I knew from my courier experience that these pallets were worth £2-£3 each.

'Are there many more of these at Longbridge?'

'As far as the eye can see,' the driver replied. He consulted his clipboard and added, 'Ask for Harry. He'll see you right if you need any more.'

'As far as the eye can see, you said?'

'Tens of thousands, mate. See Harry, he'll sort you out.'

We finished unloading and I went in to phone Osc and tell him his pallets had arrived. He told me he hadn't ordered any, which left me thinking again about the potential value. I decided to pay a quick visit to the mysterious Longbridge Harry.

Rover's Longbridge base was only ten minutes or so from our house. A monstrous complex of buildings of all sizes, it had grown over the years to cover many square miles, swallowing up rolling farmland south of Birmingham. Many of my family had worked in this warren of hideouts and outbuildings in the 1960s and '70s, part of the tens of thousands who went there every morning. In reality, such a huge workforce didn't guarantee much when it came to actual car production.

I knew where Number Two works was from my courier days. Whenever I went there at any point in the day, the person who needed to sign off my delivery was on his tea break. They say the unions ruined the car industry, but I think the tea break was as much to blame. I eventually found my man Harry, sitting alone in a poor imitation of an NCP parking attendant's hut in the middle of what looked like an airfield. There were pallets everywhere - fifty high, fifty wide, and in a pile a mile long.

'You Harry?'

'Yeah. Who are you?'

'I'm Duncan. Your name was mentioned by a driver with reference to some pallets.'

Harry eyed me for a moment.

'Come back in an hour,' he said, 'I'm on my break.'

But I wasn't for turning.

'I can't, but I am after some pallets. What's the score, Harry?'

He indulged me.

'You bring your lorry in, load up what you want and...'

'There's a nice drink in it for you,' I butted in.

'Oh,' Harry replied, warming to me. 'You can come any time you want then. I'm here nine 'til six.'

It turned out that Harry didn't know, and didn't care, who took the pallets or where; but to me this was a good chance to make some serious money. So I shared my thoughts with Harry and told him to stay put - I'd be back with transport as soon as I could.

He lit a cigarette and took a slurp of tea before leaning back in his chair and looking up at the sunshine.

'I like the sound of that,' he said, 'but can you avoid coming on my break next time?'

On the way back home, I kept going over the sums in my head and tried to contain my excitement. There had to be hundreds of thousands of those pallets in Harry's field. If I could shift them, even at £2 profit each... bloody hell. I intended to clear Number Two works of every pallet they had. It would be daft not to. All I needed was the blessing of my long-suffering folks, in particular some help with storage and transport. Maybe if I told them I just wanted to collect a few pallets - say two hundred - and bring them back to sort out because some were damaged... Then I thought of the copse next to the house. It would be perfect for storage - two acres and with trees as cover, so no one need know what I was up to. And I'd need the largest van I could hire, but... you had to be twenty-one or over to drive a hire vehicle and I wasn't. But I knew someone who was. What I needed was a convincing game plan.

Later, having rehearsed my story, I seized the moment and put the plan to Mum and Osc over dinner. Surprisingly, Osc immediately agreed to the use of the copse, but with...

'…two conditions. One, you don't damage the trees; and two, you take no more than a week, two maximum.'

Then Mum mumbled that it was OK by her too. This was a huge relief as Mums don't normally drive seven and a half ton trucks.

As it turned out, I couldn't hire a flat-bed at such short notice anyway, so I got her a van for now, using my dad's courier business account. We drove out in convoy, Mum leading in the hire van at about five miles per hour, bending back the wing mirrors on the gate post as she went. As soon as we were out of sight, we swapped over to save the mirrors and Mum's nerves. It was then that I realised the vehicle was racked out like a bread van and would only hold about twenty pallets. I was going to need that seven and a half tonner and a second driver as soon as possible.

Any entrepreneur will tell you that staff are the key to success. And on that basis, I approached Tim - twenty-one years old and just finishing university. He was the brother of a friend and we'd clicked during many a session down the pub. He was also six foot four and strong with it, so he fitted the bill perfectly. It took only a brief phone call to get him interested, but we couldn't meet at the local pub because my recent demise was still the stuff of serious gossip. I didn't want Tim to lose confidence in the enterprise before it had even begun. His parents were another reason for keeping things low key, his dad being a district judge and his mum a local magistrate. I didn't think I was planning anything illegal, but they were both disdainful of me in a way only legal people seem to be.

Tim was eager to find out what had happened to the business with Jon and, after I explained, he reassured me that all successes begin with a failure. I really liked his spirit and especially his support, something I hadn't heard from anyone for a while. I explained the plan to him.

'You serious?' he asked. 'Several hundred thousand pallets?'

'Yep, and you will be on a thirty per cent cut - and that's for just driving and lifting. Once we've sold enough, we'll be able to employ at least two blokes and get a couple of flat-beds.'

Tim's eyes lit up.

'I could buy a Porsche,' he said, 'within a month! Thanks for asking me, Dunc.'

I stressed that he must keep this to himself in case every Tom, Dick and Harry started copying us. And I was none too keen on his parents finding out what we were doing either. Tim agreed and did some sums in his head. By his reckoning, we could be making three or four hundred thousand quid a year - and that was a cautious estimate. But my chief concern was to be first in line at Longbridge before anyone else could muscle in on the idea. Making money was a powerful incentive, but I was still a young man living at home; if I could make enough to have a decent car and then blow the rest on having a good time, then that would be a good start.

Meeting over, I went back home. Mum tagged me as I headed off to bed.

'Look Duncan, whatever you're doing, you'd better make it work. It's time you got your career sorted out.'

'Mum, this is my career. This is what I do. Can't you see something big's about to happen? Can't you feel the excitement?'

'All I know,' she replied, 'is that if this goes wrong, I won't be shopping in the village ever again.'

I had a strong hunch what she was talking about but asked her to explain it anyway. I was right. In the village, I was seen as some kind of flash upstart who'd tried to cut a corner and failed. And I got the distinct impression that there were plenty of people who couldn't wait for me to fail again. But this time Mum's reputation was on the line too.

❧

Tim arrived first thing in the morning, eager to get started, so off we went to Rover where we found Harry, inside his hut drinking tea. It was ten past nine.

'All right, Harry. Come to make a start. Here's fifty quid. If things work out, that's what you'll get every day, seven days a week.'

Harry looked happy enough and for us, it was a small price to pay for exclusive access to this goldmine.

'Thanks, lads,' he said, trousering the cash, 'but do you have to come at this time? I'm on my break.'

We got to work. I quickly discovered that pallets are deceptively heavy, especially when the biggest thing you're used to lugging around is a brick-like mobile phone. But we worked like dogs that day and relocated at least two hundred pallets to the copse. The next day should be even more productive as we'd be swapping the bread van for the truck, meaning at least a hundred pallets a trip.

The following morning, Harry pointed at this fork lift truck driver.

'Give him a drink and he'll load up for you during working hours.'

This was fantastic, and meant we could clear the place in half the time. Tim was beside himself. He'd been dreaming of making enough money to get a second-hand Porsche. Now he was thinking brand new. Meanwhile, I was beside myself with relief. My plans were going to work.

We spent the next two days loading and unloading, doing about ten trips a day. The hard labour nearly finished me, but we kept going. Tim explained that if we did another five days, throwing in some night work as well, we'd be able to shift close on ten thousand pallets. Then we'd be ready to sell them to the dealers. Amazingly, Mum seemed quite impressed with what was happening. Maybe I wasn't such a fly-by-night after all. And Osc was away fishing for a week, which meant I could systematically cover every square foot of his land with industrial wood without fear of an inquisition.

Then disaster struck. A load of pallets fell on Tim, injuring his leg. It would be a while before he'd be driving again. So I decided to risk it and drive the lorry myself, even though I wasn't allowed to. But it was still slow going, with me doing most of the loading and unloading as well, and we were now down to only three trips a day. And to add to the fun, the police pulled me over for the heinous crime of not indicating. As this marked the end of my lorry-driving, we desperately needed another driver, but who? I was about as popular as a fart in a space suit, so it was up to Tim to find someone who was not just reliable but - more importantly - unconnected to anyone we knew. It took him only moments to think of Terry, or Taxi Tel as everyone called him on account of the '83 white Granada which he used to give anyone and everyone a lift. Tel adored that car and was convinced that it made any member of the opposite sex ignore his six foot three and ten stone build, and trademark long greasy hair, not to mention the tight leather trousers and cowboy boots. Tim assured me that Taxi Tel was trustworthy and would accept payment on account. His lifting and shifting abilities were somewhat underdeveloped, but he could drive a lorry legally, which was exactly what we needed. So, deal done.

With Tel at the wheel, we worked twelve hour days with at least fifteen trips a day. Tim spent most of the time moaning about his injury and the problem of driving a lorry under-age. He was worried that if I ended up in court, he'd have to lie about being part of this operation. When I asked him why, he reminded me that his mum was a magistrate.

'So, what happened to *admiring my spirit for having a go*?' I asked him.

'Yeah, that's fine, but if you get caught, you're on your own,' he replied.

He then went back to dreaming about the vast sums of money we were going to make.

༶

Taxi Tel wasn't interested in what we were doing or how much we were going to make. He had his own pot of gold at the end of his own rainbow - he was a keyboard player in a band doing quite well round the pubs and clubs of Birmingham. And when he asked me if I wanted to see them in action, I jumped at the chance as I hadn't been out for weeks. I knew Birmingham's clubs and bars well, but I'd never really hit the busy working men's pubs in the city centre before. When I walked through the door with Tel, I was hit by a wall of noise, clouds of blue smoke and a tense excitement in the air. Tel himself was engulfed by women trying to hug him. *Bloody hell*, I thought, *it must be the dim light*. He then introduced me to the band; a bass player who looked like Jon Bon Jovi, a lead guitarist resembling Jim Morrison, and a drummer with a girl on each arm and a hairstyle better than any of the women's in there.

And then the band went on stage to be met by a deafening roar of approval. All the people in there had come to see them. And they'd paid as well. Even now, remembering the moment when the drummer pressed down on his bass pedal to get things going sends shivers right through me. The crowd were captivated and those lads, playing together in such harmony, they were untouchable. I was mesmerised by the atmosphere, all those people shouting and cheering them on. I realised that Taxi Tel was a dark horse. And I realised that I really liked him and his band.

When they'd finished playing, I was introduced to the singer, Andy, with Tel billing me as some kind of golden-balled entrepreneur with the Midas touch. It was a shame I didn't have enough money for a round of drinks. I felt at home with these guys - they were alive and passionate about what they did, with an attitude to life that resonated deep inside me. Money and image suddenly didn't seem important; it was all to do with being part of something. The free drinks and enthusiastic women of all ages had their attraction, too. I got chatting with a girl in the pack. Her name was Caroline and she was absolutely stunning, so stunning that I was waiting for a boyfriend - probably tanned and with a six-pack - to turn up and suggest I relocate myself. She asked if I was the band's manager. Tel interrupted and introduced me as a wealthy businessman. I played along and started telling her about my pallets venture, until I could see how boring it sounded. She upped and left, but not before suggesting she might see me at the next gig. That was a dead cert.

Taxi Tel took me home. I was enthused by the whole evening - the camaraderie, the laughs and the sheer energy of the band. And Caroline. I wanted to be a part of it all and I made a decision. I told Tel that I'd use some of the money I was going to make from the pallet operation to help the band. I reckoned that I could help out with promotion and maybe get them some gigs. He was delighted. I was excited. As soon as the pallet business was ticking over smoothly, I was going to turn my attention to the band.

I was still buzzing the next day. Tim was fit again and I reckoned that we'd soon have enough pallets for me to start finding some buyers. I telephoned a few dealers, confident that we'd be shifting the pallets in next to no time. What the first dealer told me just reinforced my confidence.

'No problem,' he said, 'we'll take all the Euro pallets you can supply.'

It was only as I put down the phone that I took in what he'd said. Euro pallets? I'd never heard the word 'Euro' in relation to pallets. Not to worry, I thought, a pallet is a pallet. And we certainly had pallets, thousands of the buggers. I checked with Tim and he reckoned it was anything between eight and nine thousand. The copse was certainly full - our pile must have stretched back three hundred feet by then. I estimated that we could make about £3.50 per pallet. If we got the ball rolling by offloading six lorry loads' worth, we'd be able to claw back the rental expenses and earn ourselves a couple of grand profit on top. Our first pay day!

So off we went to see our first customer, crawling north up the M6 to a place just past Spaghetti Junction. It was hot and humid and we were worn out, but confidence was high. And I realised we were dealing with a big company when I arrived at a pallet yard that dwarfed Rover's at Longbridge. I jumped out of the van and went straight into the office. Pallet Guy vaguely remembered me as the man with thousands to sell. He shook my hand and there were smiles all round, before he told me they could only take up to a thousand pallets a day. Everything was falling into place. I could almost smell the money we were going to make.

'Just bring your lorry in,' I was told, 'and when you're unloaded you'll be given a ticket. Bring it to me and the cash will be waiting.'

We did as we were told and watched a fork lift drive up, ready to make us rich. The operator parked his forks under the first ten pallets and then stopped. He jumped out and shouted over to his charge hand, a massive bloke with all the airs and graces of a pit-bull.

'You two taking the piss?' he said. 'These aren't Euros.'

I smelled a rat. Was the pit-bull trying to knock us down a few quid? I decided to play along.

'What are Euros, mate?' I asked.

My question prompted a detailed lecture on pallets, the main points being:

- The vast majority of articulated lorries ploughing up and down motorways are curtain-sided.
- Having curtain sides enables fork lifts to unload the goods or produce which have been put on pallets.
- The standard pallet is a Euro pallet.
- Euro pallets are an exact fit for curtain-sided lorries.
- Any other pallet won't fit.
- If the pallet doesn't fit then the curtains won't draw.
- If the curtains don't draw then they can't be tensioned to keep the pallets in place.
- No tension, no safety, no goods.

Professor Pit-bull then ended the lesson with his conclusions.

'You, sonny, have non-Euros. They're worthless. See over there?' he said, pointing at a very large fire. 'That burns up non-Euros twenty-four hours a day. We only take them as part of a bulk purchase.'

Tim came over in time to catch the tail end of the lecture.

'We'll unload these pallets for you,' Pit-bull told me.

'Really?' I replied.

'Yeah. But it'll cost you a drink or two for the fork lift driver.'

Tim, none the wiser, watched our pallets being unloaded straight onto the bonfire. Then I asked him to lend me a fiver to pay the driver. I told him the bad news.

'You've had me grafting all week just so we can deliver pallets to a bonfire?'

'There's a good chance, yes.'

'And then we have to pay for them to be destroyed?'

I couldn't answer that. The truth was too painful to be spoken out loud. Strangely enough, the silence continued throughout our journey back to the van hire firm. All I could think about was the thousands of worthless pallets waiting for me back home. And the bill I'd run up with the hire company - a bill that would be going direct to my dad. And I'd used my last two hundred quid to fund the whole sorry venture. Basically, I'd been paying Longbridge Harry so that I could get rid of his rubbish for him.

So we drove in silence. Major mistakes or life-changing balls-ups tend to quieten people down that way. Silence allows it all to sink in; the realisation of being involved in a complete failure. By the time we got back to the rental yard, I actually felt quite upbeat. I think my mind was already refocusing on all those new horizons that still beckoned. But Tim could not be described as looking upbeat. He looked like he'd been diagnosed with a terminal illness.

I was waiting for him to enquire how we would get home when, without saying a word, he walked to a phone box. When he returned, he told me his mum was on her way to give him a lift back home. I could just imagine the aggro she was going to give me, but at least I'd get a lift out of it. While we waited, I asked

Tim if he had any ideas how we could shift the rest of the pallets. He didn't. I reminded him that he had a thirty per cent stake in the operation, so he was going to be responsible for getting rid of three thousand pallets. He didn't want to talk about that either. In fact, he couldn't even look at me when he spoke. I was a reminder of the big, fat mistake he'd just made in his life. OK, I was the lack of brains behind the mess, but I was also the one who was going to be out of pocket. Tim had lost nothing more than a bit of time and some face with his mates; mates who he'd bragged to that he was in on something big, something lucrative, something that made him feel just a little bit more important than them.

And for that he was giving me the cold shoulder.

Tim's mum arrived so I asked for a lift.

'Sorry,' she said, not looking sorry at all. 'We're not going your way.'

And off they went. Tim still refused to look at me but his mum shot me a particularly nasty smirk. It was left to Taxi Tel to save the day and get me home. He was all smiles when he picked me up. I hadn't seen a smile all day, which perhaps prompted me to spill out my sorry tale to Tel.

'Does that mean your business is shut?' he asked.

'Yep. Although I've still got nine thousand pallets to shift. My parents think they're worth £27,000. They haven't even invited anyone round for a week in case someone tries to muscle in on my brilliant plan.'

Mum sensed something was wrong as soon as I walked in. She said nothing, just let me come out with it all. When I'd finished, she went to the window and looked out at the copse. She told me that she wouldn't be mentioning this to anyone for the next few days. And then she gave me my deadline - I had a week to get rid of every single pallet.

So I was left with nine thousand pallets and no idea how to shift them. I couldn't sell them because they were quite literally rubbish. But I couldn't take them to the tip because I didn't have the transport to do it. Even if I used the family car and strapped two of the buggers to the roof, I estimated that it would take me around about 4,500 journeys all in. This equated to a year's work - a mere fifty-one weeks over my mum's deadline.

Sleep rescued me from my agonising.

The next morning, Mum was not for budging. I had my week, and then I had to go out and get a proper job. I decided that now was not the time to mention my plan to move into the music business. I went into the copse and forced myself to remember yesterday's debacle at the pallet dealers. What had they done with the non-Euro pallets? Burned them. If that's what the pros did...

So I started to build a pyre and then added a splash of petrol. Whoosh! Up went the lot. Not bad at all. I dragged a few more over until I had quite a nice fire going. I decided to leave it for half an hour, come back and then lob some more on. If I kept at it, I could have the lot cleared within the deadline.

I realised there was a problem as soon as I went back outside. There was so much smoke that I couldn't even see the top of the trees anymore. And when I ran over, the heat just hit me. My pallet pyre was burning out of control. I had two options: call the Fire Brigade or fight it myself, and I chose the latter. But with only the family garden hose to dowse it with, I got precisely nowhere. And peering through the black smoke, I realised that the fire had spread all the way down the long line of pallets.

The next forty-eight hours were the darkest of my young life. I'd turned a beautiful piece of woodland into a scene from a disaster movie. The tyre tracks of five fire engines had done the same to the front lawn. And just to kick a man when he's down, Tim's dad sent me a letter explaining that as his son had not entered into any agreement or contract, he would not be held responsible or accept any liability in his thirty per cent share of my so-called business.

The next day, our nearest neighbour popped round to see the carnage for himself. When I say nearest, he actually lived a healthy-sized field away from the chaos I had created.

'What caused all this then?' he asked.

'Just a few pallets,' I muttered, avoiding eye contact.
'Any left?'
'A hundred or so. Maybe more. Do you want some?'
'Twenty five, if possible. I'd arranged to have some delivered about ten days back. I needed them for my daughter's horse jumps. Some tosser must have swiped them off my drive while I was out.'

CHAPTER FIVE

A couple of days later, when the fire had finally stopped smouldering, Taxi Tel came round our house. He'd heard on the grapevine about my business going up in flames and was genuinely concerned. The sight of him stepping out of the Granada, the street lights reflecting off his patent leather trousers, made me smile. I trusted Tel and soon found myself describing my deep feeling of failure and stupidity. Just the fact that he was prepared to listen was a comfort, but he refused to go along with my analysis of the disaster.

'I'm impressed, Dunc,' he said. 'You've got balls… and vision.'

Even though all around me was evidence to the contrary, I actually agreed with him. It had been a bloody good idea but for one small detail; and I hadn't ripped any one off, despite what Tim's father might think. And, I realised, it had been only my second venture, so maybe third time lucky? But I was back at square one, with loads of enthusiasm and nowhere to direct it. Then Tel made me an offer.

'Why don't you help me and the band? We're always getting ripped off by landlords and promoters. Any excuse to pay us less.

We've got a gig in a couple of days. Why don't you tag along and we can have a band meeting afterwards. We need some structure, some discipline. We need someone to take us to the next stage.'

Redemption was being handed to me on a plate. And it was something I really felt a connection with. Leasing and pallets were just a means to an end, but this was the music business. Even though what I actually knew about it was second to - well, almost everything else I knew, I wasn't worried. I could feel it in my bones that this was exactly what I should be doing. It was something to do with the risk - and the reward when I succeeded at something high risk. So we agreed that I'd go and see the band play and then we'd have a meeting to discuss promoting them, and whatever else it took for me to get them to the very top.

The gig was being held in a function room and the place was packed. At least one hundred and fifty people were there, drinking and chatting noisily, waiting for the show. And as soon as I walked in I felt that buzz again, just like the last time, and was soon enjoying a free drink on the band. Then in walked Caroline, the girl from the last gig. My legs went to jelly and my stomach to knots. I offered her a drink, praying that she'd go for a half of lager as I was down to my last tenner. But no, she asked for a large Malibu and Coke. The barman, seeing the look on my face, reassured me.

'On the band's tab,' he said, handing the concoction to Caroline.

She seemed impressed. Not as much as me.

'So you've decided to manage them?' she asked.

'Well,' I chose my words carefully, 'I'm here to finalise things, but hopefully, yes.'

'What about all your other projects? Tel was saying you're on your way to being a millionaire.'

'Oh, you know… one step at a time.' A tramp with a shopping trolley and eight overcoats had more assets than me, but that kind of information was on a need to know basis.

The night was cracking - music, free drink and the company of a stunning girl. When the band finished and the lights came up, Caroline explained that she had to go. We exchanged phone numbers and I walked her to the door.

The place soon emptied, leaving only the band and several girls, clearly under the influence of Malibu, who draped themselves across the laps of the bass player and guitarist. Once in position, they just stared at these rock gods, occasionally nibbling their ears.

Eventually it was time for the negotiations. We were sat at a table. The barman placed two trays of drinks on it and left us to talk.

'Can you get a van?'

'Yeah.'

'You're hired.'

And that was it. As they headed for the exit, with the girls in tow, they shouted to the barman.

'This is our manager, he'll deal with everything.'

The barman came over and we went through the figures. We'd sold about a hundred tickets at £2 a pop. Grand. Room hire was a hundred. OK. Then factor in the drinks on account, £160, and the sound man who wanted £60…

'Just popping to the toilet,' I said and went straight out of the front door, walking as fast as I could. But thanks to the drink, I was laughing. It had been the best night for a long time; and I had direction, a task, a job. I could leave the past in the past, and it felt great.

Next morning, I was woken by a rush of cold air. It was Mum opening my bedroom window. She wanted me up and out and looking for a job. I dressed, still buzzing from last night, and went downstairs to quell the uprising. I explained my latest venture, band promotion, to Mum and Osc and their open-mouthed silence said it all. I was expecting all kinds of objections, even though they'd have known I'd go ahead with it anyway. But my enthusiasm must have rubbed off on them slightly. They had only one condition - that I pay rent. Then they added another - I had a month to prove I could actually achieve something this time. If I screwed up, I'd have to find somewhere else to live. Looking at their faces, it was clear they were serious, so I agreed. All in all it had gone well, so I thought I'd try my luck.

'Any chance I could borrow a vehicle?' I asked, 'A van, maybe?'

They must have still been in shock because they handed over some keys. They belonged to a clapped-out Ford Fiesta from Osc's car lot. OK, not a van, but it was transport. Just about.

And so my musical journey began. I was to join the band at their rehearsal venue in Newtown, an industrial part of Birmingham. The building gave no clue as to its use, but as I approached I could hear the muffled noise of instruments. Above the door, a small light shone over a sign proudly announcing *Robanna's*. I pressed a buzzer and entered. Upstairs, it was all heat and noise in a café-cum-lounge. I was greeted by a man and woman who both had strangely grey skin. I assumed it was due to the lack of daylight. Then the band arrived; we grabbed mugs of tea and went to their rehearsal room. This was down at least three flights of stairs and behind a soundproofed door two foot thick. The rehearsal space was more of a cell than a room and, like everywhere else in the building, the walls were covered in carpet. Not just any old carpet, but grimy, gaudy stuff even your grandparents would have thrown out.

Our meeting started. Everybody lit a cigarette. Within minutes, my eyes were watering so much I couldn't see a thing. Fortunately the game plan was clearer. I would get the gigs, collect the money, pay for everything and any cash left over would be saved for the band's needs and wants, including the hire of this room, which was £60 a week. I was amazed - £60 a week for this? I suggested that they might be joking. They weren't. And if we didn't pay, we were out on our arses. At *Robanna's*, there was a waiting list. So, remembering my hot-footing it away from the last gig venue, I decided to lay down some conditions - no bar tabs and we needed a friendly sound man. And by 'friendly,' I meant free. They agreed. They'd bring their own lager and a bloke that the drummer knew called Bean.

Business was over, so I stayed to hear them rehearse until the smoke drove me back upstairs to get a drink. The owners were up for a chat but the noise coming from above, below and everywhere in between made small talk difficult. It seemed like all the bands in the place were trying to drown each other out. And there were a lot of bands. The owners had converted the place themselves, creating fifty rehearsal rooms. The only problem was soundproofing, although they reckoned some more carpet on the walls and ceilings should do the trick. I also discovered why the place was called *Robanna's*. The grey-skinned pair were called Rob and Anna.

The band already had gigs arranged for the next two weeks, so I had some time to get on the phone and organise future fixtures. I found out straightaway that it was one big merry-go-round in Birmingham, with hundreds of bands on a circuit; earning a bit, losing more, and not really getting anywhere. So I decided to venture beyond into the countryside and managed to arrange a couple of gigs back-to-back for our first weekend. I swung it with one landlord by telling him the band had just signed to a major record label. I explained that we needed to be playing rooms holding up to two hundred people at £3 a ticket.

Our first gig would be slap bang in the middle of the bouncing, beating heart of quiet-end Worcester. We arranged to meet at *Robanna's*, with me collecting Bean, the soundman, on the way. He was a big fella, twenty stone plus, and wearing leather trousers with an elasticated waistband. When I asked him why he was called Bean, he shrugged and said he guessed it's because he's a fat lad who loves baked beans. We filled the car to the roof with his gear and I could see we were going to struggle with a Fiesta. When he got into the passenger seat, it was definitely higher on my side.

We arrived at *Robanna's* to be met by the band with the rest of the gear and assorted girlfriends.

'Where's the van?' they asked.

'That'll be a few weeks yet, we'll manage.'

'You're the manager.'

So, for now, we would travel in elegant convoy with the Fiesta, a Ford Granada Saloon and the guitarist's race-ready Golf, which had all its doors welded shut. We managed. Just. Bean ended up clinging to the cymbal case hanging out of his window as I prepared to drive off. I checked in my mirrors and saw two pairs of legs hanging out of the Golf - you could only get in head first, after all - and a set of keyboards peeking out of the Granada's sunroof. I could also see one of the band shouting and waving at me.

'You've forgot the drink!'

There must have been fifteen cases of lager and cider. I didn't realise they were for the band, I thought they were a delivery for the studio.

'Where's that going to go?' I asked.

'You're the manager.'

Problem solved; the Fiesta had a roof rack.

We headed off towards the M5 with the rider on the roof strapped down with bungee cord. The trip was not glorious, especially as the Fiesta refused to do much more than twenty miles per hour, and we kept getting lost. And despite sounding like a rally car, the Golf wasn't much better. Two hours later we arrived, unloaded and set up. It was total madness and I was starting to feel the pressure now. But I was still loving it. I left them to the one-two, one-two of mike checks, with the bass drowning everyone out, and set up my desk at the entrance. It was time to take some money.

We went down a storm. The place was full with well over two hundred people. But my door technique needed work as we only took a couple of hundred pounds. Each band member must have had at least six brothers and sisters, given the number of people claiming to be family and friends. We were playing in Worcester, but it wasn't that rural. I took note. This would not happen again.

After paying for the room and the tab (still over £40, even with the drink they'd brought themselves), and factoring in the costs of the petrol and all that lager, we were at break-even or slightly under, but I refused to be downbeat. This was, after all, a two-night tour and if I sorted out the problems on the door and kept the bar tab down, I was convinced we could still make a profit.

Bean offered to drive so I thought a few cans were well-deserved. The band was chuffed to bits that we had branched out and I was happy to be part of something real. And it was fun, until they realised I hadn't booked them into a hotel. I'd expected all of us to drive back to Birmingham. When I explained we only had £40 in the kitty, enough for just one hotel room, they pointed out that Bean was now the only one sober enough to drive. A compromise was called for. We'd have to find somewhere that could accommodate all eleven of us, at short notice and for bugger all. The pub landlord gave me a couple of numbers of places nearby and I managed to secure us a family room (plus breakfast) in a B&B. The owner had been at the gig and now all we had to do was get everyone and everything over there.

Bean set about driving all the gear and all the cars to our resting place. All went well, until he tried to get into the Golf with the doors welded shut. It was not designed for drivers of his size and I ended up crying with laughter as the band, by now decidedly the worse for wear, tried to force their soundman through a window considerably narrower than his waistband. Bean made it in, eventually, but only after he'd had his trousers and top removed.

At the B&B, the fight for beds began. The first casualty was Bean who was still stuck in the Golf. Nobody seemed at all interested in helping to get him out, being too worried about finding a bed for themselves. So we left him out there. The owner of the place was an ex-musician who clearly had a soft spot for us. He offered us two chairs and a settee, which were immediately grabbed, and after that it was the floor. The day was catching up with me and I didn't fancy that, so I went upstairs in search of a real bed.

The room we were actually paying for was rammed with all our equipment, a small mountain of lager tins and five bodies, already dead to the world. The bath was occupied too. Back downstairs, I tried the kitchen, only to find someone already flat out on the table, looking eerily like a body on a mortuary slab. Remembering Bean, still stuck in the Golf, I grabbed a blanket and headed outside. Bean had resigned himself to sleeping in the car but in exchange for the blanket, he passed me a pint glass full of piss.

'Can you pour this a bit further away?' he asked. 'I've already chucked two out and it'll smell.'

I walked back inside and lay down on the floor in the lounge. The offending pint glass went by the fire.

The last comment I heard before passing out was, 'Can you smell piss?'

Breakfast was light - loads of tea but only half a loaf of bread and a dozen eggs between eleven of us. I formulated a plan. We'd go to the next venue and set up, using their facilities to wash and generally spruce ourselves up. I would then get us all lunch and put it on the tab. I didn't want to do this but these were exceptional circumstances, all the more so as I hadn't eaten for a whole day. Breakfast was interrupted by news of Bean. Unable to hold on, he'd relieved himself in one of the Golf's bucket seats. I quickly settled the bill - £3 a head for bed and breakfast, not too bad. And we set off for the next venue.

After the usual lugging and plugging and testing, we were done for. At least, I was. We ordered lunch, wondering how to kill the eight hours before the gig was due to start. Someone suggested a few drinks and then a pre-gig rest, but I skipped the drinks and went straight for the sleeping option. I awoke to the sound of banging on the door of the function room where we'd all crashed out. All around was evidence of a massacre - bodies sprawled on the floor and band members asleep with their foreheads stuck to table-tops. It was the landlord the other side of the door, telling us that people were arriving at the venue. I checked my watch. It was half an hour until they were due on stage.

Well, we weren't at our best that night, thanks to sleep deprivation and a diet of caffeine, lager and cigarettes, but ticket sales were good. Then the landlord presented me with a food bill for more than a hundred quid. Factoring in room hire and petrol to get us back home, I knew someone had to go short. As soon as the gig was over, I went over to Bean to explain my problem. He was standing behind the sound desk in nothing but his pants. When I asked, he gestured towards a sink at the back of the venue. He was soaking his trousers in a cocktail of water and a selection of those toilet fresheners that look like pineapple chunks.

'Let's do a runner,' suggested Bean.

'A runner? It took us two hours to load up the stuff last night.'

'It's either that or another night roughing it.'

'A runner it is then.'

I left Bean to tell the band about our plan while I paid the landlord what we owed for the food, and explained that I was going to a cash point to get the rest of the money while the band loaded up. The landlord just about bought it, which gave us about ten minutes to make our escape. We were out of there double quick sharp, with the bass player jumping head first into the Golf as it pulled away from the venue. Thanks to extreme fatigue, morale was low when we got back to the rehearsal rooms. We agreed to meet up the following evening, refreshed and ready to discuss a new strategy. While we slowly unloaded all the gear, a group of lads came up to moan about the lack of free spaces in the rehearsal studio. They were on the waiting list, they said, but it was clear waiting didn't suit them. I was far too tired to take it in and was soon back in the car and taking Bean home. We stopped for ages at some roadworks on the M6 and, winding down the window to release some of Bean's unique smell, I noticed some signs plastered all over a building - 'To Let: 20,000 sq ft, open plan, can be converted to most uses, financial incentives available.' That's when the conversation with the three moaning lads came back to me. I scribbled down the telephone number and tried telling the semi-conscious Bean about my idea. He just groaned. My final impression of that weekend was a lasting one - the sight of Bean staggering to his front door wearing nothing but a pair of saggy pants and his cowboy boots. But my last thoughts were all about waiting lists and financial incentives. And how I was going to create my own rehearsal studios.

At breakfast the next morning, I was greeted with the words, 'Pay your rent, Mr Epstein.' I explained that the last two days had been a trial run and certain elements were in need of fine tuning. They accepted this, but warned me again that I was on dodgy ground. I told them not to worry - music promotion was just one part of my new entertainment empire.

A couple of days later, I met up with Caroline and briefly explained my future plans. I also decided to set the record straight about my current road to millionaire status.

'So you don't drive a BMW?' she asked.

'No.'

'And you don't have offices in the city centre?'

'No.'

By the time I'd told her about my pallet business literally going up in flames, the penny seemed to drop.

'So what you're telling me is I have more money than you,' she said.

I was half expecting her to get up and walk out. Instead, she kissed me on the cheek and told me that at least I had bottle. I knew she was sincere when she then said she'd like me to meet her parents. So I did, and they seemed delighted to meet me.

'Pleased to meet you. Caroline has told us all about you.'

It was then that Caroline set the record straight. This was met with a pregnant pause and then the single word, 'Oh.' I was starting to get used to this - people just seemed to be wary of failure, of how to handle it and how to treat me; whether to look away or praise me for my courage. I honestly think it would have been easier to say I'd just got out of prison. Then Caroline's parents broke the silence with the classic British line.

'Fancy a cup of tea?'

For me, failure just didn't matter as long as I had something else to channel all my energy and enthusiasm into. And now I did.

When I entered the building, I realised straight away why incentives were available. In a run-down part of Erdington, the place hadn't been used for years and was suffering serious neglect. And there was an all-pervading smell of damp. I was met by this small Indian chap who explained the space to let was on the first floor. The ground floor was being bricked up so there would be just an entrance hall and a small loading bay. Climbing the stairs, I walked into this open space which, with love and enthusiasm, was going to transform my fortunes.

Intense negotiations with the Indian man followed. I explained that I had no money but I did have a grand plan to make the landlord's building into something very special. He just gawped at me, but he knew that any work done on this building would improve it and so we agreed on one month rent-free, although he'd bill me for the electricity. He even offered to supply us with some of the materials we needed, but it would be down to me to obtain any permissions from the relevant authorities. That didn't worry me. We weren't in an area of listed buildings and beautiful views; just chimney stacks and smoke as Birmingham's industry churned out bits of metal. You could see the oil glistening in the gutters when it rained. A few people playing drums and guitars weren't going to bother anyone.

To convert the building, I needed some working capital and decided using my credit cards for starters. I also needed help, so I met up with the band and their various hangers-on to introduce them to my grand plan. As soon as I'd got the place up and running, I told them, I could turn my attention back to promoting them. And, of course, they'd have a free place to rehearse. My plan was greeted with cheers. I felt humbled. The band did, however, have one condition. They'd arranged to record a demo with a producer. It shouldn't cost them more than a couple of hundred pounds and I wouldn't even have to pay the man up front - they'd told him who I was and said I'd be passing on other bands to him in the future. I agreed, but insisted that they made sure it was £200 and not a penny more.

We then turned to the issue of fitting out the rehearsal studios. I asked if anyone had any experience of carpentry, plumbing, electrics and, most importantly, sound proofing. Nobody did, but I was told all about their DIY experiences, from kitchen re-fits to slabbing the drive and making dens in the loft. So work started, with the band and their mates providing free labour. People even volunteered to work through their holidays or phone in sick.

Timber was delivered and our new neighbour next door let us use a Coma flat-bed van. It was near scrap and only had first and fourth gears, but it moved, most of the time. I started emptying the local DIY stores of all their rolls of insulation for soundproofing. I then convened a planning meeting and allocated various jobs to my volunteer army. When someone asked about dimensions, I employed the tried and tested method of taking large strides and using the nearest object to mark the spot.

'I want to be open in a fortnight,' I declared.

Everyone just nodded like I actually knew what I was doing - which was keeping busy. I would come back home in the evening covered in dust and debris which, to my parents, was some kind of badge of honour, a sign that I was doing something positive. I'd have a quick shower and then go back out to meet up with the lads to discuss what was happening, or to fine-tune the labour force. Now and again I'd meet up with Caroline, and although she'd applied for a work exchange job in Chicago which would take her away for a year or so, that was fine. We were young and our careers came first.

As with any major project, much of my time was spent firefighting, resolving one problem after another as they came up; and my next issue was security. I visited the steel fabricators down the road and was told that a tank wouldn't get through what he had in mind for the front door. I left him to it and returned to the building. The rooms were taking shape and we'd partitioned off one area for hiding all the rubble and junk, labelled 'For Further Expansion.' Still, we had twelve rooms ready - not bad when you consider that we hadn't used any kind of architect or buildings manager. Such a DIY project did have its downsides, however. Our food and drinks counter had been built by a very short person and only came up to my waist. On the other hand, the rear shelving had been put up by someone well over six foot, so parts of it were only accessible by stepladder.

Neither of these things bothered me much. I was more concerned with sorting out the phones. One guy with some sort of telecommunications background had been going on about an amazing phone system he had stored in his garage. It was some kind of enormous switchboard and he reckoned we could have an extension in every room. I'd seen something similar before when I'd collected parcels for my dad. The receptionist would be frantically pushing banks of lights, directing calls here there and everywhere; fine for an office block, but a bit big for a twelve-room studio. I suggested this but was told it would be fine. It was, apparently, cutting edge technology. The other day-to-day essential, food and drink, worried me less. Our venture ticked all the suppliers' boxes and we'd have a captive market, open all hours and with nowhere else remotely close for people to go. The man hired to deliver Cornish Pasties was so enthused that he even threw in a free fridge and microwave.

Work was nearly done and arriving one morning, I was greeted by our new name. The building had been called Beverley House but my workforce wanted more glam than that. So they removed the letters *ouse* and replaced them with *ills Studio*. Our new front door was something else; at least twelve inches thick and sheet steel all the way. It took all my strength just to open it enough to squeeze through. The landing was awash with boxes of crisps and chocolate, and the reception area was a tribute to the Cornish Pastie and its related machinery. It was time to make a cup of tea and a pastie or two. I pressed the button on the microwave and switched the kettle on. Click. It went silent and dark. A voice came out of the darkness.

'You need to stick another pound in the meter.'

'Very funny,' I replied. 'Go and check the fuse box.'

'No. The landlord put an electric coin meter in yesterday. The bloke who installed it stuck a fiver's worth in.'

I was stunned. This would not do. I marched off to the phone box to sort it out but the landlord wasn't budging. There was nothing I could do apart from get in some pound coins. But I refused to be downbeat. The rooms, after all, were nearly finished. It was time to test the soundproofing.

I shouted for everyone to come into the reception area and then sent someone to the farthest room with my portable stereo. He was instructed to turn it up full. We stood and listened. There was definitely noise, so we weren't sound free, but all in all it wasn't so bad. Then we realised that the noise was coming from someone's portable radio two rooms away. So, we were not soundproof at all and nobody could work out why. We'd obviously got something wrong, but what? There was no option - we'd have to work around it. Onwards and upwards.

A much bigger problem was presented by the phones. BT hadn't connected us and weren't planning to for at least another three weeks. This was a disaster. I'd have to rely on potential punters making the effort to travel to Beverley Hills just for an enquiry. In the end, I needn't have worried. I'd placed adverts in the local paper (excluding the phone number but giving the opening hours) and as a result, we had plenty of people coming to look round. By the end of the first week there was only one room left. And it was then that I learned something about the music business. With musicians, there's always an issue with money, particularly the lack of it. They always claim they have no money, and with the kind of 'artists' I was working with - the odd club circuit regular, some wannabes and plenty of never-will-bes - they were probably telling the truth. The rent was only £50 a week. Between four or five band members, at least to my way of thinking, it wasn't a life-threatening amount. But nobody actually paid in full and I was left with a cash flow headache. And the cash I actually received... well, one band's seven members tried to pay with towers of one and two pence pieces stacked on the counter in reception. Even then it didn't come to a tenner. They promised the rest after they'd been gigging that weekend. I should have known. My own band weren't exactly break-even experts when it came to gigs. And they had a manager.

There were also immediate operational hiccups. The door took two to open efficiently so we tended to leave it open. This meant the place could have been warmer, so bands brought meter-draining electric fires in. Also, the microwave and kettle were in constant use - bands always seem to have money for food and drink. So the meter kept on turning and we'd be plunged into blackness and silence on a regular basis. But the place was up and running and being used. I'd stand there and feel my rib cage moving with the noise. It was absolutely deafening, distorting the brain inside your throbbing head. You could only communicate by pointing or writing. Even when the meter ran empty, you'd still have ten drummers all banging away on their kits and band members shouting at me to go and sort out the meter. It didn't matter. These were small issues. I was loving it. I'd work all week and get cover on nights or weekends so I could go and promote gigs. I still needed more enquiries so we could get on and convert the other rooms, ideally from bands who would actually pay the full price. But there was still no phone. And when winter arrived and we had to keep the doors shut all the time, I'm not sure I could have heard the damned thing ringing anyway.

The noise was so bad that I had to invest in some ear protectors, like the ones they use to park planes. This meant I now couldn't hear the door, so I rigged up a washing line with a red flag and threaded the whole thing through the previously boarded-up reception window. Visitors pulled the line, the red flag moved and that meant money for me. And it also meant a trip downstairs to drag the door open.

'Pull!' I'd shout through the steel.

'No. It's Chris!' would come the reply.

And I'd collapse, laughing. Humour was the way I dealt with everything, good or bad. Without it, I don't think I'd ever have been able to give anything a go.

Christmas was approaching and I couldn't have been happier. The only downer was Caroline getting confirmation of her American trip. She'd be off in a few months, but it still seemed so far away. I wasn't making much money. Actually I wasn't making any, what with the grimly efficient meter and the bands' consistently cavalier approach to payments. It didn't matter. I was living completely in the present and, with just enough to survive, had all I needed. I even offered to open up on Boxing Day so anyone who had new instruments could come down and bash away. We got a full house and threw a big party to round the year off. Everything was perfect.

The new year started with a visit from a massively overweight man with greasy hair waving a carrier bag at me. He showed me the contents - various bits of broken ornaments. He was bright red and frothing at the mouth, shouting and swearing and telling me he'd phoned the council, the fire brigade and the police. I just nodded and puffed and blew my cheeks out, agreeing with him while wondering which secure unit he'd escaped from. When he'd calmed down, I got his story. He ran a café from a unit at the end of our building which opened early in the morning and closed at lunchtime. This meant he'd be closed by the time I normally arrived. But the café, as it turned out, wasn't the issue. The owner rented a flat above it from our mutual landlord. And the flat was right next to one of our rooms. A new band had started using that room recently. They were into the heavier end of thrash metal. I'd had to put them in the end room because even my ear defenders couldn't combat the noise they churned out. Neither, as it turned out, could the café owner. The vibrations had bounced his precious possessions along the fireplace and off the other side. The results of their falls were in the carrier bag and he'd written to the landlord and his MP to complain.

'Why didn't you come and see me? I would have done something,' I said.

'I tried, but could never get an answer.'

I didn't think it was wise to show him the flag. I watched him waddle off and knew that I'd have to compensate him. I also knew that we needed to do more work on the insulation.

However, I didn't have time to implement a thing. The next day a clipboard turned up, held by a man from the council who served me with a noise abatement order. I didn't have permission to operate, apparently, and needed to submit a change of use application. But I could still trade while I did it. Result. But then the fire officers arrived. They were polite enough as they explained who they were and why they were here. After a couple of hours spent touring the premises, their numbers seemed to swell and by the time they huddled in reception, discussing God knows what, I counted half a dozen. They didn't mince their words.
'You're being closed down.'
It was a long time ago and I can't remember every specific reason why, but they had issues with the fire exit (non-existent), the steel door (unopenable) and the fire extinguishers (see 'fire exit'). And of course, as they were explaining about the need for back-up lighting systems, the meter ran out.
Word soon got round and the bands removed all their kit with an unprecedented speed and efficiency. What made it worse was that everyone was more sad than annoyed. The place had felt like home to a lot of them, as it had to me. And its demise had been unexpected and sudden. All that was left was my own band, looking at me for direction. They'd lost their rehearsal place. And needed the money to pay for the demo they'd done. I told them to leave it with me. The one thing we still had was the van; it was such a wreck that the landlord was happy to be shot of it. So I gave it to them so they could clear out their gear.

I locked up and went home, feeling numb. I had nothing to fall back on and no one to turn to. Everyone I knew was connected to the enterprise in one way or another. And the situation was all down to me, one hundred percent. I had no choice but to take it on the chin.

First thing the next morning, I went back to Beverley Hills to try and find everything that was worth anything. The front door told me everything. It wasn't there. Twelve-inch-thick sheets of steel and someone had nicked it. I was astonished. So I wasn't too surprised by the scene that greeted me upstairs. It was empty. Everything had gone overnight. All that was left of my efforts was the washing line and red flag on the wall outside.

I sat in my car for the rest of the day and into the evening, trying to figure out a future where I could make things work, be a success, or even just have a say in what that future would look like. But by the time I got home, it was late. With everyone in bed, I was suddenly hit with an overwhelming sense of loneliness. And, for the first time in my life, I felt real fear. I took myself to bed having decided to come clean to Mum and Osc in the morning. But by the time I was up, they were out. They'd left me a note on top of a pile of my unopened post. A music producer had been round looking for his money. Osc had paid and the note wondered whether I could reimburse him the £600. So much for the band's promise not to go over £200. I pushed the note to one side and started opening my post - all credit card bills, all to the limit and all needing paying. But there was one letter that stood out, looking very official. I peered inside. It told me I'd been summoned to court for non-payment of fines from driving the pallet lorry.

I went out for an aimless drive. The look on Mum and Osc's faces when I returned said it all. The landlord had been round in my absence. He was after the rent and had been very happy to tell them what had been going on. I was made to sit down and go through all the gory details of the past few days. I then got to listen to how I should have been doing things. I suddenly knew how it felt like to be a criminal as the judge sums up your case. The verdict was plain - guilty. The sentence - pack your bags, you knew the consequences. They were as angry as I'd ever seen them, gave me ten minutes to pack and told me to leave the car keys behind.

I didn't have anywhere to go and not that much stuff to take with me. I'd lost more than I'd ever kept. So I grabbed my only suit and a decent pair of shoes, and then put on loads of layers of other clothes to keep me warm in the sleeping bag that I'd shoved into a blue holdall. I was suddenly struck by a sense of certainty that I would, indeed, come back from this. Maybe not tomorrow, maybe not for a while. But I would not be beaten. As I stepped out into the cold winter air, I half expected Mum, and maybe Osc as well, to come rushing out and tell me not to be so stupid. To come back in and start getting my life back on a more normal track. But they didn't. I'd made a decision to gamble with that normality and I'd lost. I walked alone down the driveway and out onto the road.

CHAPTER SIX

It was dark and freezing cold and I was trying to think straight.
I knew I needed to be practical, but my mind kept wandering.
Every car that rushed past made me wish I was the person inside,
that I could swap my problems for theirs.

I had two contacts left: Caroline and my dad. I'd only
seen Dad a few times since I'd stopped working for him. We
hadn't fallen out, but we'd both been working non-stop. And
every time we did talk, he wanted to know if I was saving for
a house or whether I'd sorted out my pension plan yet. I'd
explain what I was doing and there would be a sharp intake
of breath followed by the word 'risky.' I decided to phone
Caroline. She launched straight into an excited speech about
going to Chicago and because I was pleased for her, I kept my
own news brief. When I'd finished, she didn't know what to
think.

'You could stay here for a couple of nights,' she said, 'but...
well, you know, my parents? One moment they think you're
going to be a millionaire, and now we'd be telling them you're
homeless.'

'Don't worry,' I tried to sound strong. 'I don't want your help, just your support.'

She said she was there for me and I told her I'd phone again as soon as things had settled down. I then tried my dad and got ten minutes of 'I told you so,' and, 'What about your savings?' I told him as well that I'd be in touch, and left it at that. And it then struck me I'd nowhere to go, so I just started walking with neither a plan nor a destination in mind. I walked for hours through the countryside, shuffling trance-like in a darkness only occasionally illuminated by a passing car or lorry. After a while, the traffic thinned and I was left alone in the pitch black. I came to a crossroads. The place names on the signs meant nothing to me. I was in the middle of nowhere with no idea which way to go. I was also tired and thirsty and knew that I couldn't go on much further. A few miles back, I'd noticed a lane that led to a canal and decided to retrace my steps. It seemed as good a place as any to rest until daylight. I couldn't find the lane but climbing over a low wall, I found myself on the canal towpath. Thank God, I thought, I really needed to rest. But as soon as I sat down then the cold bit into me, so I put on two extra jumpers, wriggled into my sleeping bag and fell asleep.

I'd been walking most of the night and was exhausted, but only managed a couple of hours rest before the chill and the damp woke me up. My legs ached, my back was stiff and my throat was dry with thirst. I realised I wouldn't get back to sleep again anytime soon, so I just sat and watched the night slowly turn into day, the sky brightening and changing colour, and the birds up and about looking for food. It gave me time to think and I didn't feel shame or regret. I didn't even feel any anger towards my parents. I just told myself that I would come back from this.

As soon as I could, I set off for the nearest village to find some breakfast. It was only a mile or so from Mum's house but a good two from the canal. Along the way I passed a bench and made a mental note to come back later and claim it. As a bed it would be a comfortable improvement on last night's hard towpath. I soon found my bearings and located the village shop I'd visited a few times over the years. I added up my money - £15 - and blew a third of it on cigarettes, crisps, chocolate, cans of pop and a newspaper. I downed one of the drinks in one - ecstasy - and then headed back to the canal. After all the decisions I'd made over the past few months, it was a strange relief to face just one - to stake my claim over the towpath bench. Passing a few dog walkers on the way, I tried nodding a greeting to each one, but in return I got uncomfortable silence as their eyes turned in the other direction. I spent the rest of the day smoking, reading the paper and occasionally stretching my legs. Periodically, passers-by came and went but only one, an old man with slurred speech, stopped to talk. He interrupted my reading to ask me a question.

'Are you a druggie?'

Not knowing what to say, I made up a story about coming back early from holiday and my parents not being home yet. By the time I'd finished my tale, he'd already wandered off. But it had given me an idea. After that encounter, I started playing a game in my mind, trying to dream up scenarios where every passer-by's life was in some way far worse than mine. Coming to the conclusion that I was better off than them cheered me up no end. I didn't feel homeless at all. I just felt like I was in some kind of limbo, waiting for something to happen.

Dusk arrived and the cold set in. I stripped down to my t-shirt then slowly put on everything I owned, making sure there were no gaps. When I'd put on my jeans, suit trousers, two jumpers, my suit jacket, another jumper and then my coat, I climbed into my sleeping bag feeling like a lagged boiler. It was then that I realised I needed to go to the toilet. The hours passed and I refused to feel downbeat. Instead, I tried to work out how to get out of this situation. When I finally fell asleep, I was none the wiser.

Something woke me, probably a passing animal, and then the cold really hit me. My sleeping bag was frozen on the outside and dawn was still hours away. I sat there smoking and fighting a desperate urge for a cup of tea, one of the small comforts that I was beginning to miss. I realised that I couldn't take another night of this. I had to come up with a plan. Eventually dawn broke and I had another visitor - a woman walking her dog.

'Are you homeless?' she asked. Before I could reply, she launched into a long story about how her sister helped to serve Christmas dinner to people like me at a hostel. She droned on and on about how cruel society could be until I ran out of patience and cut her short.

'I don't suppose your sister ever comes down this way?' I asked sarcastically.

'Good God, no,' she replied. 'But I can give you directions to the hostel. Do you have transport?'

'Are you serious?' I asked.

'Fraid so. It's about an hour's drive away.'

I pulled my hat over my face and she went off, calling her dog who had just pissed on my bench for the third time. I then went back to the village shop, passing friends' parents and other people I vaguely knew. Nobody looked me in the eye and I sensed that word had already got around about me and my predicament, but that was the least of my worries. Far more pressing was the fact that I was down to my last £10. I bought bread, crisps and, as an economy measure, rolling tobacco and papers. At the counter, I quietly asked the lady whether, if I bought some tea bags and milk, she could lend me a spare cup, and if she did, would she provide me with some hot water. This was embarrassing enough but the growing queue behind me, listening to everything I said, made it far worse.

'We're not a café,' came the stern reply, loud enough for the whole shop to hear. When I swallowed what was left of my pride and explained that I was temporarily homeless, she nodded and informed me that the whole village knew exactly which bench I was currently using as a base.

'So is that a yes or a no?' I said in a resigned tone. To my surprise, she disappeared for a moment and then returned, reluctantly giving me a cup of hot water. Just as I was brewing my cup of tea, one of Mum's friends came into the shop.

'Hello!' she said, all fake jolliness. 'And how are you?'

'OK,' I replied.

'Heard you got thrown out. Such a shame,' she said, without conviction.

'I'm living near the canal.'

'Yes. So I heard. I didn't realise there was anything newly built up there.'

I didn't care about her put-down. The tea was inside me now and I could feel its warmth trickling through to every part of my cold and aching body. When I handed the empty cup back to the shopkeeper, she pulled her jumper sleeve over her fingers, took the cup and threw it straight into the bin.

'I suppose,' I said, staring at her, 'you'd have to burn down the shop if I used your toilet.'

Strangely, I felt more upbeat after that episode. Yes, I was homeless and a social leper. And completely broke. But as I walked back up the hill, back to my newly built detached bench, I still thanked God I wasn't them.

And so, back to my plan. I was going to spend the day mastering a new skill, learning how to roll a cigarette. It didn't go well. Every time I tried to light it, the paper would split. I spent much of the morning covered in tobacco with a thin piece of paper hanging from my mouth.

I treated myself to a crisp sandwich and watched as people passed me by. Some would return my smile, but most gave me a very wide berth - if there had been a gentle breeze, they would have ended up in the canal. Then an elderly gentleman approached and as he got closer, I recognised him as the slurry bloke from yesterday. Our eyes met and he smiled at me.

'Still here are you?' he said.

'I am.'

He sat down next to me. Just that simple act meant a lot to me and when he asked me again how I'd ended up on a bench, I told him everything, throwing in my problems in the village that morning for good measure. This made him laugh out loud, as did my attempts to roll another cigarette. He took the tobacco and papers off me, made me a perfect roll-up and then stood up.

'I'm off for a pint. Might see you later.'

'Before you go,' I asked. 'Could you make me some more roll-ups?'

The hours drifted by and my thoughts began to go round and round, following the same sequence of questions and answers. *Should I just go home and beg for forgiveness? Would anyone be worried? Probably not, they'd be thinking I've moved in somewhere. But if they could see me now, wouldn't they see they'd made a mistake? Surely they'd give me another chance? But then, if I had to rely on them again, I'd have to become someone I wasn't. And imagine going back into the village shop and hearing them all saying, 'Oh, look, he's behaving himself now.'* And at this point in the cycle, I always came to the same bold conclusion. *Bollocks to that, I'd rather die a cold, slow death. I'm an entrepreneur. It's just that the scales of risk/reward are not quite balancing at the moment. But -* and this was more important than anything - *everything has been my doing. If I come back from this, then the rewards will be mine.*

My elderly rolling machine returned. He'd had more than a pint and was slurring, swaying and growling, and started slapping my chest and arms with a rolled-up newspaper. I couldn't understand a word he was saying, but invited him to sit down anyway. He wasn't the best of company, but at least he could roll me a cigarette. Ah, no he couldn't, missing the paper and licking his hand. I tried tuning into his ranting, which seemed to be about his ex-wife. When he staggered away some time later, he only narrowly missed a dip in the canal.

I went up the road to the phone box and rang Caroline, desperate to hear the warmth in her voice. She was pleased to hear from me and had some news. She told me about a bunch of musicians who wanted to kill me because they had nowhere to rehearse. I also learned that the van I'd given to my old band had broken down after a gig, leaving them to carry their equipment home. I laughed. They were the least of my problems. Not that I was about to come clean with Caroline. When she asked me where I actually was, I made up some rubbish about being at an aunt's house, miles from anywhere. But when she reminded me that she'd be off to Chicago in a few weeks, I realised I might not even see her again unless I could get myself sorted out.

I was now down to my last £5, cold and depressed and not ready to return to my bench just yet. There was only one thing for it - a trip to the pub. Not being exactly dressed for success, I chose the bar entrance. It was all horse brasses and open fires, the kind of place I wouldn't normally have been seen dead in. Sitting down at the bar, I saw myself in the mirror, looking like a coal miner on overtime. It wasn't a look the barman approved of.

'Sorry, I can't serve you. We have a dress code.' Once I realised he was talking to me, I unzipped my coat to show him my designer jacket underneath. Only I'd forgotten that the jacket was under a big jumper, itself over three t-shirts and another two jumpers. His reply was short and sweet.

'We do take-outs.'

So I walked out with two cans of lager, stood in the shadow of the pub and let the first beer go straight to my head. I could hear some kind of party going on in the lounge side. Cars were drawing up with well-dressed people getting out. I watched them come and go while I tried to roll a cigarette. A van pulled up and two lads got out (two lads on the outskirts of the large group who I hung around with from leaving school and through my leasing days, etc., always happy to scrounge a drink and cigarettes or expect me to pay for their curry, etc., hated the fact I was earning plenty of money but in a snide way). Seeing me, they did a double take.

'Hey! Is that you, Duncan?'

I nodded and mumbled, trying to explain the state I was in. They only listened before walking off, laughing. I concentrated on my second can and listened to the music that had started up in the bar. The lager flowed and I started clicking my fingers to the beat. I was having a ball. Then the two lads came back out of the pub and headed off to their van. When they saw me in the same spot, they told me not to move. They said they had something I'd need.

'Brilliant,' I said, walking up to the van. 'What is it?'

They handed me a piece of string.

'It's for your dog,' they said and drove off.

I stood there, holding this piece of string, thinking that if my luck ever turns and I get out of this, they're going to wish they'd never done that.

༄

It was after several more days like this that I started to deteriorate. I'd managed to stretch out my money for nearly two weeks, but now it was all gone and I hadn't eaten anything substantial for two days. I was sneaking into pub toilets to fill up my water bottle and have a wash. I'd sit in the cubicle for as long as possible without attracting attention and use the warm hand dryer on my face and hands, until someone came in through the door and jumped when they saw me. I wasn't a pretty sight. The weather was playing havoc with me. I just couldn't get warm and I kept wondering how the homeless managed to survive. And of course, the answer is that they don't. The only saving grace was my elderly friend who began stopping every morning for a chat. He was always smartly dressed and seemed on edge in case anyone saw him talking to me. But this was a man who was permanently intoxicated. I must have fallen a long way for a drunk to be embarrassed by my company. Sometimes he'd bring a flask of tea or hot water, and then collect it on his way back home from the pub. More often than not, he'd just walk straight by when I tried to hand him back the flask. I'd have to run to catch him up and hand it over. One time he was so drunk he just grabbed it, swore at me and threw it in the canal.

I didn't sleep at all that night and decided I had to go into the nearest town. I headed for the supermarket, even though I had no money to buy anything. It was now all about survival and I needed food. It took me two hours to get there, plus another ten minutes to strip down to a single layer of clothing so I didn't attract attention. It didn't even cross my mind that I'd be committing a crime. I was too hungry and thirsty, too tired and cold. I grabbed a trolley, hooked my holdall on the back and walked in. I knew what I wanted - small, light items like cheese and ham, nothing bigger than bread. Putting them first in my trolley, I then slipped them into the holdall and then just walked through the checkout area and away. As soon as I was outside, I ran. The nights sleeping rough were taking their toll and I didn't get far before running out of breath. I stopped and looked back. There was no one coming after me so I started the long walk back to my bench. It was only then I reflected on becoming a petty thief. A one-off, I said to myself, when needs must.

That night, on the bench, it was party time for me. The old fella, who I now knew as Bert, dropped by. He said he couldn't find the flask but promised to bring me something back from the pub. I was full by then and took great comfort from the fact that I'd managed to steal enough food to last me for a few days more. And it was just as well, because during those days I could feel myself weakening. My body ached all over and although mentally adjusted to the cold, I would still wake up shivering at random times throughout the night. Sometimes it would be hours before the shivers would subside. I was surviving on a diet of adrenalin and determination, supplemented by a further raid on the supermarket which didn't go so well when I accidentally grabbed some Stilton, a cheese I just can't learn to love. And this time, I was chased before escaping, which used up strength I could barely afford to give. It was now that I finally saw just how far I'd fallen...

A long, long way down, as evidenced by some credit card statements I found at the bottom of my holdall. Looking at them, I could remember each individual transaction from only a few weeks ago. But strangely, they actually cheered me up. Although they represented what I'd had and then lost, they were happy memories and in a way, a kind of achievement. I was putting the statements carefully back into the bag when a letter dropped out. It was a court summons, which I must have stuffed away and forgotten about. I was summoned for failing to produce my documents after the police had pulled me over in the pallet lorry.

And I was due in court that very day. This was brilliant news. At the very least it was an excuse to sit in the warmth and unburden all my problems. And the worst that could happen? If sentenced, I'd have a roof over my head and three hot meals a day. It had to be better than freezing and slowly starving on my bench.

The heat hit me as soon as I entered the courthouse. The clerk told me my case wouldn't be heard until the afternoon so I found an empty chair next to two people, who immediately got up and moved away. There was a radiator nearby so I took the opportunity to dry off some of my clothes. I then washed myself, and the rest of my clothes, in the court toilets. I rounded off my morning by spreading myself over three chairs and having a good sleep. Several hours later, I was rudely awoken by the usher bellowing my name. I sat up, rubbed my eyes and asked for a minute to collect up my washing.

Inside the court, the magistrate asked me to confirm my name and address. I was still half asleep and decided to play the sympathy card by telling her I was homeless and living on a canal bank. It was only then that I recognised the magistrate. I raised my hand.

'Excuse me, you know me.'

She looked up and gave me a deathly stare while everyone's eyes turned to look at her.

'Do I?' she boomed.

'Yes, you do. I'm Duncan. You're Tim's mum, aren't you? The last time you saw me, you refused to give me a lift after my pallet business closed.'

The look in her eyes now turned to anger. Her important time was being wasted, and for the accused to claim to know her was a major embarrassment. She used her most magisterial voice.

'If you say you know me then I'm afraid we'll have to adjourn this case. You will be notified of a new date.'

'How?' I asked. 'I mean, it's not like you can send a letter to my bench.'

There was no answer, just the usher telling me to step down and leave the court. Outside, it was blowing a gale and I could see the rain catching in the headlights of the cars rushing by. Any feeling of warmth disappeared as soon as I stepped onto the street, to be replaced by an overwhelming need to eat. It didn't matter that I'd just walked out of court, I was going shoplifting again. Not that I ever thought of it like that. To me, it was just survival.

I walked up and down the aisles, carefully selecting what I needed, before heading for the exit and casually slipping the items into my holdall. It was then I felt a tight grip on my arm and heard the words, 'Got you.' I tried to explain it was a question of survival, but the security man just smirked and marched me off to the store's offices. He had my bag in one hand and my arm in the other, and to unlock the office door he had to drop the bag and loosen his grip on me. I made my move, elbowing him to the ground, and grabbed my bag and ran. There was another guard at the store exit but I pushed him clear and made it outside. The pair of them then chased me, but even though I was running on empty, I still managed to pull away. In a way it was funny - one moment dreaming of a nice warm cell with three meals a day, and the next scarpering like mad to avoid it.

I managed to make it to a large housing estate, driven by my need to eat or perhaps just by adrenalin, and pushed myself backwards into a hedge. There I wolfed down a can of Coke and some processed ham while waiting for the coast to be clear. It didn't touch the sides, so I made myself slow down as I ate the rest of the loot - another can and some cheese. Then I suddenly started shivering. It was so cold and wet that I felt an overwhelming urge to get back to the security of my bench.

It took me hours to get there and by then exhaustion had taken over. On the way I could feel my spirits giving up. I didn't care what happened to me anymore. I told myself I'd given it my best shot, but I'd failed, and this was the price I was now paying - humiliation and shoplifting, along with physical and mental ruin. I looked up at the night sky and realised that my time was up. Then I cried. I cried at the loneliness of it all. And as I lay down, my holdall as a pillow, I was so numb that I didn't even feel the cold and rain anymore.

I woke up shivering. It was still dark and I was ill, light-headed and without the energy even to sit up. I'd been living through weather that alternated between frosty and wet. That night it was both and the rain was coming down sideways. I dozed off again, to be woken some hours later by a prodding in my ribs. It was Bert.

'Morning,' I managed.

'It's the afternoon,' he said.

'Sorry. I don't feel that well.'

'You don't look it.'

There was nothing new about this economical exchange, but something was bugging me about Bert. It took me a while to realise exactly what it was - he was sober. He then opened a small bottle of whisky and explained that he'd been barred from the pub.

'Does that mean you won't walk down here every day?' I asked, worried.

'No point now.'

Bert asked me again why I was sleeping rough. The booze must have erased any memory he had of my telling him before, so I went through the story again. This time I could tell he was listening.

'So you're not one of those druggies? You look like one of those druggies.'

I assured him I wasn't. Bert took another swig of whisky and stood up, ready to leave. I wondered whether this would be the last time I'd see him. He turned to me, gave me a thoughtful look and then said:

'Grab your bag. You can stay at mine for a bit until you get yourself sorted. But you pay rent and I don't like mess or noise.'

I half fell off the bench, wriggled out of my sleeping bag and caught him up. I grabbed his arm and asked him if he was being serious. He replied with a curt, 'It's a forty minute walk.'

Halfway through the journey, having asked what day it was, I suddenly realised that it was my birthday. And no ordinary birthday either - this was my twenty-first. But I soon let go of the thought. It was a measure of how ill I was that I could barely keep up with the ambling, whisky-sodden pensioner. By the time we reached his driveway I felt delirious, swaying and shaking. I could hardly take in my surroundings, just registering that Bert lived in a bungalow. The warmth hit me as I entered the house, and the heating wasn't even on. Bert, now his old self thanks to the whisky, gave me a tour of the bungalow consisting of a few slurred comments and some pointing. The key thing was that there was a kitchen, a spare bedroom and a bathroom. Luxury. Unadulterated luxury.

I went to open the kitchen door and a clamp-like pain shot through my calf, accompanied by some low growls and a gurgle.

'That's Jess,' explained Bert. 'She'll get used to you.'

Jess was a Collie-cross who, with teeth gripping my leg, was clearly already attached to me. I dragged myself, and her, to the bathroom where I ran a bath. We then returned to the kitchen and I made three cups of tea. I looked through a serving hatch and saw Bert in mid-gulp on his bottle of whisky. I asked him if he would make me some cigarettes, which he did, and to get Jess off me, which he didn't. But the roll-ups came flying through the hatch so I hobbled back to the bathroom carrying three cups, some cigarettes and one dog, who was now starting to dig her back legs into the carpet. I closed the bathroom door on my leg, finally managing to disconnect it from the dog. Free at last, I couldn't believe it when I looked in the mirror: dirty, unshaven and my face, arms and hands so much blacker than the rest of my body. I climbed into the bath but the water turned black almost immediately. I ran a second bath and then lay there drinking and smoking and soaking in the deliciously hot water. The effect was dramatic as my body finally began to relax. I dried off and gathered up my clothes. Jess was still on the other side of the door so, using my coat like a matador's cape, I warded her off while I took the short walk to my new bedroom. I threw the coat onto Jess in the corridor and went to bed. The mattress had collapsed in the middle, leaving me with the distinct sensation that I was lying on a mountain side, but I passed out almost instantly.

I slept for a whole day. When I woke up, it took me a few minutes to remember where I was but only a few seconds to find Jess still waiting for me outside my door. Seeing my clothes in a smelly heap on the floor, I investigated the wardrobe and found a dusty old black suit. I put on the jacket and trousers - no socks, pants or t-shirt to ruin the look - and climbed out of the bedroom window in a bid to avoid Jess. The garden was an unkempt celebration of waist-high grass and forty foot conifers, so I didn't feel too guilty about relieving myself in a secluded corner before knocking on the front door. Bert didn't even raise an eyebrow, just sighed, let me in and went back to the living room.

Now I was able to take it in, I saw that inside the bungalow was even messier than the garden. The dining room contained a dust-topped table and a single chair. The lounge consisted of Bert in a stained armchair, another chair with a blanket on it (presumably for Jess), a TV and a three-bar electric fire which popped and fizzed when the dust hit it. The principal theme in the house was debris, with piles of newspapers and unopened letters everywhere. In the kitchen, something was bubbling on the stove. Lifting the lid on the saucepan, I saw a massive bone with stringy meat still clinging onto it. I sincerely hoped it was for Jess. I made tea and brought it to Bert, who was watching telly. When I sat down, Bert barked at me to move; I was in Jess's chair. Once I'd settled on the floor, Bert topped up his tea with whisky and gave me the lowdown on bungalow life. He said I could use the phone and wear any clothes that I happened upon. He told me to help myself to anything in the kitchen as the milkman brought supplies every day, and meals on wheels were delivered three times a week. I smiled and thanked him. He nodded and offered me dinner.

Dinner was, indeed, the bone which Bert, having scraped off what little meat there was, threw to the floor. Jess clamped her jaws round it, much to the relief of my leg. We then feasted on ham hock served daintily between two slices of bread. Bert showered his in salt but to me it tasted fine without. By then, anything would have tasted OK to me. Just having hot food in a warm, dry house was enough.

After dinner, I made two calls. The first was to Caroline, who wanted to come over. I desperately wanted to see her as she was leaving for the States in a few days, but I wasn't exactly proud of my surroundings, so I put her off with the promise that we'd get together as soon as possible. Mum answered my other call with a torrent of questions: Where are you? Where have you been? Why didn't you phone? I didn't have the energy to explain, just asked if she would come over and bring me some clothes that actually fitted. She said she'd be round in the morning so I went back to bed, exhausted again but just beginning to feel a little bit better, a little bit stronger.

I didn't sleep so well that second night, not helped by Jess deciding to share the bed. I awoke to find her head on the pillow next to me. When I tried to nudge her off, she just growled, so I left her and nodded off, only to be woken again, this time by a loud banging. I got up and put on the suit. The banging wasn't Bert, who was dead to the world in his own room. It was the milkman handing over some bottles and a carrier bag containing another large ham hock bone.

Mum turned up mid-morning with some clothes and a look of shock at my appearance. I was still unshaven and my hair was a haystack of tangles, but it was the suit with no shirt that really did it for her. I brushed off her questions with stock replies about being ill and having no money. It was great to see her, but at the same time I wanted the meeting over with. My recent ordeal had hardened me inside. She handed me a pile of letters and a sports bag with a few clothes in it. Then she went back to the car before returning with a little something that she thought I might need. It was a lemon meringue pie. We talked for a few minutes more, but I didn't really have much to say, and then she left.

It felt wonderful to be in my own clothes again but complete bliss to be able to clean my teeth. I sat down at the table with a cup of tea and cut myself a slice of the pie. Jess stared resolutely at me until I relented and gave her a slice too. I ate while going through my post. It was not the sort of news I needed. The landlord of the rehearsal studio wanted compensation and the council had invoiced me for the removal of the truck that the band had left in the centre of a Birmingham roundabout. Then I opened the last letter, from British Telecom and dated the morning Mum had thrown me out. They apologised for not being able to connect my phone at the studio and said they were happy to enclose a cheque to compensate for any inconvenience my business had suffered as a result.

It was for just over sixteen hundred pounds. I stared at it until my eyeballs started to ache. This meant one thing and one thing only - I was back. Smiling, I looked over at Jess who was licking her lips in anticipation of another slice of pie. *I'm not just back,* I told her. *I'm back where I belong, in the speculative world of the entrepreneur.* I swear she was grinning back at me.

CHAPTER SEVEN

I finally met up with Caroline on the evening before she left for America. While we sat in the pub and chatted happily, I decided not to reveal what I'd been through over the last few weeks. Instead, I simply told her I was back in funds, and the conversation remained upbeat and positive, looking to the future. She was about to embark on a life-changing adventure, and so was I. I just didn't know when, where or what it might be. We left the pub to stroll round the local area and eventually ended up sitting on a wall, chatting about this and that. Sitting there, we were in our own little world, together and happy, but I think we both felt the heaviness of imminent separation. We tried to hide any sadness behind jokes and speculation about the future, but eventually Caroline said she needed to go. Handing me an envelope, she made me promise not to open it until she was gone. Wanting to give her something, anything, in return, I managed to remove the street name from the wall we were sitting on. We laughed but as she couldn't very well take it home on the bus, she asked me to send it on to her - her new address was in the letter. She promised to phone and I promised to visit, and then the bus took her away.

By the time I arrived back at Bert's, it was gone midnight, and he and Jess were sprawled across their chairs, snoring in stereo. I felt sad and lonely, as if I'd lost the only person who really wanted to know me for who I was. I decided to open the letter, and very quickly began to feel a lot better. I read that Caroline wanted the relationship to continue and for me to come over and visit her as soon as I could. She'd not wanted to ask me direct in case I'd said no. I was really touched by this, but although I could now afford to make the trip, it would put a serious dent in my finances. Fortunately, I didn't have to reply or make any decision immediately. My body was still recovering from sleeping rough in sub-zero temperatures so it was a relief to let life stand still for a few days. And Bert gave me plenty of space, his company being limited to a couple of words until he'd had a lunchtime drink or two.

I must have been in this state of timeless limbo for a few days when Caroline phoned, telling me she'd arrived. She said she was OK and living in the grounds of a mansion just outside Chicago. She'd told her hosts all about me and they couldn't believe the things I'd achieved at such a young age. Looking round Bert's room, I couldn't either.

Feeling almost fully recovered, I knew it was time to do something. I was grateful for the roof over my head and had money in the bank, but it wasn't enough. I needed a project, something to get me back on my feet and show the world what I could do. The local paper had plenty of vacancies in factories, packing boxes, or in offices as trainee this and trainee that. But I wanted a challenge, not a life sentence. Trouble was, my CV and work experience didn't exactly match up to the more rewarding job profiles. Still, I was beginning to realise I was blessed with what some might call stubbornness, but I thought of as resilience. I had plenty of self-confidence and just needed a little more time to pull together some ideas.

That evening, around midnight, I was waiting for a scheduled call from Caroline when Bert came back from whichever pub hadn't yet banned him. From my vigil by the phone, I watched him wobble into the front room with a plate full of ham hock, waving a carving knife dangerously close to the dog, whose eyes were glued to the bone. Bert collapsed into his chair while Jess tried to climb up. Belching and gesticulating with the knife, he carved the meat and dropped pieces into his mouth. Now and again, he'd fling a bit across the room for the dog. Then, at last, the phone rang. Caroline wasted no time in giving me all the reasons why I should be in Chicago, and looking at the scene in Bert's lounge, I didn't need much convincing. I was just about to reply when the dog, having leapt up onto the table to chase a tit-bit thrown by Bert, skidded off taking out newspapers, cups and the phone as she went. My chair tipped over and Caroline was cut off in mid-sentence. By the time she rang back, Bert's laughter at his dog's performance had evolved into a coughing fit. Jess, realising Bert was temporarily distracted and disabled, grabbed the bone and ran out of the room. Jumping out of his seat to chase after her, Bert tripped over the phone cable and flew head first out of the lounge, cutting off the phone as he went. Caroline rang for a third time and instead of trying to explain what had just happened, I simply told her what she wanted to hear. I was coming to Chicago.

A week later, having bought my ticket and some new clothes, I had to go back to Mum and Osc's house to retrieve my passport. Walking in, it didn't feel like home to me anymore, as if all the warmth and safety had gone out of the place. Perhaps I'd just grown a tougher skin in the past month or two. I certainly felt more mature. Grabbing my passport, I went into the kitchen and told them straight out - I'm off to Chicago in the next couple of days. They were stunned and speechless, and I tried prompting with all the whys and wherefores of my trip. Still nothing; not a word in reply. So I said goodbye and left. Bert wasn't much better.

'I'm going to Chicago.'
'Where's that?'
'America.'
'But where in America?'

'Dunno.'

Bert grunted, losing the thread.

'Caroline says it's great; freezing cold, but then it's cold here so it won't be so different and my first plan is to…'

Bert's pickled mind suddenly caught up with the conversation and overtook my whirlwind of news.

'Chicago!' he blared. 'It's full of them gangsters!'

That gave me an idea. With a few days to wait before my departure, I packed and re-packed, everything I owned now fitting inside my blue holdall, and with the street sign I'd promised to Caroline poking out of the top. By night I would go for a walk, but not just for the fresh air. Picking my routes carefully and varying the time, I was able to pause in front of the same house without too much suspicion, sometimes stopping to tie up my laces while I surveyed the layout and refined my plan. It would have to be done under the cover of darkness, preferably late at night.

Meanwhile, I'd arranged to meet Taxi Tel in a pub. He agreed to take me down to Heathrow in the early hours of the morning. He didn't know where Chicago was either. I noticed he'd changed. The leather trousers had gone but so had his happy-go-lucky self. The band had finally split up and he had a career now, and wasn't at all happy about it. He said he was jealous of me. The only thought going round in his head was, 'Is this as good as it gets?' He even said he was jealous of me, which gave me a bit of a guilty buzz. I knew what might cheer him up and asked him to do me one last favour before we set off for the airport. I needed to stop off at a certain house on the way to the airport, and when I explained why, he grinned from ear to ear.

The evening arrived and I left a note for Bert tucked in an envelope with his rent money, and a little bit extra. Then Tel and I set off, parking just round the corner from the house I'd mentioned. It was the dead of night and as I'd intended, there was nobody about. While it was to be a harmless prank, I wanted it to be good. So, carrying a bag of tools, I led the way up a small drive with a van parked on it. The van was a useful bonus as it blocked the view of the porch door from the road. I'd gambled on that door being unlocked and it was, sliding back silently. Once inside the porch, I got to work with my dispensing gun, starting at the top corner of the door frame and working all the way round, filling every nook and cranny with silicone sealant. When I was done, I stepped out of the porch as silently as I'd gone in. Tel appeared from the side passageway with a hosepipe and I fed it through the letter box and into the sealed-up porch. We went round the side of the house and turned on the tap. As a parting shot, I'd tied the piece of string they'd kindly donated as a dog lead to the door of their van. Tel gave me the thumbs up and we were off, back up the drive and away.

With hours to kill before my flight, I phoned Caroline as promised to let her know I was on my way, but she wasn't there. Instead, I got the lady of the house, a loud, brash woman who punctuated her sentences with 'goddamn' and 'awesome' and, now and again, 'goddamn awesome.' Having shouted highlights of the conversation to her husband in the background, she finally rang off telling me I was a real knight in shining armour, a true romantic. I was completely taken aback by this exuberance, especially as I was a complete stranger to her. And I didn't really understand what she meant either, but the activity of the airport soon distracted me and I turned my thoughts to the flight ahead.

If Heathrow was busy, it was nothing compared to Chicago O'Hare. Having passed through passport control, I waded through the noise and madness and headed for the exit sign. Outside it was blowing a blizzard. Visibility was down to just a few feet, and the wind instantly numbed my face. Peering ahead, I noticed an official-looking man waving his arms around and relentlessly blowing a whistle. I went up to him to ask if this was the taxi rank. He was so wrapped up it was hard even to make out his eyes, and instead of giving me an answer, he just blew his whistle in my face. Suddenly a guy jumped into view through the snowflakes, took my holdall and threw it in the boot of his taxi. Whistle Man pointed to the door. I climbed in, beaten already by the wind and cold. I told my taxi driver the address and off we sped through snow so thick that I couldn't see where we were going. I wasn't sure he could either so, sitting back, I crossed my fingers and hoped we'd survive the journey.

Progress was slow and an hour later we finally hit the suburbs, driving past outrageously large gates protecting outrageously large houses. We found the right house and after decoding the intercom controls, gained entry through the powered gates. We drove through, stunned into silence by the enormous house in front of us. I paid the driver and approached what I thought was the front door. It wasn't. After a few more wrong doors and a lot of bouncing up and down to glimpse through windows, I was noticed. A smartly dressed woman greeted me with a huge cheer, 'Duncan, all the way from England!' and then gave me a massive hug. I followed her through to a kitchen that was the size of Bert's entire bungalow, where she got me a drink and started shouting through to various people to come and meet me. A procession of friends and family duly appeared, all very enthusiastic in their welcome. One of them said how touched they were by my decision to come all this way to see Caroline. They marvelled at how romantic I was, and were sure that Caroline would be won over. Not quite sure what they meant, I showed them my street sign, explaining why I'd brought it with me.

'Oh,' they cooed, 'Caroline will do a U-turn when you show her that.'

I just nodded. Everyone was being so nice and friendly, but they didn't seem to understand about me and Caroline at all. Eventually I was shown to my room. It was stunning; vast, richly decorated and with fabulous furniture.

'Duncan,' I thought to myself, 'you have finally arrived.'

I politely enquired about Caroline, but the lady of the house finally seemed lost for words. She muttered something about how sure she was that we would be able to sort things out and then told me to unpack, settle in and come down for dinner whenever I was ready. So I had a shower, changed my clothes and then headed back downstairs, clutching my street sign. I was ushered into a ballroom-sized lounge and introduced to the lady's husband, who shook my hand and offered me a drink. We talked about business. Caroline had clearly told them all about what I'd done - but not about how each of my ventures had ended - so I just went along with it, pretending to be some kind of trainee Donald Trump. Finally, I noticed Caroline enter the room and went straight over to give her a hug and a kiss. Because I was nervous and excited, I didn't catch on to her embarrassed and slightly chilly welcome. Nor did I notice the man standing behind her.

Caroline walked me over to the corner of the room, her gaze fixed firmly on the floor. I knew instantly that there was a problem and my stomach tightened as Caroline finally looked me in the eye.

'I can't believe you're here,' she said. 'Why did you come?'

'What do you mean, why did I come?'

'I phoned and left a message. And I phoned the following day to make sure you'd got it.'

'What message?' I asked, feeling increasingly uneasy.

'You must have done. He said he'd told you.'

The room went quiet and the penny dropped. I sighed.

'You've met someone else, haven't you?'

She nodded and pointed to the guy she'd come in with. I was lost for words. I'd been travelling for two days, with a road sign and to another continent, just to sit in some stately home and get dumped. Caroline left the room. Stunned, I finished my drink, hoping she'd come back in and say it was a mistake. She didn't, so I quietly walked out and began climbing the stairs. The lady of the house called up to me.

'Gee. Didn't work out then?'

I just shook my head.

'You're welcome to stay.'

I thanked her but explained that, under the circumstances, it would be best if I just packed and went. Nodding her agreement, she said a servant would call for a cab to take me back to the airport.

When I was done, I sneaked a final look at Caroline sitting next to Mr America, all hunky and clean cut. A large grandfather clock in the hallway told me I'd been there for slightly less than three hours. Caroline came through to say my cab was coming up the drive. I forced a smile, not sure what else to do. She gave me a hug, wished me luck and told me how sorry she was about how things had turned out. With a shrug I opened the door and walked outside, straight into a blizzard of horizontal snow.

'What about the road sign?' she shouted. 'Can I have it?'

I couldn't think what to say and just carried on walking.

Sitting in the back of the cab, I realised that it wasn't Caroline's fault. She'd been a good friend to me, a real port in the many storms I'd found myself in. All I wanted to do now was go back home and curl up in a ball. But I didn't have a home, just some money and a bottomless reserve of positive thinking. I rallied myself; by the time the plane touches down, I thought, I'd have a plan and be back in business. Fate, however, had other ideas.

'What do you mean I can't change my ticket?' I asked. The woman at the airport desk explained. All I could do was buy another ticket for next day travel, but that would wipe out all my funds. And the snow was getting worse, threatening major delays. Wandering over to a row of seats to have a think, I noticed a Greyhound Bus ticket desk nearby. The only place in the States I knew anything about was Florida, so I asked if it was anywhere near. The Greyhound woman's silence and raised eyebrow made it clear it wasn't. She showed me a small framed map and pointed to Chicago.

'Aah, that's where we are,' I said. Her eyebrows shot up again. I then spotted New York a bit to the right of Chicago. It seemed really close, and my head immediately filled with images of the city that doesn't sleep. I was an entrepreneur. It was a match made in heaven. I booked a return trip.

There was just enough time to phone Bert and I wanted to know if Caroline really had left a message with him. But all I got was a semi-conscious, 'Ay,' 'Ay' and occasionally, 'What ay.' I resorted to shouting down the phone, causing people to stop and stare.

'Have there been any messages from a girl for me?' I boomed.

'Yes,' he said, his fuzzy brain at last tuning in. 'You're not to go to America. You need to phone her ASAP. Why? Is there a problem?'

I hung up and headed for my bus.

☙

As we were about to depart, the driver announced the ports of call on our sixteen hour journey to New York. I just laughed. It could be sixteen days as long as it took me somewhere warmer than Chicago. Then we were off. Occasionally we'd stop to change bus, or to grab a drink and a snack, but otherwise we kept going, hurrying through small towns and along the big, empty open road. I spent hours looking out of the window, with plenty of time to think about what I was going to do. Whatever hand was dealt me, nothing could ever be as hard as the past. I felt I could do anything I wanted. If anything, I had too much choice. I decided not to focus on the future, and just to enjoy the next few days. Then, eventually, I dozed off.

When I woke, I sat bolt upright and looked at the bus clock - 09:35, a total of two hours sleep. But it didn't matter at all. All around me was New York! And it was exactly as I'd always imagined: skyscrapers, steam coming up through manhole covers, policemen standing in the middle of the road blowing their whistles at vehicles, drivers blasting their horns, sirens everywhere. And people everywhere, of all sizes, fashions and colours, walking or running as if their lives depended on it. Total mayhem.

As we crawled into the bus station, a fellow greyhounder gave me directions to Times Square, whatever that was. I was told it was only a few blocks, whatever they were, and assured it was where it all happened, whatever that... So I got off the coach, clutching my street sign which I was now firmly attached to and which had proved a useful conversation opener on the bus. During one of several amiable chats with other passengers, I'd learned many facts about New York, including summer temperatures which could top one hundred. Not today, however. It was so cold they could have called it Chicago. I put my chin down and stepped forwards, almost carried by the wave of people around me. Reaching a corner, I stopped. To a young Brummie from The Land of Drizzle, this was like a fairytale. The noise, the billboards, the buildings stretching forever upwards, the smell of the restaurants and the hot dog stands, everything was captivating. The cold, however, reminded me I needed a place to stay. Picking a side street at random, the scenery changed within a few footsteps. I was suddenly surrounded by filth, litter, porn cinemas and sex shops. The look on people's faces said it all - this was deprivation of the highest order.

'Sod this,' I thought. 'I'm on my holidays,' and headed straight back out of there and walked a few blocks before coming across the Plaza Hotel. There was no messing - I went straight in, took the lift up to reception, paid cash and went to my room. And then it hit me, the accumulated effects of all the travel, the emotional hits and the excitement of the Big Apple. I fell on the bed and pretty much passed out with exhaustion.

Waking early, I did the sums again. Well over twelve hours sleep this time. Fully recharged, feeling on the wave of opportunity and lifted by Manhattan, I decided to explore. But first I stopped for a coffee and people-watched. A quick survey revealed that here you either slept in a doorway or you made it big time and travelled in a limo. There was a madness that appealed to me. By lunchtime, I'd been all over town and had noticed that on most street corners there were vendors selling the usual tacky souvenirs off foldaway tables or small stalls. Plenty of people were stopping and buying this stuff, but I noticed that the sellers looked and dressed worse than I had when I'd been sleeping rough. Then, when I saw someone approach to relieve them of their takings, I understood what was going on. Pretty much everything I've done in my life has been driven by a combination of instinct, 'Why not?' and 'Who knows where this might lead?' And it was this that took me over the road and up to one of the larger street stalls. An idea was forming in my head.

The street vendor was in mid-discussion with what I took to be his area manager. My initial inquiry produced nothing more than a suggestion, in a thick Spanish accent, that I check out the stall's wares. I shook my head and asked who was in charge. The older of the two guys, standing tall and pigeon-chested, said it was him.

'No, no,' I went on. 'Who is in charge of you?'

'Who are you?' he replied.

'I am from England and I have something for your boss which will make us all lots of dollars.'

It was a simple enough pitch, but the conversation that followed dragged on for an hour until a small chap, considerably better dressed, turned up. Then all three of them started arguing in Spanish, occasionally pointing at me and pulling faces, until I was invited to explain once more. At last the new arrival seemed to grasp the situation and shook my hand. He told me his name was Gee. When I told him mine, he kept repeating it back as 'Dunecoon.' I smiled and suggested they all just called me D. After another ten minutes of batting things back and forth, Gee left, telling me to follow him. We took the subway and emerged in a residential area straight out of Kojak, but I was so busy keeping up with Gee that there was no time to feel fear or apprehension. I asked him where we were.

'Hell's Kitchen.'

'That sounds like a description of my last landlord's cooking,' I replied, but the joke went over his head.

He led me into a run-down apartment building and up some shabby stairs, before stopping to knock on a door. A well-dressed man opened it and stared at me throughout his conversation, in Spanish, with Gee. I offered some smiles and thumbs-up even though, for all I knew, they were discussing how to dispose of my body. But I think my innocent enthusiasm worked because Gee and I were at last invited into the apartment. And what a contrast to the shabby surroundings! The place was beautifully done out and had to be where all that street-stall money ended up.

I was offered a drink and asked for a cup of tea. Instead, I got a small black coffee and a shot glass full of a mystery liquid to be downed in one. The drink made me cough, and the coffee was no comfort to my burned voice box. So, with my voice no more than a hoarse whisper and having not a single word of Spanish, I was reduced to playing charades in a bid to cut a deal. My aeroplane impressions just didn't cut it, for me or for him, and eventually, having tired of my theatrics, he shouted for someone to come in and help out. In walked a gorgeous girl, about my age and with beautiful olive skin. She was, to my excited eyes, pretty much perfect in every way, and my mouth just dropped open as I swiftly fell in love with her. In perfect English, she explained that her name was Marisol and her family were originally from Puerto Rico. If I'd paid more attention in geography, I would have had some idea where that was, but it didn't matter - I was mesmerised. And even another round of drinks, served by a lady who I was already regarding as my future mother-in-law, failed to dampen my desire.

Now that I could actually explain who I was and what I was there for, I could see the main man warming to me. I came straight to the point and told them about my idea to sell British street signs to American tourists. There followed a round of creased frowns. Eager not to lose my new momentum, I started mentioning all the London roads I thought a typical American might have heard of - Baker Street, Downing Street, all the famous touristy places - and thank goodness this registered with Marisol, who then took over the negotiations and fought my corner for me. We eventually agreed to meet up again the next day, when I would bring them a sample sign. Finally, Gee took me back to Times Square.

I learned something from that first meeting which has stayed with me ever since - doing deals is all about instinct and trust is a handshake, no more, no less. Back at the hotel, I was on a serious high, so proud of myself for seeing an opportunity and just throwing myself at it. I felt like I could take on the world (once I'd bought myself a map).

The next day, smartly dressed and with my street sign, I met up again with Gee. He'd arranged for me to meet up with half a dozen people at a local restaurant a few blocks from the hotel, and once inside, we all exchanged handshakes and then each downed a glass of the same fiery liquid that had stripped my teeth of enamel the previous day. I barely noticed though, my world suddenly brightening when I saw that the increasingly lovely Marisol was also there. She smiled hello and told me the drink was a type of clear rum, which explained a lot. Formalities over, I stood up to sell my idea to the folks at the table, with Marisol translating when required. I showed them my sample and told them that they'd need to manufacture the signs as exact replicas of the London originals, with every detail correct down to the postcode and borough. I added that I'd provide all the names and on the job training, but it was sales flannel; I'd need as much training as anyone else.

They all nodded and seemed interested, leaving just one wrinkle to be ironed out - the money. Instinct told me that while these guys were probably very tight with the stuff, they'd understand the concept of speculating to accumulate. If anything, I think their only issue was whether to trust a complete stranger from abroad who'd popped up unsolicited with a comprehensive business proposition. Through Marisol, I told them that if it worked, I'd still only have about six days here before I had to return home. All I asked for was enough money to live on until then.

'And not like your street sellers,' I added.

Their loud laughter broke the tension, definitely a good sign. However, the meeting went on through lunch and into the evening, but the hospitality was second-to-none. We were served traditional dishes – calf's kidney, beef tongue - washed down with different coloured rums and strong coffee. My insides and my head were taking a battering, and when I nearly collapsed face first into dessert, I knew I had to leave. Staggering upright, I thanked Marisol for her help and gave her the street sign as a gift. She smiled that smile again and told me to go round to Gee's the next morning.

Outside, the bitter wind sobered me up just enough to amble back the half mile to the Plaza. But by the time I got there, I was wide awake again and deciding it was far too early for bed, I headed for the famous Broadway 49 bar and ordered a beer. Two men sitting at the bar invited me to join them. Normally I'd have been on my guard, but I picked up the Brummie accent immediately and guessed they must have heard mine. Sitting there in New York, that sound from home was too hard to resist and I immediately got chatting. They turned out to be a couple of executives from a brewery and proceeded to drink me under the table, and all on their expense account.

Next morning, I woke up on their bathroom floor, still fully dressed, having been drinking my way through the hotel's entire cocktail menu. After trying several rooms, attempting to locate mine, they'd eventually given up and dragged me by my legs into theirs. Now I was awake, they invited me to join them for breakfast. I just nodded and staggered off to my room to shower and change my clothes before joining them in the dining room. I couldn't face the bacon, eggs, waffles and gallon of coffee, and just sat staring bleary-eyed at a pillar, trying to follow the conversation. Suddenly, through the fog, my brain latched onto something they were saying about the fortune I was going to make.

'I'm sorry,' I said, 'but I don't know what you're on about.'

'The bar you want to open!' came the reply. 'It's a brilliant idea. It's you who'll make it the place to be. And 'Ridler's' is such a great name.'

The fog closed in again fast.

'Erm, could you explain it to me again?'

'No time. Let's meet again tonight at about 9 o'clock.'

I agreed, hoping they didn't mean a bar in Manhattan. I was, after all, only going to be there for another six days.

Meanwhile, back on the day job, I visited Gee at his Hell's Kitchen apartment, a cramped place full of children. His wife and Marisol were also there offering treacle-coloured coffee along with the customary shot of throat anaesthetic and extra strong cigarettes. I began to wonder whether my taste buds would ever recover from this trip. We worked for most of the day; I'd describe what the signs looked like and Marisol would do the design. They'd already sorted out the manufacturing side, so I added some additional colour by explaining where the streets were and what their names meant. To be honest, I was making it up as I went along, winging it, but that was pretty much how I lived my life. Finally, having agreed to meet up near my hotel and go over any loose ends, I got up to leave. As Marisol was showing me out, I dared myself to ask if we could meet up again later on. She nodded and suggested 11pm, giving me the name of a bar, and my confidence rocketed to skyscraper heights.

Earlier that night, I met up with my new brewery friends and at last I found out about the mysterious Ridler's Bar. Immediately I spotted all kinds of problems with the concept such as finance, premises and how to pull a decent pint, but they brushed these 'mere details' aside. They were well ahead of me in their thinking, with plans to find a run-down building to renovate and the promise to help fund the enterprise. They had even provided for my bar training, scribbling down the details of a man who worked at a hotel near Gloucester. He could offer me a half decent salary, accommodation and training.

'Duncan,' Barry went on, 'we're deadly serious. The drinking scene is changing from pubs to bars selling fancy bottled beer, dance music and themed nights. What have you got to lose? In five days' time, you're out of here and back home and unless you've a better plan, you'll probably be back living on that park bench.'

God, I thought, I must have told them the whole story the night before! Mind you, put like that, their offer did seem very persuasive, so I took their business cards and agreed to give it all some serious thought. Truth be told, their enthusiasm had already won me over. But my mind was now on other things, as it was almost time to meet up with Marisol. I located the bar and found her with a few friends. I'd hoped to be her sole companion, but guessed she wanted them to check me out. All fine by me, my intentions were honourable. Over drinks, I learned that this was only the second date she'd ever had, hopefuls having to be approved first by her father. I must have made a decent impression on him, but the time went so quickly and an hour passed in what felt like minutes. Before I knew it, Marisol was heading off for a cab. But before she left, she turned and kissed me on the cheek. That was it. I was in love.

My last few days were spent overseeing the street sign business as it grew from concept to reality. Every stall started stocking them, and I also suggested that they have blank signs so a customer could have the design of their choice. A side-line in American signs would massively expand the market. In the early evenings, I'd meet up with my brewery friends for cocktails. Their business plan was convincing enough, but something was holding me back. Could I really swap Manhattan and the most beautiful girl in the world for sleepy old Middle England? As if being given the answer, I'd then meet up with Marisol and we would chat for hours like old friends who share a secret sense of humour. I skirted round any talk of my return to the UK for as long as I could but now, being my last night, it was unavoidable. One last meeting with her father so that he could pay me for my living expenses, and then I'd be off. I didn't want to go, and Marisol didn't want me to go, but with no money, what else could I do? I checked out of my hotel, using the rest of my money, and left my holdall with the concierge while I headed out to Hell's Kitchen for the final time. Drinks were served as usual but Marisol wasn't there, and when I politely enquired, her father didn't explain, talking instead about my journey home and subsequent plans. I couldn't really answer that so he sat back in his big chair and looked me straight in the eye.

'You stay in New York,' he said.

Well, of course I wanted to! But I told him my money had gone and I knew the street sign venture had been a long shot. His response was to throw a thick envelope over to me.

'You stay now,' he said. 'Your idea very good, make us all money.'

I wanted to get outside and see if this was dollars or ripped-up newspaper. As I left, he shouted out that Marisol would meet me at the bar, same time as usual. I smiled, thanked him and went outside. The envelope was full of fifty dollar bills. Six thousand dollars all in. I checked back into the hotel and upgraded. I'd come a long way in a short space of time - from my freezing bench to a New York hotel suite. Looking out of my window across Manhattan, I was ecstatic and decided to celebrate with a good cup of English tea. All I needed was a kettle and some tea bags. The bellboy claimed not to know what these were but when offered a hefty tip, scurried off to track them down. I was loaded and for the next few days was living the dream, doing a little work with my partners but mostly spending time with Marisol. With things between us getting pretty intense, I was nervous but not surprised when she told me one morning that we were to meet her father, just the three of us.

The meeting started with the customary firm handshake followed by drinks and food. We talked about me and my future, and a bit about my family. Then he asked me if I had considered making my move more permanent.

'Who knows?' I replied, thinking *where is this heading?*

'It's down to money,' I went on. 'Plus, am I allowed to stay in America?'

According to him, neither issue was a problem. He then whispered to Marisol, who blushed and nodded, before addressing me again.

'I want you to move in with Marisol.' I don't know what I was expecting, but it wasn't that.

'You mean I come and live here with Marisol?'

'Yes. You will be looked after and we need you for the business.'

Marisol was now nodding at me, but I was totally taken aback. Mumbling embarrassed thanks, I said I'd need to give it some thought. Marisol's father sat back in his chair with a look that told me I hadn't given him the right answer. However, as I left the restaurant, I thought *this is it!* I felt proud and honoured that in such a short space of time I had met a group of people from a totally different culture and way of life and, out of mutual respect, we had formed a bond. And I had met a fantastic, wonderful girl. And...

...then my bloody instincts kicked in. This wasn't right, I just knew it - but what exactly was *wrong*? Why was there a loud, clear voice in my head telling me not to do this? I had various theories - I was too young, I needed to continue devising my own journey, create new deals, not settle down and help run someone else's company. Maybe I even missed something about home? Probably a bit of all of these, but more than anything, I knew I should trust this instinct. Even if it meant losing the gorgeous Marisol. I went straight back to my hotel room and sat staring out of the window. It was a long way up and I felt like a kid on a diving board looking down with his stomach churning as he prepared to leap into the unknown. Suddenly the answer became clear. I knew the right thing should be to see Marisol and discuss my reasons. She deserved that, at the very least. But with her father in the picture, a clean break was the kinder option. So I packed, settled my bill and was leaving the hotel when I saw the bellboy. He shrugged to indicate his lack of success in finding me a kettle, but I had an idea.

'Do me a favour,' I told him. 'We'll call it quits if you get me a cab and if anyone asks after me, you haven't seen me leave. Deal?'

'Deal.'

I jumped into the taxi.

'Airport please,' I said.

'JFK?' asked the cabbie.

'No, London,' I replied, not realising New York had more than one airport.

At the airport ticket desk I handed over most of the money from the envelope. For just one brief moment, I hesitated. Here I was, paying through the nose to leave behind a place that was truly magnificent: the people, the buildings, the extreme weather, the way everyone seemed to move in the same direction. But it didn't matter. I had made my decision. And in a few hours, I'd be on the plane back to England. I would phone Marisol just before boarding.

CHAPTER EIGHT

I opened the front door and walked in slowly. With Bert's memory so unreliable, I needed to be on my toes. The first time I'd been gone for a day he'd forgotten who I was; God knows how he'd react now. To me, it felt like I'd never left. As ever, it was the odour that hit me first, and in spite of the world of smells I'd experienced in the past few weeks, there was nothing quite like Bert's house; the blended cologne of dog and booze and, above all, the true smell of being back at square one. I'd be warm and safe, but I'd also be bored shitless.

I pushed open the lounge door - situation normal, man and dog both snoring - and went to put the kettle on. This was the moment I'd been looking forward to for days, a proper cup of tea, and the first cup didn't touch the sides. After another two, I sat down at the table waiting for Bert to resurface, and looked around me. The dog on its back with its tongue hanging out and its owner fast asleep wearing a blanket of old newspaper, covered in pipe tobacco and bits of gristle. It made me glad I still had ambition and focused my mind on my own future. Tearing my eyes away from the sight, I pulled out the brewery executives' business card; on the back was written the contact details for the hotel they'd suggested for my work experience. Back in the cocktail-fuelled buzz of Manhattan, it had seemed like a brilliant idea, but now it didn't look quite so clear cut. Could someone used to making his own decisions really adapt to working for a boss - and for how long? Six months? A year? It felt like a huge step backwards and all to what - someone else's dream? It began to feel so unreal, I started thinking about staying put now I was back, get some stability, a job, a career even. I could make contact with some of my old friends from the village - even if they knew what had happened to me. We're all on one level now, I told myself, the past is the past.

Tossing the card onto the window ledge, I came to a decision. I'd get in touch with my old friends in the village. Yes, they'd hardly been sympathetic in the past, but we'd be on an equal footing now, just getting on with life. I started to dial various people but the conversations were one-sided, no one mentioning anything about my past exploits or about me being homeless. So I didn't mention it either, instead spinning my US adventure as a trip to see my girlfriend. It slipped out that a big group of them were meeting at a large country pub that very night, so I asked for a lift. No one had any space. I understood and said I'd meet them there. But when I put the phone down, I felt a wave of sadness which I couldn't quite diagnose. Maybe I was grieving for my lost life of fortune-making at the click of a finger. Or was this just a temporary U-turn?

Eventually both dog and master woke up and Bert turned his head very slowly round to me, then frowned a little and sat there, staring.

'How are you Bert?' I said, smiling.

Nothing. Maybe the dog would remember me, I thought, but she just growled and danced back and forth, trying to make her mind up whether to bite me or not. Bert turned, ignored this and seemed to be trying to get his tongue and lips back into action. I watched his eyes and could see the cogs slowly moving in his head, dispersing the whisky fog. Finally, Bert recovered the power of speech, his opening comment finally putting me in my place.

'Did you get any milk, Darren?'

Faced with an evening of confusion with Bert, I decided to chance it at the pub. When I got there, I saw about twenty people taking up a whole alcove in a corner of the pub, amongst them some familiar faces. I felt wary, unsure of my welcome, and then noticed one of my old mates waiting to be served at the bar. I went up and tapped him on the shoulder.

'How are you?' I asked.

'What are you doing here?' he replied.

'I made a few phone calls and found out where you all were.'

'Oh, right. Heard you were skint, parents kicked you out and were sleeping rough.'

I half smiled and brushed it all to one side, which was fine by him. He told me he had to get his girlfriend a drink and said we'd talk later.

Clutching my pint, I approached the alcove and nodded and smiled at the group. Most of them went quiet, others smirked and there were various comments as I sat down facing the crowd. I tried making conversation but soon exhausted my topics. They were more interested in their own lives, their plans, romances and holidays. But suddenly the conversation turned back to me when one of the girlfriends shouted across.

'So, still living in a box on the canal?'

'Yeah,' said another. 'My dad even saw him asleep in the pub toilet.'

That got a laugh, as did, 'A BMW to a cardboard box? What a twat.'

Then, when the whole alcove erupted to the remark, 'Wanna buy some pallets?' I tried to join in the laughter. It was funny, even if it was at my expense, and I hoped it might be an ice breaker. But it wasn't. Comments were coming thick and fast, with people throwing one and two pence pieces at me. There was no humour attached to it now, just humiliation. To get a break from it all, I finished my pint and went up to the bar for a rcfill. By the time I got back to the table, people were getting ready to leave.

'Where's everyone off to?' I asked.

They mentioned another pub so I downed my pint and tried to tag along.

'Any chance of a lift?'

'Sorry mate, we're full.'

Finally I got the message, and as their cars sped out of the car park, headlamps momentarily blinding me, the place went dark and quiet. Pulling my coat around me, I made my way to the bus stop. As I walked, however, I realised it had been the right decision to try the pub, and the sadness I felt earlier had completely gone. In its place was a stimulating rush of renewed determination.

The next morning I phoned the hotel recommended to me by the brewery executives. The person I was passed to was Gordon, the restaurant manager who, having accepted my explanation for calling, spoke at length in a very broad Glaswegian accent about Rangers FC. Football not being my strong point, he might as well have been talking to Bert's dog, or even Bert himself. Had I understood the accent, I'd have realised he was also slipping in information about the hotel and its operations. In the end, I did establish that he wanted me to come down and see him the next day. I agreed straight away, hung up and then phoned the hotel's reception for directions. My last call was to Taxi Tel who agreed to help, even though it meant phoning in sick.

Sweeping through the picturesque gateway and on up the driveway the next morning, we both looked at what had originally been a beautiful country mansion, at least two hundred years old. Tel parked carefully alongside the manicured lawns and I walked through the front door into an interior every bit as magnificent. A receptionist directed me to a conservatory where I sat down and waited for Gordon, taking in the amazing views, well-tended lawns sweeping down to a golf course on one side and the Gloucestershire countryside on the other. Eventually a waiter appeared and poured me a cup of tea with great elegance.

'You're the new barman?' he asked in a rather high voice and then, before I could answer, introduced himself as Steven. I opened my mouth to say hello but again he got in first, shooting a look at me. 'And please, do not call me Steve,' he flicked his head back. 'It offends me. Bricklayers are called Steve.'

And with that, he flounced off like a model down a catwalk, pausing midway to turn and add a final piece of information. 'Oh, and Gordon is a real bitch.'

Right on cue, Gordon entered the room briskly, immaculately dressed, very pale and with jet black hair. He exuded an air of authority and wasted little time on pleasantries before launching into my interview. To my relief, he wasn't interested in my past history, merely that I came highly recommended. That was good enough for him. He got up and gestured for me to follow.

'And this is your bar,' he said, 'not very big but fully functional.'

I was no expert but it certainly looked the part, so I just nodded.

'Maybe you can introduce one of your cocktail menus?' Gordon added.

My brewery friends had obviously laid it on thick, but I was willing to play along. He then mentioned my salary, which was very low, but added that accommodation, food and tips were included.

'Any questions?' he said. 'No? Great. See you Sunday.'

And that was that. I was hired. Before I left, I called Barry from the brewery to say thank you.

'Didn't I say you'd walk it?' he said.

'Yes, but they think I'm some kind of Manhattan bottle-spinning, cocktail-barman who's decided to up sticks to Gloucester.'

'Don't worry about it,' he told me. 'The most complicated drink you'll have to serve will be a Bloody Mary. Keep your head down, learn the ropes and in a few months, you'll be opening your own place.'

We arranged to meet up in a few weeks.

Back at Bert's, I packed my holdall and while waiting for Taxi Tel to arrive, I reflected on the turn of events. It had been another rollercoaster ride, from the anguish and loneliness I'd felt when I first arrived home, to the fully restored self-belief I now experienced. In a way, that evening in the pub had been the turning point. Although I was the butt of their mockery for being a failure, each of my 'friends' presented aspects of what, for me, would be true failure - a nine-to-five job, time off to decorate a bedroom and Friday nights round the same pub table. I wanted to carry on and achieve my dream of becoming a successful entrepreneur. If I failed, it would be my own doing, but at least I was still prepared to take risks. I knew at that moment that I would open this bar, it would happen. I just didn't know how or when.

Then it was time to go, and time to say goodbye to Bert. From the very first time he'd stopped to talk to me on my canal bench, Bert had been a true friend. Loyal, uncomplicated and, once you knew his ways, totally reliable. I wanted to find the right way to thank him for everything, but communication between us had always been pretty economical. So we shook hands and I mumbled my thanks. He didn't reply until I was halfway into Tel's Granada.

'You will come back, won't you?' he said.

I was touched, but it was one question I didn't have the answer to.

My new home was in number three bungalow at the back of the hotel, well away from the grand public areas and surrounded by an eight foot concrete fence. Before I could open the door, Steven flung it open wearing a black satin dressing gown that didn't leave much to the imagination.

'Oh 'ello!' he said, his voice even camper than when we first met. 'I always get the newbies. Make yourself at home. Let's put the kettle on and then I'll show you your room.'

Inside there was another guy lying on the settee and wearing a matching dressing gown.

'Roger, my partner,' explained Steven.

'Er - maybe I should unpack first?' I suggested.

They both sighed in unison, looking up at the ceiling, and then Steven agreed to show me my room. It was small. Very small, with its one little window giving a detailed outlook onto the concrete wall. I unpacked and we headed off to the hotel for staff dinner. The rear was a stark contrast to the front, a warren of beer crates and food waste bins, concrete floors sticky with God knows what, and extraction fans chucking out the invasive stench of cooking grease. Dotted around were staff, smoking and gossiping. Steven led me through to the kitchens to show me where our food was kept. Staff lived on heated-up leftovers and today's feast was a full English breakfast. Fine by me, although Steven warned I'd be fed up after five days of the same thing. I had just begun to help myself when a roar erupted in the room. It sounded like a bear and, looking round, I saw someone who did indeed resemble a bear.

'That's Chef,' whispered Steven, 'don't mess.'

Chef came over, followed closely by half a dozen of his kitchen cubs. I smiled and said hello.

'You're the Brummie barman,' he bellowed at me in a Scottish accent.

'I am.'

'And is it true that all Brummies are fuckwits who only drink Vimto?'

I guessed I was meant to say, 'Yes, Chef,' but opted instead for a bit of friendly banter.

'No,' I said. 'I think you mean the people who work in kitchens.'

The other staff took a sharp collective intake of breath as Chef swooped in close and clamped a great big shovel of a hand round my neck. Before I had time to let go of my dinner, he lifted me off my feet and sent me flying through the air to land in a heap somewhere beyond the kitchen. Steven followed me out of the kitchen.

'Come on,' he said, as if nothing much had happened. 'I'll show you where the tea and coffee is.'

Gordon appeared and tapped me on the back.

'You've met Chef, then,' he said.

'I have, indeed.'

'Don't worry about it,' said Gordon, shrugging his shoulders. 'His name's Jeff, but we call him Chef Bad Bastard. Just remember that as far as he's concerned, it's always the kitchen versus the restaurant.'

A tall, thin, young man then appeared, and Gordon introduced him as Thierry from Paris. He was on work placement to improve his English, but rather than demonstrating it for me, he kept his greeting to a silent nod. We then stood there, looking at Gordon.

'OK, team,' said Gordon. 'This is Duncan, our new cocktail barman. He'll be in charge of the bar and all the surrounding rooms.'

My eyes flickered from left to right, expecting to see the rest of the team; but no, this was it - a Brummie with nil experience of bar work and a reticent Frenchman in need of English practice. As I didn't officially start until the next morning, Gordon invited me to tag along with him to the pub. It was a classic village inn full of hanging tankards, rosy cheeks and green wellies. When I was introduced to the landlord as the hotel's new barman 'straight from mixing cocktails in Manhattan,' I knew that if I didn't come clean I wouldn't even make it to my first shift. But Gordon's only interest was in making me down pints and shots of Drambuie. When we hit the second round of drinks, I decided to go for it.

'Gordon, there must be a misunderstanding. I'm not a cock-tail barman.'

Gordon took a massive gulp from his pint and looked at me.

'You are a barman though,' he stated, wiping his lips with the back of his hand.

'Not really,' I paused. 'But I'm willing to learn.'

'You mean you've never worked behind a bar?'

'No.' Now it was all out in the open, my optimism about the job was weakening.

'But you're supposed to know all about cocktails!'

'The only cocktail I know is a Mickey Mouse - half lager, half bitter. Sorry.'

Gordon, now looking totally confused, was quiet for a moment.

'But you came highly recommended,' he said eventually, before walking to the bar to order more drinks. When he returned, he sounded more positive.

'Tell you what,' he said, 'you're here now, so I'll give you a week. If you survive that then you're hired.'

Next morning, the first in my new job, I woke up in a clapped-out Nissan with the sound of seagulls bouncing off the roof. Gordon had dragged me to the clubs of Weston-super-Mare and we clearly hadn't made it back. But I was half dead and due on duty in half an hour, so I roused Gordon and we made our way back. Steven greeted me at my bungalow in a bright pink satin number. I hadn't even unpacked from the day before but luck-ily for me, Steven had. Everything had been put away and my clothes were on a rail, my shirts were ironed and ready, and my uniform was laid out on the bed. I was gobsmacked but grateful. Steven instructed me to have a shower while he made me some tea and toast.

It was mid-morning and the hotel seemed dead, except for a bubbly blonde receptionist who was laughing and joking on the phone. I went over to her and waited patiently for her to finish up her call. Ten minutes later, I finally managed to catch her eye, which stopped her in mid-conversation.

'Can I help you?'

'I'm the new barman. Is there anyone supposed to meet me?'

Without a word, she put the receiver down on the counter and passed me a large bunch of keys and a till tray with about £200 in notes. Then she picked the phone up again and carried on with her conversation. As I headed for the bar, she shouted, 'I haven't had time to sort the till.' Not having a clue what she meant, I just gave her the thumbs up and went on my way. Plenty of time later to ask questions, I thought. There was bound to be someone who would help me.

Apart from the floor, sticky with spilled drink, everything about the bar reeked of quality. But even without any experience, I could tell something wasn't quite right. I quickly realised it was the stock - rows and rows of tomato juice and bitter lemon and plenty of Martini Rosso, Galliano and Advocaat, alongside a whole shelf of peppermint cordial. But that was it. The rest of the shelves were pretty much empty, apart from a hundred or so half pint glasses with chunky handles - just the thing for exotic cocktails. Stock check over, I spent the next half hour trying to open the till. There must have been a hundred keys on this bunch but none of them fitted. I stuck my head round the door towards Reception but she was still on the phone, so I decided instead to sort out the gummy floor. Moments later, the receptionist came through to tell me that the beer delivery had arrived. As I still couldn't open the till, I had to take the cash tray with me as I tried to find the cellar. The Reception phone was busy again and all I got was a vague nod in the general direction of a doorway. I asked if I could leave the cash with her but she mouthed that she was off shift in five minutes.

My quest to find the cellar took me all over the place, through a magnificent ballroom, a conservatory, and in and out of the kitchens along the way. Finally, catching sight of a delivery lorry driving off, I located some barrels of lager and bitter, and yellow crates stacked six high by a door. Of course it was locked, but through trial and error I eventually selected the right key from my bunch. The door opened. Inside, the floor was covered with yet more barrels and yellow crates containing either tomato juice or bitter lemon. As I took in the sight, the receptionist re-appeared.

'Customer,' she said.

A customer. My first customer! She was an old lady dressed in white and sporting a very large tartan beret. Definitely a golfer.

'How can I help you?' I asked, praying she just wanted a half pint of Advocat.

She explained that she'd just finished a round of golf with two friends, and then ordered a Moscow Mule, a Pink Gin and a Henry. She placed ten pounds on the bar and wondered whether I would be a sweetie and bring them over to their table. I played for time, moving glasses and bottles about until she sat down, and then hot-footed it to Reception where, to my relief, a different girl sat behind the desk. And she wasn't on the phone either. But when I asked her about the drinks, she replied in a broad Gloucestershire accent that she only drank cider and black. My shoulders dropped. I had no choice but to return to the bar and come clean with my customers, who were initially sympathetic, until I discovered that we had no vodka or ginger beer for the Moscow Mule nor any gin, pink or any other colour. I said I could check the barrels for the Angostura Bitter and that just left the 'Henry' - orange juice and lemonade - only we had no juice.

'I can offer you a nice peppermint cordial.'

Silence.

I apologised and offered them three teas on the house, which they accepted, saving me any further humiliation. After that, there were no further customers, so I busied myself learning how to pour a pint without a six inch head of foam and then set about cleaning the bar to within an inch of its sticky life.

At dinner, I collared Steven, Thierry and Gordon to discuss the problems I'd encountered, from having no change through to the bizarre stock. Their answers were so nonchalant that I realised, of course, I was just another employee now - no one lost any sleep over each other's problems. But being used to taking responsibility as a boss, I felt the buck stopped with me anyway. If there was a problem, however small, I still took it personally. I'd let those three ladies down at lunch and it bothered me.

༄

Day two, and I got to work by nine, even though my shift didn't start until two. I bumped into Gordon.

'Let's do your induction,' he said, 'and I'll give you a guided tour.'

We went straight to a small door and then down a concrete staircase to the hotel wine cellar, which also housed the spirits I couldn't find the day before. His eyes lit up when I asked about all the wine that was laid down in the cellar. The standard house wine aside, every other bottle was like a child to him. Reaching for one after another from different years or vineyards, he explained in great detail why each was so precious. I couldn't knock his enthusiasm, but wondered how someone who habitually downed pints and chasers, accompanying a diet of fried food, could possibly be such a wine buff. The rest of the tour was less detailed.

'You can drink through there, eat through there and sleep up there,' he said, pointing in various different directions.

Within a few days, I'd grasped the basics of how a hotel operated and why everyone was obsessed with GP - gross profit. It mattered to all staff from the general manager, Chef Bad Bastard and Gordon all the way down to me. If you got over sixty percent GP, it triggered your bonus, and with basic salaries living up to their name, this meant everything to these guys. I also learned about the hotel politics. At its heart was restaurant staff versus kitchen, while front of house would just take on anyone. Then there was the back office, which included accounts, sales and the general manager, although the furthest they got was the noticeboard where all events and internal memos were posted. And then there was the temporary conference and banqueting manager who everyone used as an excuse when things went wrong. The kitchen hated him as they had to cook in bulk, and Gordon hated him as his clients only ever ordered house wine. Reception hated him as people attending his events were always asking for directions to the toilets, where to hang their coats, etc. Meanwhile, I got on with running the bar. I wanted to get it running smoothly, mainly to make my life easier, but also remembering why I was here. I often phoned Barry from the brewery and sometimes we'd meet up so he could make fun of my situation, but he was right on the money; I was gaining invaluable experience for running my own bar.

By the time spring came a couple of months later, I'd settled into a routine, starting mid-afternoon and then working straight through until close. This could be as late as two in the morning if residents decided to stay up drinking, but I'd end up selling them the good brandy or the expensive malt whisky. This kept Gordon happy. I would then stagger back to the staff stalag and plan my own bar. I had piles of brochures and costings telling me two things quite clearly - it was going to be a very expensive venture and it was going to take a mound of work to pull off.

One day, grabbing a quick smoke out the back of the kitchens, I noticed a black and white dog out of the corner of my eye. It was a Collie cross, leaving the kitchens at speed with a string of cooked sausages in its mouth. I shouted to the chefs but it was too late. I did, however, learn that the dog was called Hobson and belonged to Nicola, the front of house manager who had been off on leave. She was Scottish and apparently rather feisty, and she lived in the farmhouse a quarter of a mile away at the edge of the hotel grounds. Only long-standing and highly-regarded employees were allowed to live there. I didn't think any more of it at the time, except for the occasional sudden and strong desire to be a top employee living the life of Reilly in that farmhouse. My thoughts were firmly on my future bar.

On my days off, I would explore the local towns and cities looking for a suitable venue. The brewery had made a provisional business offer providing I could find a good site, and the bank was prepared to back me with the rest of the money. So, apart from the premises, I just needed to stump up ten per cent of the total funds. Seeing as I was living for next to nothing - my wages and tips were just waiting for me in the bank - this wouldn't be a problem.

And all the time my bar experience was growing. In fact, my duties at the hotel were being extended and I was now in charge of the banqueting bar which served the magnificent ballroom connected to the hotel. With summer almost on us, it was fully booked every weekend for weddings or parties, and thank goodness there was going to be a new conference and banqueting manager. His responsibility would be the staff, leaving me to make sure the bar was well stocked and any bottles of wine that had been ordered as part of a package were brought up from the cellar ready for him to put on the tables.

I'd also started building a good rapport with the golfers and by mid-afternoon the bar would be packed. Eighteen holes generated a strong thirst, which wasn't a problem, but the equally strong appetite was. By the time the golfers were hitting the bar, the breakfast and lunch duty staff had gone and the kitchen was closed. I had nothing to offer the hungry pack other than bar snacks. I approached Chef and we negotiated simple plates of assorted sandwiches which went down a storm with the golfers - and with Chef - as we ended up taking more money from these than from the entire lunch menu in the restaurant. Chef loved me after that, and I charmed the rest of the staff by sorting out a drinks order for them once they'd finished service every

Saturday. A cold pint of lager after a long week's work proved a real morale booster.

The golfers themselves began seeing me as more than just a barman. Most days I'd have one or two members popping in to ask a favour, typically wanting VIP treatment for an important client they were meeting. So I'd reserve the best seats, offer drinks and sandwiches and explain that so and so would be along any minute. This always impressed the client, and the golfer would slip me a ten or twenty pound tip. It went down well in the hotel too as the golfers provided a vital revenue stream.

Once I'd got on the right side of Gordon and Chef, my hours improved. I only had one full day shift, Sunday, and was then off 'til Wednesday afternoon. On a particularly quiet Sunday, I was just walking past reception at five to six when I heard an unfamiliar Scottish voice demanding, 'Where the hell are you bloody going?' This voice was female and I immediately put two and two together.

'You're Nicola, with the dog who steals sausages,' I said.

'I am,' she replied. 'And you're not meant to be finished until six. Better get back behind your bar.'

Because I'd already locked up and really didn't want to open up just for five minutes, I kept her talking until six. But by then I didn't want to leave after all and ended up chatting with her for the next three hours. She wasn't nearly as feisty as she sounded; she just knew how the world turned and had a wicked sense of humour. As I walked back to the staff stalag that evening, a warmth and contentment flowed right through me and I wondered if this was what people called love at first sight. But I knew for now I'd have to sideline any feelings of that sort. I couldn't contribute anything to a relationship, not while I had grand business dreams to fulfil.

I sat watching TV with Thierry while Stevie (I was now allowed to use the diminutive version of his name) got on with the cleaning. Suddenly our little vision of domestic bliss was interrupted by someone pulling a large trunk backwards through the front door. He turned round, totally out of breath, sat down on the trunk and introduced himself in a broad Yorkshire accent as Richard, the new conference and banqueting manager. We told him he wasn't meant to be here, but in the farmhouse with the other management types. 'Besides,' I added, 'you wouldn't hit it off with Stevie, what with you being from Yorkshire.' 'I heard that!' came an outraged falsetto voice from the kitchen. Richard, however, was dithering, so we made up his mind for him by dragging his trunk back out of the door and gently pushing him with it. About an hour later, we heard a loud thud outside. It was Richard again. This time he was lying on the floor holding the handle of his trunk. It had snapped off and sent him flying. Looking up at me, he launched into a passionate speech.

'See that trunk? It's been round the world and survived two World Wars. Me grandad's going to kill me and the farmhouse is full 'cos they're expecting some student tomorrow who's due the last room.'

'You can live here,' I replied, 'but the trunk stays outside.'

Then, hearing the commotion, Stevie came through into the lounge and immediately ran out again in a panic. He was only wearing marigolds and some extraordinary ladies' underwear. Richard was struck dumb.

Early the following day, I was summoned into the back office for only the second time ever.

'Duncan, this is Max. He's joining us on a placement.'

Max was about nineteen and wore brogues with a pin stripe suit that looked as if he'd left the coat hanger in the back. He lived in Wimbledon, was at university doing a degree in business management and was most definitely upper class. His father, no surprise, was a close friend of the hotel's owner.

'You'll be showing him all about how the bar operates, and he'll be helping in conference and banqueting, too, so make sure he is OK on that front. Oh, and you two will be sharing a room.'

I was just about to protest that I already had a mad Yorkshireman on the floor when I was told that the room we'd be sharing was in the farmhouse. This was fantastic news.

Life was definitely on the up. I had the bar running perfectly, my relationship with Gordon was good, I got on well with all the other staff and the sun was shining. I even liked Richard, although his style was not to everyone's taste. He shared an office with Chef but treated it like it was all his. He'd have his feet up on the desk, smoking a cigarette and barking instructions on the phone. The guy was mad, but I loved his sledgehammer attitude, his confidence and his accent. And now I was off to the farmhouse. Packing my holdall, Stevie was flapping around, holding onto my shirt sleeve and pleading for me not to leave.

'I'm only down the road, pull yourself together. You can take care of Richard and Thierry now.'

He wasn't convinced.

'Look, if someone leaves I'll put a word in for you. I promise.'

'You will?'

'I will.'

The farmhouse was indeed a serious step up: open fire, Sky TV, games room with snooker table, and a massive kitchen. And even though I was sharing, the room had plenty of space. I sat on the bed watching Max take off his suit and put on his smoking jacket. He asked me for the low down on the staff and how I operated in my job. As I started talking, he opened his briefcase and pulled out sheets of paper and a graph he was working on.

'The small pale Glaswegian who looks like Tin Tin is Gordon. He's the restaurant manager. Treats all customers with utter contempt unless they're ordering a hundred pound plus bottle of wine. The reason he's so pale is he spends most of his time in the cellar talking to the wine and working out his gross profit.'

Max nodded approvingly, hearing a familiar financial term.

'The Chef is Scottish as well. He runs the place unofficially - cross him and he'll physically flatten you, then get you sacked.

'Nicola - reception manager from Edinburgh, bark worse than her bite but has to stand up to the others so cross her at your peril.

'Lower down the ranks you have Stevie. He can serve forty people, all à la carte, without breaking into a sweat. Thierry follows in Stevie's slipstream, usually whispering *pardon monsieur*.

'Richard is in charge of banqueting, calls a spade a spade, from up north, anti-European, slightly homophobic, living with a gay, part-time transvestite and a Frenchman.

'And me, I'm just passing through. I can show you how the place operates but I can't tell you how to get on with these guys. That's something you will only learn with experience.'

With the summer season well and truly here, the place was now packed with guests and golfers. We also had at least two weddings a week, massive earners for the hotel as they each brought in between one and two hundred extra guests. I had the bar running efficiently, which was fortunate as I always ended up helping Richard with one impending disaster or other. For all his lack of subtlety and tendency to leave everything till the last minute, I still couldn't help liking the guy. What I didn't know, however, was that he was colour-blind.

One Saturday, we had two weddings back-to-back, each involving two hundred sitting down - the full works. And, to add some spice, the first one involved the daughter of some local dignitaries. When I walked into his office, Richard was the picture of calmness - feet on the desk, smoking and wearing a terrible green suit. Hotel rules insisted that we wore good dark suits on wedding days. He told me he had everything covered, and when I checked he'd booked the casuals to work a double shift, he laughed and pointed at the booking sheets. I had to explain that they were not duplicates, but two separate events. He sat bolt upright and picked up the phone to his assistant, Colin. Colin was over fifty, an ex-facilities manager who had been on a six figure salary and drove a Morgan. He'd been made redundant but was a workaholic who needed to do a minimum of a hundred hours a week just to keep his life on track. This led to the exhaustion that caused him to drop everything, and earned him the nickname 'Colly Wobbles.'

As Richard waited for the phone to be answered, I asked him what colour his suit was. He felt his suit lapels and frowned.

'It's brown,' he said.

I just nodded. Colin burst through the door, having decided that running to the office would use up more energy than answering the phone. Richard pushed him back out while shouting, 'Double everything!' at him. He put the phone on hands-free and frantically dialled the numbers of local temp agencies and then the temporary staff themselves. Only one answered .

'Cover me while I go out and collect more staff,' Richard told me, 'just for an hour, yeah?'

'OK, but who are you getting to cover for me?'

'Tania.'

'You don't mean Tania Jam, the jam maker?'

'Yes,' Richard said, rather abruptly.

I raised my eyebrows.

'What about her nervous tic?'

'She'll be fine as long as she doesn't get flustered, and she's bound to know other people as well.'

Just then, Tania's answer machine message cut in.

'Hello, if you're in a jam and you want some jam, then you've come to the right place.'

'Bollocks!' shouted Richard, grabbing his car keys and running out of the door.

To be fair, Richard had made some preparations, like shifting the white wine up from Gordon's wine cellar to my beer cellar. But when I went to check it was nicely chilled, I realised he'd mistaken the red for the white. I remembered being told that the client had ordered the good stuff, but had no idea what it was called. Making a snap decision, I grabbed Colin, who was already leaning up against the wall nearly dead with exhaustion, and told him to get down the wine cellar.

'Just bring up anything decent - a hundred and fifty bottles - just as long as it's white.'

Then it was time for the cavalry, so I rang down to the farm-house and got Max out of bed. Soon the casual staff turned up, stating immediately that they were only here for half a day. Max came waltzing through the door, wearing black tails and looking like the groom, making a fine contrast with Colin, now drenched in sweat.

'Richard better have a plan,' I said, 'otherwise there'll be three of us serving a wedding breakfast to two hundred people, and that's before Gordon finds out his best wine has vanished on my orders.'

The first sitting went perfectly. Nicola, standing in as acting host, directed events perfectly and the bride's father was a happy man, not at all upset that his original wine choice hadn't been available. He even gave a generous tip and I handed Colin his share and asked him where Max had got to. Colin pointed into the ballroom where Max was sitting down talking to the guests, eating cheese and biscuits and drinking the wine.

'Colin,' I said, 'go and get him. He can have his lunch later.'

'What do you mean later? He's been in there since the start.'

I marched in and dragged him out.

'When I said can you help out at a wedding, I didn't mean by attending it.'

Completely dumbstruck, Max helped the casual staff clear down the room and re-lay all the tables ready for the next seating while I sorted out the wine. Three hours had passed by now and still no sign of Richard. I was beginning to worry but my only option was to get Colin on the case. He enthusiastically slipped on his leather driving helmet and fired up the Morgan. Following him outside, I summoned my only remaining member of staff, Max, and explained that for the next wedding it was just us two serving a couple of hundred guests. He stroked his chin and declared that this was a hundred guests each.

'Not quite,' I replied. 'I'm serving the wine.'

But this bad news didn't seem to register as he started fretting about the menu.

'Max!' I shouted. 'We're working this wedding, not attending it!'

As the first guests began to arrive, we'd just finished getting everything set up, including the welcome drinks. Running into the chef's office, I was grabbed by Gordon, his eyes popping out and his mouth foaming.

'Where is my fucking wine?'

Before I could say anything, Gordon worked it out.

'Richard! I'll kill him! Where is he?'

I wished Gordon good luck finding him and legged it.

The conservatory buzzed with guests full of joy, happiness and Pimm's. Nicola informed me we had about forty minutes before they sat down, but she could stretch that to an hour as she knew the photographer. That sounded like a plan to me. Then Max came running through to tell me Colin was on the phone. I could sense doom ahead.

'I've found Richard,' he told me.

'Where?'

'In the middle of a ford. Looks like he drove through too quick.'

'Any passengers?'

'Yes - three.'

'Get them all back here as quick as you can.'

'But Duncan,' he shouted, 'the water's above his car grille and I'm in a two-seater.'

'Just do it!' I shouted, slamming the phone down.

By the time the guests started making their way through to the dining room, Max, reverting to form, was standing out on the lawn drinking Pimm's with the guests. It was then that I heard the distinctive sound of the Morgan's exhaust. All the tension of the day drained out of me as I watched four adults struggling to exit a two-seater classic British sports car. I couldn't stop laughing.

When we finished, at five in the morning, I was exhausted. The sun was rising. Time for bed.

'Where's Max?' I asked.

Nicola pointed to a suite in the hotel. He'd pulled a bridesmaid.

⌣

Throughout my time at the hotel, there had been a huge building site in the grounds, concealed by twenty foot boards. It was referred to as the new block but I'd just ignored it, assuming I'd be well away before it was completed. But now the boards were coming down and I was still there. A meeting was called - the first one ever - by the general manager, who told us we were going from sixteen bedrooms to a hundred and sixteen. The block would be ready in eight weeks and an extra one hundred staff and management were to be recruited.

By now, Nicola and I were spending nearly all our spare time together. I loved everything about her. When she was around, the room would light up and an invisible barrier shut out everything and everyone else. In the end, I told her all about my plans, and my past. She and I both knew this meant it was not a great time to start a relationship. But I also knew I couldn't expect her to hang around to see if I made a success of things. A few months ago that wouldn't have mattered. Now it did. I'd fallen in love.

As I wound down one Saturday night, she came through to ask if I wanted something to eat, which gave me an idea. I said I'd get us dinner and offered her a menu. She was intrigued but made her choice. I then told her to lay the table back at the farmhouse and left, saying I'd be back in about twenty minutes. I had some fine wines stashed away in my wardrobe, and by writing the words 'VIP Bar' on top of the order pad, I knew the kitchen would present the food exquisitely. As soon as it was ready, I took the lot up to the farmhouse and we ate. The kitchen had done us proud but Nicola couldn't stop laughing about the deception. We both imagined Chef shouting at his staff to make sure the order was correct and up to VIP standards. She was still delighted, even when I confessed it wasn't the first time I'd done it.

The new block was still not in commission but new senior management had begun to arrive almost daily, and all with their own deputies. Meanwhile, the hotel jungle drums were banging away. Who was getting promoted? Who was getting replaced? Any doubts I had about my position were dismissed in a letter promoting me to bars manager, in charge of ten bars and fifty staff. My salary would be trebled. Nicola was also to be promoted, in charge of front of house, and we were given a week to decide if we'd accept the positions. I knew Nicola would. She'd get the best room in the house, Hobson the dog was allowed to stay, and there was a large pay rise in it.

Gordon had been very quiet about it all, so I went to see him.

'You're going to leave, aren't you?' I asked him.

He nodded.

'It's time. Big corporate hotels are not my scene.'

He explained he was taking Stevie with him, but Thierry was going back to France.

'Where does that leave me?' I asked.

'Hah! I'm not daft, you know. You've got your own plans.'

He'd obviously overheard me talking on the phone.

On Stevie's last day, I popped in to see him. Thierry was leaving that night as well. Although his English hadn't really improved, his waiting skills had. He just oozed style in all departments and would be a loss to the hotel. The stalag's usual banter and laughter wasn't there, just Stevie helping Thierry pack, each layer carefully wrapped in tissue paper. I gave Thierry a hug just as Richard burst in, cigarette in mouth.

'Bastards! They've only gone and replaced me,' he boomed. 'It will all go tits up now. And if they think I'm divulging my systems, they can piss off.'

We went out for a last drink together. Tomorrow we would all be heading in new directions. Even Max was coming to the end of his placement. I had no idea what he'd learned, having left him to it long ago. Apparently he'd attended every wedding as a non-invited guest; networking, he called it. Which just left Nicola. And me.

That was when I realised what I'd achieved. I was at a crossroads; I could stay at the hotel, the easy and safe option, or I could stick to my plan. I was damn good at this work, so why shouldn't I make my own career out of it? I went into the office, decision made.

After my shift, I went back to the farmhouse and sat in the kitchen. For the first time ever it was empty, just me and the dog. Then I heard the latch and Nicola came in looking as sad as I felt. She was part of the hotel's special team, but things between us ran deep so I knew her own decision would not have been easy. She asked me what mine was. I felt it was the hardest decision I'd ever had to make, and wanted to explain it to her properly.

'I've decided to leave,' I said and started to tell her why.

But of course, she'd worked it out already. She had also worked out something else that I could never have predicted.

'I've decided to leave as well.'

I was totally shocked.

'Where are you going? What are you going to do?' I asked.

'I'm going to open a bar,' she replied.

'How come?' I asked, confused and not sure where this was going.

She smiled at me. She looked nervous, but was definitely smiling.

'With... who?' I eventually managed to ask.

'You.'

My mouth dropped open.

'Just one condition,' she added, coming over to sit on my lap.

'Yes?'

'If we're getting a licensees' nameplate above the door, it would save money if it had the same surname on it.'

CHAPTER NINE

We had our eye on a picturesque village on the River Severn just outside Tewkesbury, a fifteen minute walk from the hotel. Nobody had a bad word to say about the village and, indeed, we spent most of our nights off in one of its two pubs. So, when Nicola had said it would be the ideal place to put down roots, I didn't even question it. We were planning to get married, buy a house and open a bar, all within the next six months, but we just took it all in our stride and started with number one on the list, the wedding. The obvious venue was the hotel and, checking the diary, we saw there was a gap in seven weeks. When we asked, hotel management said no, but I told Nicola to block the dates off anyway.

She started drawing up the list of what we needed to do. Although Nicola really wanted the full white wedding, she didn't want to jeopardise our business plans either and after adding up the items required for the wedding, it became clear the whole thing would run into thousands of pounds. But I knew how lucky I was to be marrying Nicola and was more than willing to put my future plans on hold. Business plans could wait, but the wedding bills couldn't. It was time to call in the many favours I had accumulated with the hotel's golfing fraternity. And they rose to the occasion. Word had already spread and handshakes and congratulations were the order of the day. As were offers of help covering everything from invites and stationery to all the flowers, music, a vintage Rolls Royce and all the food. I even knew a golfer who had a shareholding in a formal outfitters and another who was a jeweller. I was as overwhelmed as I was grateful. They would all be invited, of course, but there was still the problem of the venue itself. Then, out of the blue, Nicola and I were called into the general manager's office. There had been a silly misunderstanding, we were told, and the management would be delighted for us to use the hotel. Misunderstanding - or the persuasive influence of the golf committee.

It was now time to inform my parents. I'd only seen Mum once since I'd been living and working at the hotel, so when I phoned her she was speechless, and I thought it best to call back another time. My dad, having initially reacted as if I'd told him I was going to jail, then digested the information and advised, 'Keep your head down son, keep working and keep saving.' He hadn't changed, but I reckon I earned a star when I mentioned I was buying a house.

We were working eighteen hour days and any time off was devoted to wedding planning. Even though we knew the venue inside out, it still required a lot of thought and organising. Much of this involved the guest list and fending off predictable comments from distant relatives - 'I'm not going if he/she is going,' 'There *will* be overnight accommodation?' and, 'Obviously with a family discount?' And we hadn't even sent out any invites yet. We did, however, receive good news about buying a house. A colleague tipped us off about a relative who was selling a house in our dream village. These properties didn't come up very often so we knew that we needed to view it as soon as possible, and it was perfect. Our mortgage was finalised and we agreed a completion date for the day after the wedding. This fitted in with our last working days at the hotel. I was the luckiest man alive. I had met someone who was not only beautiful but was strong and made me laugh out loud. And she didn't *need* me to be a success to be happy herself; she just understood what made me tick. Everything was falling into place.

The evening of the wedding was suddenly upon us. There had been only one choice for best man - Max. I knew he would deliver a great speech and he had attended more than enough weddings to know what was needed. Walking up the aisle to make the biggest commitment of my life, I focused on only one person and was completely unaware of anyone else. 'Blink' and it was over, and we were on our way back to the hotel.

Two hundred people were in that ballroom and two events stood out. One was Hobson, Nicola's dog, wearing a big pink bow and sitting in his bed at the side of Nicola's seat. The other was my brief meeting with my new father-in-law, Bill, who had flown in from Spain with his second wife, Marguerite. He was in his mid-sixties with white hair, perma-tan skin and an easy confidence. And he was smart, I could just tell. Marguerite, at six feet tall and not a day over thirty-five, was an elegant companion, a definite crowd stopper. Nicola didn't see them much, so all I knew about Bill was that he'd made millions from property development in the late 'eighties before retiring to Spain with his new wife. In that first meeting, I could tell he had the rare qualities of someone whose wisdom and encouragement can be completely captivating.

The rest of the evening went by in a blur. But the one thing I remember clearly is how well my parents responded to Nicola, and to us as a couple. With her in the picture, they reckoned they could at last see a more settled and predictable future for me.

Next morning, I woke up a married man with a new house to move into. While Nicola sorted out all the people attending our big day who had stayed overnight at the hotel, emptying the mini-bar and ordering what they assumed was free room service, my job was to collect the furniture and the rest of our belongings. These didn't amount to much, my worldly belongings still fitting in the blue holdall and Nicola's amounting to what little furniture she had in her bedroom in the farmhouse. But word of this soon spread and I persuaded a hotel colleague with a Land Rover and a trailer to help collect all the furniture which people in the village were kindly donating. It was soon overwhelming. At the second house, a little old lady lifted the garage door and pulled a large blanket off a sideboard. I was so grateful for her kindness that I kept quiet about the sideboard we already had on board, donated by the first house.

At the third house, we filled the trailer up with a six foot chest freezer, a wall clock with massive spikes coming out of it and an old push-pull lawn mower. Back at our new home, I unloaded everything into the garage and went back to the farmhouse to collect the rest of our belongings and the bed. Closing the door, I realised I was leaving behind one of the happiest places I had ever lived.

Eventually Nicola arrived, worn out from dealing with the freeloaders. Looking around the empty rooms, she asked if I'd actually got any furniture. When I explained it was all in the garage, we decided to leave it there till the next day, balanced the TV on the brick fireplace and prepared to crash out for the evening. But there was a tap on the front door. It was Bill, who'd come to see how we were getting on. Marguerite had gone to visit relatives in Scotland and he was staying on at the hotel. We moved the TV so he could sit on the fireplace, and as we got chatting it soon became clear that he wasn't too happy. He started to reel off his problems, describing how bad his current situation was, and ended up asking Nicola for a small loan.

'I thought you'd made your fortune in property, married Pamela Anderson's sister and done a body swerve to Spain,' I said.

'It's all gone,' he replied. 'Everything. The company went bust last year and I'm just left with my state pension. We can't even afford to move back to the UK.'

He then said something that struck a real chord with me.

'The few people who know just seem to have deserted us, so we've not told most of our friends.'

We spent the rest of the night hearing about his past and touching on mine. He seemed relieved to get a lot of this off his chest, and I told him it would be a pleasure to help him but it would have to be a gift, not a loan. Then we chatted the hours away as new friends exchanging ideas - my helping him to settle back in the UK, and he coming up with new business ideas for us both in the future.

Settling into the new house was easy but the villagers' generosity continued, creating a few problems along the way. Each time I came home, there'd be some furniture or bin bag left on the drive and a note pushed through the door from someone we'd never heard of. You name it, we were given it - sets of curtains, old plates and cutlery, tables (including one you could slide open to reveal a roulette wheel inside). Even a fish tank. Sticking a polite note on the door didn't halt the flow so I ended up throwing it all in the garage, which was now overflowing.

At last I held my first proper meeting with Barry and a couple of his juniors from the brewery. My own preparation was a few months behind so I was grateful for his advice and motivation. In my mind, the plan was simple. I'd find a building and convert it to a modern dance bar, but this time I'd use professional contractors, anything rather than repeat the music studio experience. The bar would open up five nights a week and take the serious money on Fridays and Saturdays. We looked at the figures and worked out that to make it pay, I'd need a capacity of between three hundred and fifty and five hundred, and a turnover of approximately £7,000 to £9,000 a week. With £6,000 a week to cover running costs and repayments, I'd be able to give myself a small wage.

We examined the details of the properties I'd viewed. There seemed to be endless reasons why these places didn't fit the criteria - ineligible for licensed premises, too small, wrong area, too expensive - which meant that after all the searching over the months, only one building in a side street in Worcester city centre ticked all the boxes. Barry told me this street was ideal, a drinkers' alley. Every Saturday night, the eighteen to thirty age group thronged here, and this building would be right in the centre of the action.

Then we talked money. I was asking for a brewery loan of £30,000 over ten years. Barry explained that it undercut a bank loan, but it did tie me into the brewery for all my stock purchases. Their prices were a lot more than we'd paid at the hotel, but I wasn't too worried. I'd budgeted for the loan to be repaid in three years, after which I could choose from any independent supplier. Barry then informed me that if, for any reason, the venture failed, the debt was secured on my house in the form of a second charge. That was fine by me. I signed the forms.

Next stop was the bank to raise the rest of the money. One of the wealthier golf members had put in a good word for me with his bank manager on my needs, and told me I would be well looked after. The branch manager showed me into his office and explained it would be his area manager looking after me. A few minutes later, a large man came in, placed himself behind the desk, picked up the phone and barked an order for two teas. I handed him my business plan and the summary notes, which he glanced at briefly before he tossed them all into the in-tray.

'How much do you want?'

'A £30,000 loan,' I said. 'You see...'

'How about £15,000 loan and £15,000 overdraft?'

I didn't want an overdraft as I wanted to use my own money for working capital. But before I could explain this, the door opened and our two teas were delivered by the obsequious branch manager. Getting up from the desk, the area manager told him off for taking too long and, leaving the tea undrunk, went to the door. He told me that all the details and administration would be dealt with by the branch - and then left. Not even a goodbye or a good luck. I went through the agreement, questioning the interest rate, arrangement fees, life insurance, medical insurance, loan and overdraft payment protection insurance. But I didn't have a choice. I was in a new business, and in a way I was glad it was all so organised. As I filled out the forms, I noticed that the bank was also securing the loan and overdraft against our property.

Back home, I asked Nicola about her day - she had taken an office job to tide us over while I set up the bar - and then relayed the day's events to her. I also had to explain that her signature was needed on the forms as well as mine. Given that we'd paid £60,000 for our house with a £3,000 deposit, and the bank and brewery were securing another £60,000 against it, I wouldn't have been at all surprised if she'd said no. But she signed them.

I'd made an appointment to view the one building which ticked all the boxes. Standing outside, I could see the position was perfect for a bar, although the whole frontage would need to be changed. Walking in, I was hit by the smell of neglect and could see it hadn't been used for a number of years. Ignoring this, I explored. There were two wide open spaces separated by a staircase which led through a small archway and up to the second level. Here the ceiling had Velux windows and I realised that knocking down the wall would let in natural light, and I could fit in a twenty-five feet long bar on this level to give a full panoramic view. So far, so good. Back in the main area, at the front was another archway, this one leading down a set of stairs into a basement - perfect for a chill-out room. Another set of stairs led into a sub-basement which ran all the way under the building - perfect for a cellar and general storage. Finally, yet another staircase led off the main area, this time to a flat which could be converted into toilets and a kitchen. This place was right on the money for my needs.

I explained my plans to the agent who didn't see a problem, but advised that the owners would have the final say. I'd taken some good advice in readiness for this moment so when we talked figures, I requested twenty-five percent discount on the annual rent. This effectively gave me three months' rent free. And I'd want the keys immediately - even while the negotiating was taking place - so I could start planning properly and finalising quotes. However, the next two weeks of negotiation nearly strangled me with red tape. Firstly, the property, owned by a division of Kay's Catalogues, hadn't been let for years and some key people within the building's management company didn't even know it existed. Meanwhile, the council required an application for planning permission regarding the frontage and the change of use. Then I had to make friends with the alcohol licensing department (part of the courts), which itself involved permissions from the fire brigade and approval from the police. And everyone I needed to speak to was either in a meeting, ill, on holiday or at lunch. When I did I eventually get to speak to anyone, I was told, 'I'll need to check that with my superior, and you'll have to put it all in writing.'

I'd have pulled out there and then if it wasn't for my determination not to be beaten by faceless, unaccountable bureaucracy. I was driven by my need to create my own enterprise, by the desire to know what success feels like, to get it right. And so, from that moment on, I created my own solutions. Anyone 'out to lunch, on holiday, away training or attending funerals' would be met head-on or simply bypassed. My date for the bar opening was now only twelve weeks away, and things were going to happen my way. So, at the large executive offices of the commercial building management company, I walked straight past the receptionist and pushed open the double doors to confront a woman behind a desk. It was clear she was unsure if I was someone of importance. I sat down, apologised and then explained the facts. I was prepared to lease their building and spend tens of thousands of pounds on it, but not if the lease took months to sort out. She admitted she didn't even know where the building was, but agreed I could have the keys if I paid a holding deposit. I was also allowed to go ahead with minor alterations immediately, if I had approval from the council and other departments. The lease, she told me, would be ready to be signed as quickly as my solicitors could deal with it. Result. Now I could start.

I instructed an architect. My plan was simple: replace the frontage, open the archway up which separated the two floors, knock down a couple of internal walls upstairs and create toilets and a kitchen. When I received the architect's quote, it was way over budget, but I should have anticipated this. He was held in high regard by the council on account of re-designing a doorstep in the cathedral - very fine but not much use to me. So I found someone who, although not an architect, could still draw up plans. He did them in a day and submitted them to the council.

The money was also falling into place with both loans confirmed. The bank's was available immediately and the brewery's just needed signing off, which was a formality. The conversion from start to finish was budgeted at £55,000. When I threw in the £15,000 of my own money, it left me with plenty in reserve for emergencies.

All that was left was to recruit my workmen. I spent two days in the murky world of contractors, meeting up with builders, plasterers, electricians, carpenters, plumbers, labourers and a shop fitter for the bar and frontage. This proved more of a challenge than the red tape I'd finally escaped. The work wasn't rocket science, so in the end I nominated myself as project manager and bypassed anyone who wanted to be on site for months with a six-man team eating up most of the budget. Instead, I settled for independent tradesmen, one man one job, agreeing on a start date and price.

At last, I collected the keys from the agent. The council informed me I'd get approval if I amended the drawings slightly on the frontage. And the licence hearing had been set.

❦

First day of work on site; I'd telephoned everyone the night before saying we will go for a 9am start. They all agreed but by lunchtime, the only person to arrive was the skip man, who just swore at me and drove off because I hadn't organised a permit. Skips were to become a constant problem. One would be delivered at the crack of dawn, but by the time we got round to using it at 10am, it was already full with other people's rubbish, usually tyres. We'd then have to clear it out, chucking all the rubbish into the alleyway at the side of our building. Alternatively, the skip didn't arrive until 5pm, blocking the road during rush hour.

Late afternoon on the first day, the builder eventually arrived to tell me he'd be starting first thing the next morning. He told me to make sure the electrician was here first so he could get power to his Kango hammer. Of course, the electrician should also have been on site on day one, so I went straight round to his house.

'Why didn't you turn up?' I asked.

'I would have been there but I was getting a lift with the carpenter, and he didn't show,' came the reply.

I told him I wanted them both there for nine the next morning and then drove round to the carpenter to deliver the same message. His excuse was that he'd left his tools in his brother's van. His brother was the plumber and he hadn't turned up either.

The following morning everyone turned up except the builder. We had lift-off! Well, at least for an hour before they all disappeared to have breakfast. Then, once back on site, everyone had their mandatory half an hour each in the toilet. Finally, there was a lot banging and rushing around and I began to feel more optimistic. But they were just getting the water and electric supply sorted for the kettle.

The first few weeks were painfully slow. The only person who used to turn up on time and work non-stop, only breaking to have a quick drink, was a guy who I called Yeah Yeah. He'd enquired about the vacancy for the doorman's position but said he could do odd jobs and some labouring until we opened as he needed the money. He was enormous, with hands like shovels, but quite shy and never keen to enter into any type of conversation. I'd ask him to do all sorts of jobs and all he ever said was, 'Yeah, yeah.' But with everyone else, it just took a van to break down, the wife or child in casualty or the fatal words, 'Just nipping out for some materials,' and you knew someone was gone for the day. What with breakfast and lunch breaks thrown in, I realised I needed to introduce an incentive. So, gathering everyone together, I stressed the need to keep to the schedule and the only way to do this was if everyone turned up and did a full day's work. From now on, I told them, everyone turned up and did a full day's work, or was fired. As everyone had transport issues of some sort or another, I hired a van and Yeah Yeah's job was to collect everyone and bring them to work.

Everything went to plan for about a week and an outline of what I'd planned was at last beginning to emerge. But it wasn't to last. The electrician went first, causing an uprising, and work was downgraded to a go-slow. By the next morning, there was a lot of leaning up against walls, smoking and drinking tea. The talk was very negative - they'd priced too low for the job, the place wasn't going to work. I can put up with most things, but grown men whining and whingeing is not one of them. But instead of losing my cool, I just gathered everyone together. I then fired the lot of them.

They thought I was joking, until I told them any monies that were owed would be paid only if the replacement contractors came in at the same price, or less. Grabbing a wrench, the plumber assumed group leader position, backed up by the rest of them. They were not leaving until they were paid in full - even for the work they hadn't done - otherwise they would undo every cable, pipe and brick, and then take me apart. At this point Yeah Yeah came through, went straight up to the plumber, grabbed his hand, twisted it round behind his back and marched him out of the building. He then returned and in his usual whisper said to the others, 'It's time to leave,' and they went along with all their tools. I closed the door behind them. They were still shouting insults and abuse an hour later. They'd overlooked the fact that the person who had just chucked them out had driven them all in that morning. We carried on for the rest of the afternoon and then I told Yeah Yeah that we'd start recruiting tomorrow. Privately, I wasn't too confident, having just fired what I thought was the elite of the local tradesmen.

When I arrived for work in the morning, there were two vehicles parked by the premises - a small van with a snarling Alsatian hanging out of the window and a VW camper van which had clearly been painted as a tribute to Bob Marley. Yeah Yeah was already there, chatting away to two men. One was an electrician who was covered head to toe in plasterboard dust. I couldn't quite catch his name as he had a serious speech impediment. Leaving him stuttering, I turned to the other guy, a white Rasta called Lee who apparently could turn his hand to most jobs. He came over to me, walking like the Bionic Man in super slo-mo. I went to shake his hand and he clenched his fist for us to tap knuckles then started to Rasta talk, which doesn't really cut it in a Worcestershire accent.

Looking to Yeah Yeah for some kind of explanation, all I got was a nervous smile and then Lee took over. We negotiated costs based on a finishing date. If it wasn't ready by then, they would be penalised. As Lee was the only one who spoke, I appointed him Charge Hand while I agreed to do all the fetching and carrying of materials, and organise the painting of the interior and exterior.

It was time to chase up the shopfitters about the frontage and the bar.

'No problem, we will be installing it next week.'

'Great,' I replied, 'and you got the amendments from my planning guy about the pillars between the front windows that need to be rounded off, not left square?'

'I think so but don't worry - any alterations can be done on site.'

'You sure?'

'Stop worrying. The place will soon look a million times better.'

I let it go as I had something else on my mind - money. The loan from the brewery hadn't arrived so I phoned Barry who didn't know anything about it, but suggested that the finance department were on a go-slow. It wasn't that urgent as I had my own money in reserve.

Soon the building work was complete. It was now time to transform it from a building site to a bar, and I soon realised that several months of running the hotel bar clearly hadn't rubbed off as much as I'd thought. I'd overlooked little bits of equipment from my budgeting, small things like glassware, optics and just about everything else you need to serve drinks, and it all added up to several thousands of pounds. And there were a few nasty surprises, too. The cellar was like an oven so I needed to install a cooling system, but it was so big that this doubled the price. The ice machine would also need to be twice the size to deal with the heat. Then again, more ice equals less drink equals more profit. Permission for an extraction fan from the kitchen was turned down, which threw a wooden spoon at the catering plans. The clientele we wanted to attract after a night's drinking wouldn't be ordering a ploughman's; they'd want deep fried anything with chips. But these were all little niggles that I could overcome. Everything else I needed was on its way: furniture, music and a lighting system that would be the best on the street. I also wanted speakers that could make your ears bleed, strobe lighting that would blind you and an enormous ceiling mirror ball. Things were coming together and to cap it off, the shop fitters arrived with the new frontage on the back of an articulated lorry. Within a day, we'd ripped out the old black, metal-framed frontage and had the new one installed.

The non-appearance of the brewery money was now beginning to cause me serious concern. No one in their finance departments could see any reason why I hadn't received it, and I eventually got through to someone in the legal section. Apparently there wasn't any problem with the money, but they wanted to guarantee it against my property and be first in line ahead of the bank if things went wrong. With the brewery money making up forty percent of my capital expenditure, I was worried. All the legal man could do was insist I get the bank to swap places with the brewery in the 'who would repossess my house first when it all goes tits up' league. I spent days trying to sort something out. I visited the bank. They wouldn't budge, and why should they? In fact, the only thing I achieved was to alert the bank to my financial predicament.

By this stage, my mentor, Barry, had left the brewery and his replacements wouldn't help. The only thing they offered was a better purchasing tariff, which wouldn't be any use if I didn't have anywhere to serve their products. I told them I wasn't interested. Then they sent some representatives to visit. They were impressed but still didn't want to be behind the bank if things went wrong. All they offered me was a £10,000 loan with a charge on my house and much better purchasing power. I sat down with Nicola and we went through what we had spent and how much we still needed to spend to get the place open. I was just under £20,000 short, so we'd now be relying totally on at least hitting or exceeding our turnover. We both applied for personal loans and planned to raise the remaining balance on credit cards. Finally, I got everyone at the bar together, explained the situation and said that's why everything must be completed on time and on budget. I didn't get much response. Yeah Yeah just said, 'Yeah yeah,' the electrician stuttered, and whatever I said to Lee always prompted a knuckle shake and, 'Total respect to the Boss-man Dread.' Even when suppliers came to visit he would refer to me as Head Dread. He was definitely on the Jamaican Woodbines.

It was now two weeks from opening and I'd already taken out full page adverts in the local papers, invites for the opening night had gone out, promotion was in full swing and I had the DJs booked for the next two weekends. But I was still plagued by people in suits, usually either some official person on a nose-around or somebody selling something. However, I recognised the next suit at the door as that of the council planning man. He was accompanied by several other leather elbow patch-wearing assistants and they were doing a lot of staring, checking the drawings and reeling out the tape measure. I ignored them until they called me over.

'Mr Ridler, you haven't kept to your side of the agreement on the frontage pillars.'

'I have. They're round not square, as agreed.'

'We are not disputing that, it's the width of the pillars; they are not wide enough. It's not in keeping with the area.'

I pointed out that there was a vacuum repair shop whose shop front was held together with massive stickers of the Henry vacuum cleaner, next door was a hot pork roll shop and all down the street it was either bars or restaurants, none of which had the same frontages and all of which were in different stages of disrepair. But they were having none of it and said I'd be in breach of planning regulations and if I didn't comply with those, they could have me closed down. I summoned the shopfitters, who were also building the bar for me, and the guy who'd drawn and submitted the plans. During a heated exchange in the street, I said I wouldn't pay the shopfitters unless they altered the frontage. They replied by threatening not to install the bar unless I paid for all the work, including the shop front, in cash. So, it was stalemate. Inside things were going well, with people installing the beer lines, sound system, lighting and toilets. The only thing missing was the bar, so I went back to the shopfitters and said I'd pay for the bar when it was installed, and if I got over the planning hurdle. Still no deal. So I approached the largest shopfitting company we could find. Yes, they could build us a bar and install it within our time frame, but they'd have to interrupt work already lined up which meant paying extra for their staff's overtime on building it, transporting it, then fitting it. If I agreed, it would swallow all my capital and any reserves. But I was way beyond the point of no return and had no choice. With money now such a critical issue, I had to hold off paying everyone until we opened. So if I didn't open, nobody would get paid. Time was also critical. The bar would be delivered and installed two days before opening, which gave us just enough time to fit it out and get the beer taps connected. I was now fire fighting on all fronts, buying time with the suppliers by paying a third of what I owed while explaining the situation. Most of them agreed, reluctantly, but with the threat of court action and repossession of equipment if I didn't pay. It was the final push.

I thought I'd avoided horrendous legal fees until the day I was in court to get the licence. The police were opposing the application so I'd had to hire a barrister. Talk about jobs for the boys! The police's legal team never showed so the licence was granted, and I had to fork out a thousand pounds for the barrister who did nothing more than bow a lot and flick his cape about. However, back at the bar, even though I was totally exhausted, frustrated and broke, I hadn't lost my sense of humour. In the centre of the ground floor was a disused chimney breast. Instead of removing it, we hollowed it out and inserted reinforced glass to create a twenty foot high fish tank. It had glass shelves with bits of coral and sunken galleons and looked absolutely stunning, especially with the lights bouncing off it.

Cash flow problems meant we didn't have any fish, but someone brought in a big rubber shark and then I added an Action Man, putting his head in the shark's mouth with a sign stuck on the front: "Man from Planning Department." It turned out not to be my smartest move. A man walked through the door with sensible black, rubber-soled Dr Marten-type shoes and thin lips, clearly a man brandishing unelected power. I knew I was in for a hard time as he had a brown leather briefcase, open at the ready and brimming with colour-coded files. Showing no emotion at all, he tapped the fish tank and announced:

'That's my brother-in-law you've inserted in that shark's head.'

What could I say?

'I don't remember giving you permission to hollow this chimney breast out,' he went on.

'Pardon me, but who are you?' I asked.

'Building Control for the owners of this building. You're due to sign the lease and I'm here to check you have done the work as agreed.'

He pointed to the chimney breast.

'That's black mark number one. The frontage, I hear, will need to be rectified as well - black mark number two. Goodness me, Mr Ridler, and we haven't even got started yet.'

I bit my lip and offered to show him round but he declined, so I left him to it. Some time later, I noticed he was standing at the front door waiting for me, indignant that I was keeping him waiting. I asked Lee over for technical support while the man went through his list. All the black marks were trivial points, Lee said, and could be easily corrected. However, Mr Building Control was offensively patronising to Lee and it became clear he expected us to beg for mercy and forgiveness. By now, I'd had enough of this guy so I grabbed his briefcase, which was still open, and threw it out of the door. His colour-coded files spread out all over the pavement and he ran out to try and restore order to his world. I followed him out and gave him a parting shot: 'You're barred.'

Two days before opening, I interviewed for staff and was overwhelmed with people wanting a part-time job. So, to make my life easier, I just asked them each two questions: a basic mathematical sum (adding two amounts together) and then what ingredients went into, say, a vodka and coke. I was amazed how many got one, or both, questions wrong.

The place was in a state of organised chaos. The bar was being finished off, we were still painting and the drink, the glasses and the furniture had arrived. In spite of a few teething troubles with power and plumbing, I was proud that I had got to this point still on schedule, and delighted with the lads I'd employed to do the work. They weren't professional tradesman but they'd delivered exactly what I wanted, and on time, too. There was no way I could have opened at all if it hadn't been for them.

Nicola, who'd been trying to keep ahead on the finances and balancing the books, was overwhelmed with the number of invoices arriving on a daily basis. And the bank had been in touch, demanding to see something go into the overdraft account. I worked out that night that my extended overdraft of £25,000 had grown now to nearly £35,000, and I still had to pay suppliers and the brewery for the first delivery, a huge order as we needed to carry an initial stock. I had fourteen days to pay but had reached my credit limit, so the next order would have to be cash on delivery. That was something I hadn't budgeted for. I also needed to pay the contractors and the bar staff, and the bank and brewery loans were due their first payments. And, of course, there were now personal finances involved with loans, credit cards and a mortgage needing servicing. To me, it was all numbers on sheets or paper. I was confident that even if we only hit seventy percent of our targeted turnover, we could pay everything and still earn a nice living. And tomorrow was opening night.

Unable to sleep the day of the opening, I went in at four in the morning. The building smelled of paint and newly laid carpet. The lights twinkled off the mirror backed bar and onto the optics. In a few hours, people would be sitting on my furniture, dancing and drinking. The place looked magnificent, surpassing all my expectations.

As lunchtime arrived, I was starting to get nervous. Nicola came to help me out and all around us final preparations were completed one by one as the lads finished off, the staff came in early to set up the bar, and the DJ arrived to test the sound system. I looked round. We were ready.

There was a knock on the door. It was the fire officer, who I had totally forgotten about. My throat went dry as I waited for him to deliver a hammer blow.

'Mr Ridler,' he announced. 'Everything's fine, but I can't give you the go ahead as the side entrance is a main escape route and it's currently blocked up with debris. Tyres, mostly.'

I swore to myself.

'Tell you what,' the fire officer went on, 'me and the lads are going to get a bite to eat. We'll be back in hour. Just make sure the tyres are nowhere to be seen.'

I gathered the staff into the yard and we stared at the mountain of rubbish, wondering how and where to shift it. Then I noticed our stuttering electrician, pointing at something up the road and then back at the tyres. He made several attempts to outline his plan, but they all started and ended with, 'T.. t.. t...' Frustration drove him to opt for action over words and he grabbed a tyre, ran up the street to a tipper truck, threw it in and then ran back. Then he mimed the actions of someone eating and someone sleeping. I got it at last. I shouted through to everyone to grab two tyres each and head for the truck, a good two hundred feet away. There were ten of us and we had to make five trips each. Yeah Yeah even jumped on the back of the tipper to stack them neatly. The driver, meanwhile, was sound asleep in the cab. It was a council truck. It was nice to be able to give them something back for all the help they'd been.

Opening night was intended to be ticket only, but the size of the crowd outside meant that wasn't going to last. The staff were ready, the music was blasting and finally the doors opened. We were mobbed all night right up to closing time, and once we'd cleared them all out, I switched on the main lights. The place was wrecked. There were bottles and smashed glass everywhere and the toilets had flooded. The carpet - supposedly fire-resistant - was covered in hundreds of cigarette burns. But we were open. I left everyone to clean up while I counted the takings. They came in at just under £4,000, a brilliant outcome, although I knew the place wouldn't be mobbed like this every night. Still, I was delighted. Certain teething problems needed addressing, like running out of change and the ice machine giving up, but I was still delighted. Tonight was my night and everything else could be sorted out tomorrow.

The next day, small problems like repairing damage and replenishing stock all needed to be addressed, but opening time came around again. I told Yeah Yeah that as soon as it got shoulder-to-shoulder, he was to operate a 'one out, one in' system. The staff arrived and stared at the fridges, asking why I hadn't restocked back up on Mad Dog 20/20 and Hooch. These were the first brand of alcopops and I'd ordered a few cases as the brewery rep persuaded me they were going to be massive. The staff explained that it was all we'd sold until they ran out, which had been within minutes. Soon we were full again, but the staff were right - everybody was asking for these drinks and looking let down when we told them we'd run out. They ended up ordering something else, drinking it quickly then leaving. Apparently, a few places up the road had plenty in stock. But it was still another great night and I couldn't ask for more. Well, maybe a cellar full of a lemon-flavoured alcopops, but it was on my list. The takings were just under £3,000 so I was just on target to meet my payments and start paying everyone back.

The first Monday morning after opening, I arrived at the bar to find an official-looking man waiting for me on the step. He looked quite glum and, to judge from his smart suit, definitely wasn't a council official. He was from the bank and handed me an official demand giving me fourteen days to reduce my overdraft back under £25,000. What with my overspend and their charges, they wanted nearly £15,000. I explained that I was open and trading and had taken £7,000 over the first weekend. I added that I'd only spoken to his boss last week.

'He's been transferred. We have a new manager now. Now, that seven thousand pounds - are you banking it, Mr Ridler?' came the reply.

'Some of it, but I need stock and a larger cash float for change.' He wasn't at all interested.

'I will leave it with you, Mr Ridler,' he said and walked off.

I read the letter thoroughly. If I didn't get my overdraft back under £25,000 in fourteen days, they would call in the complete loan. There was nothing I could do about it right now. What I needed was stock - a few pallets of Mad Dog and Hooch would shut the bank up. I phoned my order in and was told we were limited to only five cases of this drink. The stuff was hot and even the brewery had low stocks, and were reserving it for their own venues. They also reminded me the order was cash on delivery as I'd reached my credit limit. I phoned the bank, hoping to speak to the manager, but got the same guy I'd met that morning. At least, he assured me, they would exchange my notes for change.

The day went from bad to worse. I was now seriously worried and could see my business was starting to unwind. Because word had spread that we'd been full to bursting over the weekend, every supplier who was owed money now turned up wanting payment. I managed to delay them but it would only be for a week. If I could make it to the weekend and keep this level of turnover, I could trade my way out of it. So I decided to stay closed until the Friday to keep my powder dry. And besides, every other bar was doing weekday promotions at £1 a bottle. I needed more profit than that.

Driving to the bank on Friday to collect my change, I was feeling more upbeat; the weekend had arrived and I'd avoided any more threatening letters, phone calls and visiting creditors. I told the cashier I had a £3,000 change order and gave her the business name. She told me to wait one moment and went off to make a phone call. When she returned, I placed the cash on the counter. She counted it. When I asked for my change she asked if I'd mind going round to customer services. I could see the assistant manager walking over. He recognised me so I explained what I needed.

'I'm afraid we seem to have a problem. We are unable to complete that transaction as the money you paid in is required to offset your unauthorised overdraft facility.'

I tried to make him see reason, to understand that I needed the money to continue trading so that I could pay the bank back. His face remained totally devoid of emotion but he told me to wait. He disappeared behind the cashiers, and then came back.

'We can help you out on this one occasion but it will only be up to the maximum of two hundred and fifty pounds.'

I was staggered and asked how I was supposed to repay the bank if I couldn't have any change to trade with? Try running a bar with no change, the wrong drinks, an ice machine that could only churn out ten ice cubes an hour and a carpet that was turning into one big cigarette burn. And I needed to re-build the toilets every day.

In spite of this, I still loved what I was trying to do, but everybody I owed money to wanted paying yesterday. Trouble was, without an endless stock of alcopops, we were losing customers and takings had dipped by a third. Word was spreading that we were doomed and, looking back, I can now see it was crisis management at its best - or worst. One of the girls behind the bar told me her mum dealt with the change at the local Tesco's. So I would dispatch her off there halfway through the night. Another bar girl had a relation working at McDonalds who started supplying us with bin bags full of ice. I could still pay the staff and cover the small drinks orders in cash, but the direct debit for my original big drinks delivery was due. And both at home and at the bar, the legal debt letters were starting to arrive.

We still closed during the week, giving me valuable time to get things ready. I was now getting quite good at fixing things. But one day, there was a knock on the front door. I'd heard more than enough of these to distinguish between the knocks of friends and those of creditors, or so I thought. This one was loud and, expecting a creditor, I was surprised to find the man from the planning department serving me with some sort of legal notice concerning the shop front alterations. I read the letter, screwed it up into a ball and kicked it in the air. It bounced on his head before dropping to the floor. I then shooed him out, locked the door and got back to my DIY.

The door knocked again, a friendly tap this time. It was an area manager from the brewery.

'I see you've pissed off the council,' he said.

'How do you know?'

'Just read the notice.'

The bastard had picked up the scrumpled letter, smoothed it out and sellotaped it onto the window. That was it for me; I decided just to come clean and tell him everything. He said it didn't sound good and then went quiet, deep in thought. After a minute, he said he could help. Pulling out a brochure, he told me about this special offer - buy so many cases of lager, get a bottle of gin or vodka free. Some help.

I'd had enough now so I locked up and went home, waiting for Nicola to come back from work. I wanted to walk the dog, clear my head and shake off the day's frustrations. Hobson now had a canine friend, a black labrador by the name of Benson, inherited from a hotel colleague who'd split up with her boyfriend. As well as her dog, we also acquired two terrapins called Nigel and Arnold. About halfway round our walk, after chatting about trivial matters, I stopped and took a deep breath.

'Nicola,' I said. 'The bar is finished. It's over.'

She knew already.

'How bad is it?' she asked.

'Nic, it's bad. Really bad.'

CHAPTER TEN

The next few days were made up of fitful sleep and false dawns. I'd wake up in the middle of the night feeling doom-laden, dreading the clock ticking round to the morning and the certain defeat the new day would bring. Then, occasionally my mood would flip and I'd dream up some fantastic idea or other, only to realise that as dawn approached, so did reality.

So, I devised a plan. I decided to trade for one more weekend. I'd reduce all drinks to a pound, keep the staff levels the same, and I had just enough money to hire a DJ, which would bring enough people through the door to shift the last of my stock. Then, after closing on Saturday night, I'd pay everyone in cash and anything left over would go towards paying the contractors. It was either that or use the money as credit against the amount I owed the brewery and the bank - sums I couldn't pay anyway. And on Monday, I'd phone the suppliers of any of the free-standing equipment and tell them to come and collect it.

The weekend trade was good but didn't bring in the revenue I'd hoped for and, having spent every last piece of energy trying to make it work, those last hours of trading were the hardest of all. The last customers left and the doors were locked. As usual, the staff rushed round cleaning up and re-stocking, so I asked them to stop and gather round the bar. I then explained that tonight was our last night trading and we were closing. Instead of condolences, all I got was, 'Can I have my wages?' 'It was shit here anyway,' and, 'How am I going to pay for my boyfriend's MOT now?' Then the mops hit the floor and they were gone.

Nicola and I started calculating how much we owed to suppliers and creditors. Added together, the invoices for the multitude of small items amounted to a lot more than the loans. When planning this project out, I just didn't realise how easy it was to overspend, but the error of spending the money before it was all signed off and sitting in my bank account was now painfully clear. Then my efforts to adjust the turnover upwards in a bid to fit the borrowing costs made things worse. Including our mortgage, which we hadn't paid for three months, we were not far off owing £200,000. I couldn't see it at the time, but there had been other lessons to learn too. Lessons to do with my trust in people and processes. Had I known the brewery and the bank would move the goal posts so drastically, or that the council planning people would strangle any creativity with their red tape, would I have gone ahead with it? Who knows? For now, I had to deal with the very real fall-out, starting on the Monday morning when I found people standing on the pavement demanding their money, a warning that this failing was going to be the toughest challenge I'd faced so far. As I unlocked the doors and felt the tension and anger building against me, I knew that anything I said wouldn't make the slightest bit of difference.

A tough challenge requires a tough attitude, but I found the next few days a blur. Vans would pull up full of angry creditors, I'd try to find a way to apologise and explain there wasn't any money, and they'd shout their accusations back - I was to be sued for every penny, what I'd done was illegal, I should be locked up, and so on, always ending with the warning that I hadn't seen anything yet. Or worse, 'Wait till I tell the wife.' This alone couldn't articulate their anger so they also took out their aggression on the very items they had come to collect, throwing and kicking them into the back of their vans. Even when I thought they'd had their say, they'd come back in and repeat everything again. And when they finally went, it was a question of when, not if they would be back. Or they just sent the wives, and they were right, I'd never seen anything like it; kids in tow, screaming into my face then turning to explain to their children that it was all this man's fault, pointing at me. It was *his* fault there'd be no dinner, no new school shoes and definitely no holiday this year. Normally, I would have challenged and dealt with this kind of situation, but after days of constant abuse at the bar, on the phone and by letter, mentally, I didn't have any fight left in me. I was shot.

At last, everything that could be picked up and hauled away had been. All that was left was some nut-vending equipment in the cellar where I'd let their owner store them when he installed ours. Figuring he could collect it from my home, I loaded it into a van along with some personal belongings and took one last look round before turning off the electrics and water for the last time.

❦

During the next few days, it was as if my vision was blurring and my focus diminishing. I started to doubt my own judgement, even on the smallest everyday problems around the house, and I didn't want to commit to doing anything or discussing what needed to be done to sort out the problems I'd caused. To do so would mean making a decision and just thinking about that produced a physical reaction in me, making me drowsy and feeling like my whole body was aching all over. In the end, I would just lie on the settee, unable to do a single thing. I was mentally paralysed and would spend hours staring out of the kitchen window without actually seeing anything, not even the garden or sky. I had failed. My future, my ambition, my ability to make decisions based on my instinct - the one thing I had always been able to rely on when all else had failed - everything had gone.

Every morning, I'd wake up to the sound of the postman struggling to get all the mail through the letterbox. I'd listen to the thud as it landed on the mat and then a silence before a second or even a third thud. If I dragged myself out of bed to look over the landing, all I'd see would be a mass of white and brown envelopes. Then the phone would start ringing and I'd somehow scrape together the energy I needed to unplug it. And that was my day until Nicola came home from work. She knew how bad our situation was and it was starting to affect our relationship. Nicola was the one getting up and walking the dogs, going to work and then coming home to a person who, in her eyes, was giving up on all the things in life she had married me for. But what could she say to make it better? She had tried but I'd dismissed all the small talk.

The next Saturday morning, a week after the bar had closed, it finally came to a head. Nicola got up as usual, ready to take the dogs out for their morning walk. I stayed in bed and listened to the rain battering against the windows, waiting for the usual first thud of post on the mat. Instead, the doorbell rang and the postman handed Nicola a pile of letters that all needed signing for. When he'd left, she came back upstairs, sat on the bed and gave me a long, hard look.

'Is this it?' she said finally. 'You're just going to lie there and give in to your failures? Let everything we have as a couple go to shit because some building you converted into a bar didn't work out?'

She paused, as if waiting for me to answer. I didn't, so she went on.

'OK. You have two options. You can lie there wallowing in your self-pity and thinking 'why me?' and in a few weeks you will still be lying there, but by then you'll be on your own. Or you can return to being the man I married - and still want to be married to.'

Nicola went over to the wardrobe and picked up my holdall.

'See this? When I met you, all your possessions fitted in this bag. And today, they still fit in this bag. You haven't lost anything apart from a few months of your life. Yes, we owe hundreds of thousands of pounds. But the damage is done. Surely even you can see the only way is up.'

She was right. What a stupid, selfish arsehole I'd been. I jumped out of bed and hugged her. I kept repeating, 'Thank you, you're right,' and as I did it, every knot in my body started to untangle. I got dressed and we went out with the dogs, walking for hours, talking about what had happened and what the hell we were going to do. I arrived back home drenched but actually feeling happier than I had before starting this latest enterprise. Some people might say I was suffering from depression, but to my mind it was self-pity. I'd believed in my own greatness and couldn't accept my fall. Thank God it just took a long walk in the rain and a good talking to by the one person I loved and respected more than anything to put me right again.

I spent the rest of the weekend opening and sorting the post, and with every letter the total amount I owed rose with interest, late payment fees, bank charges, solicitor fees, legal fees, court fees and arrears fees. The vultures started circling and when I invited them round to see for themselves that I didn't have a penny, they just grew more hungry. Our own finances were in just as dire a state, thanks to the personal debt to cover the shortfall in the loans and the general overspend. Looking through all our bills, it became apparent that we hadn't really paid anything for the last few months. And although Nicola's salary would just cover the basic repayments, it didn't even touch the mortgage. We decided that she'd carry on working while I stayed at home for the next few weeks fending off the creditors. Things settled into a routine. I would get up in the morning and go off hiking with the dogs. It was the only way I could deal with what was happening. I'd come back home feeling positive and ready to deal with the post, which was now getting horrendous and more threatening by the day. Added to demands for money were new demands to work on the building. The owners wrote to give me fourteen days to return the premises to their original state or they would start legal proceedings. The council's planning department didn't bother with the fourteen days, going instead for the court action against the shop front fitting that was never given planning permission. Everyone wanted blood. The game was well and truly up. The bank and the brewery were coming after the house, as was the mortgage company, and we now had more than fifty separate court actions filed against us. At least half of them I could have disputed, but realistically I could barely afford the stamps, let alone the petrol to get to and from court to defend myself.

So, I'd go off again with the dogs to enjoy a simple pleasure, stopping to pass the time of day with other villagers. Until one day, when I came across an elderly gentleman who was chairman of the village committee. Normally, we'd have a quick chat, but today, when I was expecting the usual jovial hello, all I got was, 'You've got a nerve.' I was shocked.

'Hang on a minute,' I said. 'What are you going on about?'

He gave me a look that said if he was twenty years younger he'd have gone for me.

'What you've done is despicable, taking all that money off those hard working families.'

I sighed and started to explain, but it was too late. He marched off, only stopping to shout that one of my creditors was a relation of his. I ran after him and pulled his arm. He looked round, his eyes full of anger, and suddenly I couldn't think of anything to say that would make things better. I let his arm go and headed for the newsagents. The morning paper hadn't arrived for the last two days, so I asked the girl behind the counter if there was problem with the paperboy. She blushed and shouted for the owner who promptly arrived, gave me an arctic look and opened a massive ledger from which he ripped a tiny ticket. He flicked it at me and launched into a rant.

'You're not going to have one over on us. You're blacklisted. And you can settle your bill while you're here.'

Having paid my bill last week, I was bewildered by this but picked up the morning paper and handed him the money I owed. He took the money and snatched back the paper, opening the door and telling me, 'We don't need custom from the likes of you.'

I sloped back home with my head down to find the usual pile of post clogging up the hallway and with a card sticking out of it. It was from the electricity company, notifying me they'd be calling back to disconnect the supply. Pretty much everything in the house was electric. Our situation got even worse. The phone was the next thing to be cut off and every day I was being informed by the county court of another judgement entered against me. Not a single person in the village would now speak to me, most crossing the road to avoid me.

The postman did bring one bit of good news - a letter from Bill, Nicola's dad, who, having borrowed some money, was moving back to Edinburgh. He couldn't wait to come and see us and have a drink at the bar. The letter must have got lost at the sorting office, as that same day he phoned from a call box to say he was just five minutes away. He'd stopped off at the bar on the way down and, having peered through the window, was concerned that we seemed to be way behind schedule. It was a real tonic to see Bill again. He told us he had a little part-time job at his brother-in-law's garage, and he looked so much better now that he was back from Spain. Despite having split up with his second wife, he was happy, healthy and, after hearing about what had happened with the bar, very supportive. It had been a long while since someone, apart from Nicola, had shown me an ounce of sympathy. And his solution was simple: move to Scotland. We would have him nearby, as well as various members of his family, and Nicola knew the area well. It sounded good and I was open to any suggestions, but we had nowhere to live up there. He just told us to leave it with him.

If we had any doubt, the next moment it evaporated. The doorbell rang and peering through the curtains, Nicola reported that it was the milkman with his float. We weren't accustomed to him visiting at ten o'clock at night, so I went to investigate and was told to settle up the outstanding fortnightly bill there and then. And there'd be no more deliveries. As I didn't have any cash, Bill kindly stepped in and paid. After that, Nicola and Bill talked about nothing but Edinburgh and soon he'd convinced us. It felt wonderful to have someone giving our problems some thought and coming up with a solution, however vague it might be. For me, the thought of moving so far wasn't daunting but it would mean admitting defeat and running away from unresolved problems. Up until then, I'd always had a solution and a door opening to a new challenge. Now I was just backed into a corner. And the money issues were snowballing with all the county court judgements, and the bank and brewery showing absolutely no mercy. At least the electricity board offered a crumb of comfort. When they changed us over to a top-up card meter, they kindly left a pound's worth of power for us to consume.

Once Bill was back in Scotland, he undertook a quest to find us suitable accommodation in or around Edinburgh. But every newspaper cutting he sent down to us involved properties way over our budget of slightly-above-nothing, and none of the places would accept pets. However, a leaflet fell out of the cuttings which immediately caught my eye. It was for a caravan park which was just opening in East Lothian on the outskirts of Edinburgh. The place was set in woodland, surrounded by countryside, ten minutes away from the beach, had plenty of facilities (including a swimming pool) and accepted pets. I showed it to Nicola and we were straight off to the phone box. I dialled the number and after waiting an age, it was answered by the most upbeat voice I'd heard for months. I explained our situation, which didn't bother the woman at the other end in the slightest. In fact, she said, she would be delighted to have us stay. It was a brand new site and we would be the first customers. And if we helped her finish off the site at the weekends - a bit of painting, sweeping, nothing too strenuous - she'd only charge us £35 a week for a six-berth caravan. After the call was over, I stood outside the phone box doing a little jig of delight.

'That's our accommodation sorted,' I told Nicola.

'Look at it this way,' she replied, 'we could treat it as a holiday. A delayed honeymoon even.'

My dance was seen by one of our neighbours who'd taken great pleasure in my downfall and had been the leading gossipmongerer. I waited for him to make eye contact and wished him a good morning, adding what a great day it was to be alive. This certainly shook him but was nothing to what I had planned to mark my departure.

So, the die was cast. It was time to jump, not wait to be pushed. Autumn had arrived and having to ration electricity and unable to afford solid fuel, our house was getting colder than the village atmosphere. Nights were spent sitting in the dark in our hats and coats, watching the TV, drinking lukewarm tea from a flask and eating anything that only needed hot water added to it. We made arrangements for Bill to hire a van and drive down to collect us. It was tempting to up and leave there and then but we decided to wait for Nicola's final month of salary, which was due in three weeks. The wait didn't seem much of a problem anyway. I was past caring and very much in 'what else can they do to me?' mode. 'Bring it on,' I thought.

And they did. All the court action against me that had seemed at arm's length now took on a more physical, here-and-now urgency. The ringing and banging on the door was a constant soundtrack to my day. And I'd open the door and know straight away from the shiny shoes and the clipboard that it was a bailiff. He'd start reeling off his official spiel explaining who he was representing, and I'd stop him halfway through, offer him a seat and a cup of tea. Completely stumped, he would usually decline. I would then invite him to look anywhere he liked and take anything he found of value. I'd even offer to show him the 'antiques' in the garage. He would walk around the house, come back into the kitchen and ask for the cup of tea after all, which we'd then drink while I told him how I'd got into this position. In turn, he would explain that he was paid to carry out creditors' instructions via the court. On his way out, to justify his visit, he'd slap a Walking Possession Order on the Calor gas fire, the only thing of value he could find in the house.

For the next three weeks we'd go through the exact same process for different sets of creditors. If I was out walking the dogs, I'd leave a note on the door and the bailiff would be sitting there on the drive when I returned. He'd end up drinking tea or eating his packed lunch, and we'd chat for an hour or so before he slapped another possession order on the gas fire. In the end, that fire had more than a hundred grand secured on it. It was a legendary piece of furniture. And if it wasn't the bailiff knocking, it was the generous people who had donated us house-warming furniture asking for it back. I just left them to sort out all the collection arrangements. At least the post had slowed to about a dozen letters a day, but that didn't stop one letter from putting us on the brink of disaster. With only a few days to go and on the very day we were expecting Nicola's final salary cheque to clear, the bank had frozen our account. Apparently a number of the creditors believed we were hiding money. So, we needed to revise our plans. We downgraded the hire van and sold Nicola's car, Bill having kindly lined us up a replacement in Scotland. I then decided to bite the bullet and go and see Mum and Dad.

They knew I was in trouble financially after the bar had closed but didn't know of my imminent plans; but financial disaster is not unlike someone dying. You need the same kind of verbal support and encouragement, but people seem to approach failure in the same way as an untreatable or contagious disease and stay well away. So, even though they were my family, it was very hard to look them in the eye. I met Mum at my aunt's house. I told her that I was moving, not through choice, but because my house was being repossessed.

'Well, maybe losing your home and business will make you realise that just living a normal life does have its advantages.'

'Like what, Mum?' I asked.

She went into deep thought but came up with no reply.

'I know,' said my aunt. 'It means you can book your holidays a year in advance knowing you can actually go on them.'

There was no point arguing with that, so I gave Mum a hug and let myself out. She caught up with me on the drive.

'Duncan, is the situation that bad?'

'Yes it is,' I said, 'but I'm trying to see it all as me just back at the starting line.'

'So, you still genuinely believe you can make something of your life? That you can succeed in business?' she asked.

I nodded. Mum gave me a half smile and said, 'I do too.' She then opened her bag, pulled out an envelope and told me to take it. It was full of twenty pound notes. I thanked her and handed it back. I could really have done with the money, but this was my mess and I took full responsibility for it. Dad was even less chatty.

'You mean you haven't got anything in reserve?' he asked.

'No. I haven't got any savings, pensions, TESSAs, life insurance, PEPs, shares, gilts, premium bonds, endowments. I haven't opted out of SERPS and I haven't made a will either. I do still have a mortgage, but not for much longer.'

He rubbed his chin and looked at me deep in thought. When it became clear he wasn't going to say anything else, I said my goodbyes and moved on.

On our last night, we packed what was left of our belongings. Mine could still fit in my holdall, but we agreed to take the microwave and a few other bits and pieces that would pack into a few crisp boxes. And then finally, after all that we'd been through, we had our first disagreement. It was over the dishwasher. Nicola wanted to sell it as she knew we couldn't install it in a caravan, but I didn't want to wash up by hand. 'They can strip me of dignity and a future,' I said, 'but I am not washing up by hand.'

'OK, fine,' she said, 'but if the dishwasher's coming, you're not taking that stereo.'

The stereo in question was the one I'd taken from the bar - two five hundred watt speakers, a CD player and an amp - which I'd kept tucked away in the loft, far away from prying bailiff eyes. I had no intention of taking it; it was part of my legacy to the village.

'What about these nut machines?' Nicola shouted from the garage.

I'd never heard back from the vending man who'd left them at the bar. I went into the garage and shook one of them. It still had money in it. I started searching for the key but was interrupted by what sounded like workmen digging up the road. Lifting up the garage door, I watched Bill reverse a four-ton pick-up onto the drive. He jumped out enthusiastically.

'What do you reckon, eh? Fifty quid. And it has tax and MOT for two weeks,' he said.

'Will it last that long?' I asked, 'And how are we supposed to get three people and two dogs in the front?'

'I'd forgotten about the dogs,' Bill said. 'But fifty quid isn't the hire cost. I've bought it. You wheeler dealers always need a van. And can't the dogs sit in the back?'

'Bill, we're going up the M6, not across the tropics. They'll freeze to death.'

Ignoring this, he gave Nicola a hug and went inside to put the kettle on while I started loading up our belongings - three holdalls, the quilt off our bed, dishwasher and the dogs' bed. I then showed Bill the nut vending machines. There were ten in total, and several thousand tins of nuts. His eyes lit up as he told us of a few places in Edinburgh that might install them. So we loaded them on the pick-up, and it was time to go. Almost.

I asked Bill to pull the Transit off the drive and told Nicola to get the dogs and wait by the van with her dad. I went upstairs and then remembered. Bloody hell, we'd almost forgotten the terrapins sitting in the hall. We loaded them onto the back of the pick-up and then I set up the stereo, placing a speaker in each bedroom at the front of the house. I opened the windows and made sure they were on the latch before plugging in the CD player and amplifier on the landing.

'Nearly done,' I said. 'Bill, fire the van up.'

I made one last dash up the stairs, pressed play and repeat on the CD player and smiled to myself. The song I'd chosen was a nailed-on bar emptier and, I thought, a fitting tribute to all the understanding and kindness the villagers had afforded me when times were hard. Slamming the front door and checking it was locked, I could feel the glass in the door vibrating with the din from the stereo. I ran up the drive and opened the van door to find the cab packed with Nicola, Bill and a pair of panting dogs.

'Shit! Where I am sitting?' I gasped.

They pointed. I climbed onto the back of the pick-up.

'We ready?' Bill shouted from the cab.

'Born ready,' I replied.

We bounced off the kerb and trundled down the lane to the deafening sound of Agadoo on permanent repeat until the meter ran out.

CHAPTER ELEVEN

If I'd saved even just £100, I wouldn't now be wedged between boxes on the back of a clapped out pick-up truck, with two terrapins for company. And judging by the assortment of vehicles overtaking us, the lack of style and comfort was matched by its lack of speed. Even at forty miles per hour, the noise was deafening. I was tired and battle weary, and desperately wanted to go to sleep, but instead my thoughts wandered to the past. As much as I wanted to feel guilty about some of my disastrous decisions and their impact on others, the sadness I felt was rather more selfish. To date, I'd encountered some cracking people during my adventures and I didn't know if I'd ever meet their type again.

The sound of tapping on the glass that separated me from the cab interrupted my thoughts. I cricked my neck but at first couldn't see anything. Then Nicola wrote the word 'fuel' in the condensation. We pulled into a filling station and I scrambled over the side, bumping heads with Bill as I landed. He looked pale and drawn and he was breathing deeply.

'What the hell have you been feeding those dogs?' he asked as he sucked in the fresh, petrol-soaked air.

His mood didn't improve when I filled the Transit with fuel and then asked him to pay. Apparently I was using up his pension. I knew the nut vending machine was full of coins, so I promised to break into it once we'd got to Scotland.

'We will make it to Scotland?' I asked.

'Not with them two hairy mutts as passengers. The stench'll make me go blind.'

The journey was turning into a real test of character for us all. I would just manage to get comfy and my eyes would start to shut when there'd be a tap on the window and we'd stop. It would either be because the van needing filling or Bill's bladder needing emptying. And the dogs weren't exactly holding back either. We soldiered on through the night and into the inevitable Scottish rain, making me wet as well as cold. Eventually, pulling into yet another services, Bill announced that this would be our last stop before getting to the caravan park. I couldn't wait to get into my new home, have a hot shower and climb into bed. We huddled together in the cab, drinking tea and talking about the caravan site's fantastic facilities. The future hadn't seemed so bright in a long time, but as we got going for the last time, brightness was something we needed right there and then. Instead, I had to stand up in the back of the van, looking over the cab into the wind and rain, trying to spot the caravan site. Nicola kept shouting, 'It has to be round here somewhere,' from the window while Bill just got on with driving, believing he knew where we were going. Eventually, we stumbled upon an old driveway which led up to an even older cottage. Had it not been for the smoke coming from the chimney, I would definitely have thought it was awaiting demolition. At least we could ask for directions so I jumped down and gave the door a quick tap, sending flakes of paint flying everywhere. There was no reply so I walked round the back. Here, there was nothing but a big field divided into areas of hardcore, a modest building made out of breeze blocks, a red telephone box and a small caravan.

The place seemed deserted but I could hear the phone ringing in the phone box. Going over, I saw it was full of brackets with hanging baskets. All very odd. Then, when I walked back round to the front of the house, I was greeted by a little old lady, very weather-beaten and wearing several coats, all buttoned up wrongly. Up top, she had a hat which, but for the lack of a spout hole, could have passed for a tea cosy. I glanced over to Nicola and was met with a piercing look - not a good sign. So, I pulled the shrivelled leaflet from my damp jeans pocket.

'Do you reckon we're far away then?' I asked Nicola.

'Not really, Duncan,' she replied through gritted teeth.

'So which way is it then?'

'It's here,' she growled quietly.

'It can't be,' I insisted, waving the leaflet. I then showed it to the old lady, who smiled.

'You're the couple from down south.'

'Are you sure it's us?' I said eventually, hoping there was a mix-up.

'Duncan, isn't it?'

I was now speechless and just slowly nodded, still showing her my leaflet. She smiled again.

'I'm Agnes, welcome to my home.'

Finding my words again, I suggested that things were looking a bit different to what was on the leaflet.

'Och, I know. My son, Hamish, is in the process of finishing the site and the printers told me to go ahead with the details of the finished site. It saves on reprinting costs, you see? But that doesn't matter.'

It did, but Agnes was in full flow now.

'You're here, so let me get the key and if you drive past my gate, you'll see the site entrance just a bit further up. I'll shout for Hamish to help you unload.'

Bill was less than impressed.

'What about all the facilities like the swimming pool and the shop?'

'The shop,' I said, pointing into the far distance, 'will be over there. And the swimming pool's the other way.'

'But that's the North Sea,' he said.

'Precisely,' I replied.

Nicola and Bill were leant up against the van in shock, but I was past caring. As far as I was concerned, things couldn't get any worse so the only way was up. And anyway, we didn't have anywhere else to go.

We waited in vain for Hamish, and eventually I opened the gate and we drove across the field to our caravan. Nicola and Bill stayed in the van while I opened the door to take a peek. When I looked back at their disapproving faces, I couldn't help but laugh. Nicola wound down the window.

'Just tell me,' she said, 'Have you seen worse?'

'No.' I couldn't lie. It looked like a disused mobile air raid shelter.

We unloaded, leaving everything outside as it would need careful planning to work out where all our stuff would actually go. I was cold and damp from spending a whole night in the back of a pick-up. All I wanted to do was get to bed. So the three of us, along with the dogs, the terrapins and the vending machine that Bill was clinging onto, crammed ourselves into the living area. Watching Nicola opening drawers and cupboards and trying one of the two internal doors, I decided it was my job to instil a bit of hope.

'It's actually not that bad,' I managed, but Nicola gave me that look again.

'We have no cooker, no toilet, no heating, and do you see any lights?' she said.

Suddenly there was a massive cracking sound, followed by Bill falling off his seat. Coins flew everywhere as he finally broke open the vending machine.

'Tell you what,' I suggested. 'Let's leave him to the cash and go and sort this out with Agnes.'

We eventually found her by the breeze block shed. She walked over, beaming, and asked if there was anything we needed. I could tell Nicola was about to start so I held her back.

'Could you confirm a few minor points?' I asked.

'Of course.'

'We have no cooker.'

'Ah, yes, Hamish can sort that.'

'A toilet? Anywhere to have a wash or a shower?'

'In here is a shower,' she said, pointing to the shed, 'and next to it is the toilet. Unfortunately there's no hot water yet.'

'A job for Hamish, perhaps?' I suggested.

She smiled and went on.

'But the toilet works perfectly.'

'What about electricity?' asked Nicola.

'Come with me.'

We followed her back towards the caravan and round the back where there was a large wooden box with two doors. Pulling these open, Agnes twisted a few knobs and tugged a starting pulley. Instantly, we were covered in a belch of black smoke from the exhaust. The noise was deafening, but by lip-reading we learned that through a small door we could connect electrical items from the caravan into the generator. I gave her the thumbs up and off she went, still smiling, passing Bill who now stood outside looking startled. We shouted at the top of our voices, explaining that it was the generator. He nodded and then, stepping closer, held up a coin a few inches from my eye. It read 'diez pesetas.' He took me inside and pointed to a heap of coins on the seat, all looking like 'diez pesetas.' So much for his pension, I thought, unless, of course, he goes back to Spain.

For the next few days, we just adapted to our new environment. We needed to lay the foundations for our new life, starting with the caravan. The Calor gas fire (which still had a hundred thousand pound bounty on it) would keep us warm, and we found an old barbecue to cook on, fuelled by charcoal topped up with the plentiful pine cones that lay all around the site. The generator ran the kettle - useful for keeping ourselves clean although this involved filling two buckets with hot water, running over to the showers, pouring one bucket over, lathering up and then rinsing off with the second. Communication with the outside world was via the hanging basket phone box, and to keep warm in the evenings we'd go walking with the dogs up the pitch black lanes until it was time for bed. Our situation was bad, but we were surviving. And although Nicola had every right to complain, she just got on with it all.

Nicola wanted to register with the local recruitment agencies, so Bill gave us a lift into town. There, we met up with Bill's brother-in-law, Colin, who owned a garage right on the sea front just outside Edinburgh. Colin had a very soft Scottish accent and I immediately felt totally at ease in his company. His business partner, Dave, was all smiles, and between them they were genuinely sorry for our circumstances. They'd both been in the same position as me and, if anything, had fallen a lot further. Their ticket out of the mess was to buy a Mini Metro at an auction and then do it up by the side of the road, before selling it on. Within eighteen months, they'd progressed to owning a garage and pushing out at least ten Metros a week. Business was booming and they were making the most of it.

Colin put a set of keys down on the table. I couldn't believe it, I now had the use of a silver Metro. I don't know what Bill had been saying, but Colin seemed to think I was in the vending machine business. And I wasn't going to argue, especially as Colin was prepared to let me store the machines at the garage and use his tools to fix them up.

'If you come back tomorrow,' Colin added, 'I'll have a list of places in town you can try.'

'Thank you so much,' I said, not sure what else to say in response to such kindness.

'Just remember - we have all been there,' he replied.

I went to pick up Nicola. She'd found a job in a bank processing centre, starting the next day. And, passing me a phone number, she told me about a vacancy for a night assistant serving groceries. We headed back home to find our dishwasher, left outside for Hamish to install, still standing in front of the caravan. I didn't mind. We'd had a good day. While Nicola started the barbeque, I went over to the phone box to enquire about the job vacancy. I found myself talking to Charlie, of Uncle Charlie's Really Convenient Stores. With a gruff Scottish accent, he tested me with a few calculations which I answered, and then asked if I knew the difference between certain types of fruit and veg. I asked why and was told that the last person he'd employed had never seen broccoli and got grapes and strawberries mixed up. Then, interview over, Charlie hired me, giving me a road name where I was to meet him. It was great news, although I wondered why he'd told me a road name but not a number.

I came out of the phone box and walked straight into Agnes, all smiles as usual. I asked about Hamish doing the dishwasher and was told that he had been busy today, but it would be done. So we chatted for a while until the plumes of smoke and the roar of the generator told me that dinner was ready. Sitting on a rickety bench eating burgers and hotdogs, Nicola and I reflected on what a fantastic day we'd had. And tomorrow she'd start work while I'd cracked on finding sites for the vending machines. Then I'd collect her and bring her home before going straight off to my new night job. Things were looking up.

The first contact on my vending machine list, a pub landlord, was a bit wary, never having seen anything quite like it before. The machine was just over two feet tall and held about a hundred small tins of various nuts and sweets. He was also dubious of the mad, fast-talking Brummie who didn't really know what he was doing. But when I explained that there was no cost to him and that I would give him twenty per cent of the money taken, it was a deal. So I filled up the machine and left it on the bar. I was definitely rusty but with what I'd learned from my leasing days coming back to me, I quickly grew in confidence. I just mentioned the first landlord's name, which usually did the trick. And by the end of that first day, I had installed six machines.

Then it was off to the night job. I was soon lost in the concrete jungles of Edinburgh's council estates and when I finally found the right road, it didn't look right. It was all houses and no shops. Turning off the engine, I felt disappointed that such a successful day was going to end in a wild goose chase. Then I noticed a large blue van coming down the road. It sounded its horn and within seconds, lights came on in most of the houses. Front doors opened and people of all ages, sizes and stages of undress spewed out of their homes. The van reversed to a halt and a hatch was opened and propped up with a sawn-off clothes line. I could just make out some tiny writing on the side door, the words 'Uncle' and 'Store.' The other words had been defaced, changed to 'Uncle arse is a con man.'

A queue formed and my heart sank. I seriously considered just driving off, but I couldn't. I owed it to Nicola to get us out of this mess, so I locked the car and joined the back of the growing line of people all wanting sweets, ice cream, pop, cigarettes and alcohol. I didn't see anyone asking for broccoli. It was like feeding time at the zoo, and Uncle Charlie was like a deranged keeper. People would swear their order at him and then there'd be a stand-off with Charlie trying to take their money before they ran off with the goods. He'd shout and swear back and for the ones who tried to do a runner, he'd be ready with a wooden mallet. Bang, straight over the back of their hands with no one else taking a blind bit of notice. After nearly twenty minutes, it was my turn. By now, the road was silent and the houses dark. I was about to open my mouth and introduce myself when kindly Uncle Charlie barked at me.

'We've only got Regal in twenties and no half bottles of vodka.'

'No, I'm Duncan. We spoke on the phone about the job? Last night?'

He didn't look any the wiser.

'Remember? I know the difference between grapes and strawberries.'

He smiled in recognition and told me to come to the back door.

'Duncan, it's dead simple. We drive to about thirty streets a night, stopping at half ten. Weekends we do fifty streets, or until we run out of stock. You'll do the selling. The men want lager and cigarettes, the women want spirits and cigarettes, and the kids want sweets, pop and cigarettes. And they'll usually ask for alcohol as well, saying it's for their mum or gran. Don't serve them because mum is usually in the queue behind the little bastards.'

I nodded.

'I'll be behind you handing you the goods with this hand. The other one's for my mallet. Any questions?'

'Why did you ask me about fruit and veg?'

'That? Well, I introduced a few lines a couple of weeks ago. Big profit margin. But it didn't work because the last girl got all mixed up. I'd ask people if they wanted some fruit or veg, a bag of grapes or a punnet of strawberries, something like that. I was more or less forcing it on them and they'd just give in so they could get back to their houses. My girl didn't know what she was giving them and the daft bastards didn't know the difference either. They'd just take it and come back the next week complaining about eating boiled grapes.'

For the rest of that night's round I just watched and learned. As the evening went on and Charlie's customers got progressively drunker, the swearing and shouting got steadily worse until the last few punters could barely stand, let alone state what they actually wanted to buy. After the final stop, Charlie drove me back to my car and when he asked if I wanted the position, I accepted without hesitation. I hadn't had so much fun in ages. In an odd sort of way, it also boosted my confidence. It didn't matter how low I sank, I'd never be in the position of those people, depending on Uncle Charlie to turn up so I could get some alcohol to put me out of my self-inflicted misery. Then suddenly he was off on one again, pointing and shouting, and it took me a few seconds to realise it was me he was shouting at.

'You daft bastard! You shouldn't have left your car there!'

We pulled up alongside my Metro. The wheels had gone. So had the interior, the seats, dashboard, even the wiper blades. Everything but the bodywork.

'I'll give you a lift to the taxi office,' Charlie said.

My next Metro was brown with bucket seats and made the sound of a rally exhaust. But as long as it got me to the pubs to offload the vending machines, and then on to the night job with Charlie, nothing else mattered. I managed to site the rest of my machines quickly enough, even though the bright red contraptions looked completely out of place in the standard pub décor of brown walls and nicotine-yellow ceilings. With well-honed patter, I'd tell each landlord that I wasn't here to sell him anything, just to offer a simple business opportunity where we all could make a few pounds. Sometimes it drew the attention of the regulars, so I'd include them in my sales pitch by giving them a sample. And the landlords, once they realised they'd earn a commission without having to pay anything, quickly took to the idea. I'd often get a dig about being English, but I'd simply say we'd saturated England with these machines so why should Scotland be left out. Job done.

Although I didn't have to re-visit the sites for a couple of weeks, I had plenty to be getting on with. Top priority was plumbing the dishwasher into the shower block. I'd given up waiting for Hamish by then. We'd politely enquired several times as to his whereabouts, and Agnes always pointed into the far distance.

'He's over there.'

'Where?'

'There.'

But he never was. I didn't care that I'd have to walk across the field with the washing up bowl full of dirty crockery to load the dishwasher. Everything else had been taken away from me but for as long as I didn't have to wash the dishes by hand, I still had a life. I was loving my time with Charlie; the humour, the shouting and the banter, and the sight of him half falling out of the van trying to batter people who attempted to do a runner. But I could also see how easy it could be to end up like some of our customers. Occasionally, on a quiet night, I'd stand at the hatch staring into the cold night and would suddenly be enveloped by a deep sadness and regret. I still couldn't discuss how I felt with anyone. It was as if I'd been beamed down from a different world in order to suffer in silence. The only person who understood this isolation was Nicola, and I didn't want to put more pressure on her. And it was clear that any conversation with my parents would avoid the topic until I could report that our situation had improved. And who knew when that might be?

Soon winter had well and truly set in. And this was in Scotland, and in a caravan. Arriving back at the site one day with a boot full of charcoal and Calor gas, I heard the phone ringing in the hanging basket box. I was always hoping for a call from one of the pub landlords reporting that the machine needed a refill, but all I ever seemed to get were enquiries from holiday-makers and the tourist board, prompted by Agnes's misleading campsite leaflets. Telling them that the site was full simply triggered their life story about little Jimmy being so excited after seeing the pictures, and what with Mum and her leg, and the list of family ailments. So I'd tell them they were on a standby list in case of cancellations. I didn't want to add mass suicides to my conscience. But today it wasn't a landlord or a tourist, it was Bill and he was excited. He'd seen an article in the paper explaining the council had built three houses specifically for start-up businesses. Each development involved a two-bedroomed house and at the end of the small garden, a small industrial unit about the size of two double garages. I phoned the council immediately and got through to the business department. There was one still available but with six people already on the list waiting to be interviewed. I was the seventh. The lady on the other end of the line just needed to confirm a few details: name, address and was I self-employed? Yes. And my line of business was manufacturing? I didn't even flinch: yes. And what did I manufacture? This time I did flinch and, not sounding too convincing, replied, 'Nut vending machines.' There was a long silence before the next question. And my company name? 'My company name?' I parroted, trying to buy myself time. 'Yes, of course - Nuts About Vending.' She seemed happy with that and gave me a time and an address for a formal interview, adding that a letter of confirmation would be posted out.

When I collected Nicola that evening, we went on a detour to view the house. It was in Prestonpans, an old mining village set right on the Firth of Forth which, to my eyes - now watering from the freezing cold wind - was bang on the North Sea. The place was still producing coal for the enormous power station which stood at one end of the High Street. Eventually, we found the row of three houses, mercifully at the other end of the High Street and separated by the chip shops and various pie and cake outlets which seemed the norm for this part of Scotland. We pulled up alongside the sea wall and had a look at the house. Standing in the postage stamp, grassless garden, without saying a word, we both knew this place could be perfect. We gazed out to sea and imagined living there, just a few feet away from a pebble beach. It was an achingly-close opportunity to re-enter civilisation and a true oasis, not just for us but also the dogs.

'Wait 'til the facking waves hit that facking wall and the spray hits the facking bathroom window, which some dozy bastard has left open just when you're soaking in the facking bath.'

Turning to locate the source of the not-very-Scottish voice, we saw a large woman with huge arms, one of which sported a tattoo of an anchor.

'How the fack are you? I'm Debs. I don't know if you can tell by my accent, but I'm originally from Tooting. The lazy bastard in there,' she went on, pointing to her kitchen window, 'is my husband, Keith.'

She shouted at the top of her voice for Keith to get out there, which he did, followed by two greyhounds.

'Get back inside,' roared Debs.

Keith and the dogs turned in unison.

'Not you, Keith, I'm talking to Charles and Di.'

Keith was the complete opposite of his other half. He looked like a matchstick, super thin and with red hair. He looked at us and said, 'All reet,' in a very deep, very gruff Scottish accent.

I spoke for the first time, explaining that we were up for an interview.

'I hope you facking get it, especially you being English. We're outnumbered up here by all them Jocks. And you look better than the last family. Three months they lasted. Made facking garden furniture, the stupid bastards. The sun only comes out once a year and that's to let the facking midges dive bomb you. But oh no, they wouldn't listen to their Auntie Debs. Only one person round here any good with wood, and that's my Keith.'

Speech over, Debs pushed her Keith back into the house. We got back into the car and I turned to Nicola.

'Leave it to me, love; we *will* have one of those houses. And what brilliant neighbours.'

'I thought you'd say that,' said Nicola quietly, looking out of the window.

Our day-to-day existence had been getting a lot harder, mentally and physically, and more so for Nicola than me. While I got some relief flying around in the mobile store four or five nights a week, she'd stick out the evening shift in the caravan on her own. At times, I could physically feel the strain she was under. At other times, I had felt myself trapped in a slow spiral of impending doom. The nights had been getting colder and darker, with the temperature dropping to below freezing at night and only rising a few degrees above in the day. We were still cooking outside on the barbecue, and inside the caravan the only warmth came from directly in front of the Calor gas fire, a precious space usually hogged by the two dogs. We'd perch together on the edge of the caravan seat watching the condensation build up. Then, eventually, thanks to the methane from dogs - who were now on economy food - we'd rush to push the door open and gulp in the fresh, cold air, leading, of course, to total heat loss.

Keeping clean was also a task we dreaded. Still using the twin buckets, we now shared the chore, one of us stripping off while the other stood on a chair to pour lukewarm water over you. There'd be a quick scrub before the other bucket rinsed you off, and then you had seconds to dry and get dressed before running back to the caravan and scrambling into bed fully clothed. I'd then wake up the next morning with a dead leg or arm, having been trapped by fifteen stone of dogs. And then the daily routine began, firing up the generator for the tea and thawing out the frozen milk.

Nicola deserved so much better than this, something brought home one morning when I drove her to work while it was still dark. As we passed under a streetlight, she pulled down the vanity mirror to check on her make-up and screamed. Her reflection revealed that her face was covered in patches of soot she'd missed during the previous night's ten second shower. I couldn't put her through this any longer. We needed that house so I needed to crack the interview with the council.

I entered through two massive double doors into a room of some grandeur. In front of me, at the end of a long table, sat the five people who held our future in their hands. And they didn't hold back, interviewing me for nearly an hour about every aspect of my business. I'd updated the trading name to Knutz About Vending, but that was about the only thing I had done. So, did I lie at the interview? Yes. Through my teeth. None of the machines had yet been emptied or needed refilling, and anyway, I didn't have a clue where I'd obtain more stock or how I would pay for it. But my vision wasn't outside the realms of reality. At least, I didn't think so, but did they? I was told to wait outside while they made a decision.

Sitting in the corridor, I was lulled into a mindless state by the central heating and lost all sense of time, but eventually was called back in. As I entered, the lady on the end of the table smiled. Then they all looked up, smiling. I felt a ten ton weight being lifted off my shoulders. I was in. We were going to have a house to live in. I was told it would take a week to process every-thing before we could move in. And I was also told that if I filled out a few forms, I should be entitled to a £1,000 European grant. I shook everyone's hand and thanked them profusely. My thanks were noted and mention was made of a visit to ensure I got all the support and advice I'd need. And that was it.

I was about to leave when I decided to ask why they had chosen me over the six other applicants. The question left them looking embarrassed.

'Only you turned up.'

Outside, Nicola leaned over to open the car door for me. I didn't say a word, just smiled and that was enough. Punching the dashboard, she let out a loud 'Yes!!!' We decided to go straight round to Bill's flat to share the good news. I also had a proposi-tion to put to him, inviting him to help me to run the business. I knew he'd leap at it.

'No problem,' he said, 'I'd love to.'

'That's great,' I replied. Then, trying not to look at either of them, I added, 'There's just one other thing, Bill.'

'Yes?'

'I told the interview panel that you're blind.'

'What?'

'I'm sorry. I had no choice. I had to go in strong to convince them of my need. And anyway, it's not a complete lie. I mean, even you say everything's a blur when you're not wearing your glasses.'

'What happens if someone visits officially?' asked Nicola.

'Don't worry - I've thought of that. We'll get him some Stevie Wonder specs and a white stick.'

'I'm not sure about this,' said Nicola.

'And you both won't believe my genius,' I went on. 'We stick a fluorescent coat on Ben, what with him being a black Labrador, and we've got ourselves a guide dog.'

I chose to take the silence that followed as the sound of approval.

Until we received that letter telling us everything had been processed, we couldn't settle. We didn't even visit the house just in case, and instead continued with our life as it was. By the third day after the interview, I felt so battle weary I didn't know if I could pick myself up to fight another round in life. My body felt like jelly and my mind was just a haze. Having dropped Nicola off at work, I drove slowly back to the site knowing that if the letter hadn't arrived, I would have to make a phone call to find out. I was greeted by Agnes standing outside and waving an envelope. Without even looking at her, I jumped out of the car, grabbed it, ripped it open, scanned it and then sat down on the step. It was all confirmed and relief flooded over me. Agnes didn't say a word and I decided to carry out some chores for her to keep myself occupied. Hamish had gone into town, apparently. Not that I ever minded helping Agnes - she had adopted our terrapins by then as we couldn't keep them warm enough in the caravan.

When I went to pick up Nicola from work, she was the most upbeat she'd been since our time at the hotel. For my part, I was still stressing about what would have happened had the council changed its mind. But she was having none of that.

'Duncan, I married you because I love your outlook and your vision. I love the fact that if something has a ninety-nine percent chance of failing, you will always hang your hat on the one per-cent. OK, everything you touch turns to dust, but have you quit? No. I made one major decision in life and that was to marry you. And look what happened - I'm living in a tin hut, I shower in temperatures below freezing, go to work with a charcoal face and get gassed out of my damp bed by the dogs.'

I laughed and was about to reply, but she put her hand on my knee and continued.

'And if that's not enough incentive for you to make things better, try this.'

Looking straight into my eyes, she said, 'I'm pregnant.'

CHAPTER TWELVE

Walking into the new house that was about to become our home, we were hit by the smell of fresh paint, by how clean everything was and, after weeks in a cramped and freezing caravan, by the sheer amount of space. Then, just as we were contemplating our complete lack of furniture, in walked Debs, our soon-to-be next door neighbour, shy and retiring as ever and followed in by her three children, their faces covered in chocolate.

'How the facking hell are you both? I'm so excited you pair got the house.'

She numbed my arm with her version of a gentle punch and explained why nobody else had turned up for the interviews.

'Any people that came to view, yeah? Well, I'd blast some music out and send the kids out, telling them to shout and scream. And then Keith would start up some of his tools and all that, with a bit of my cockney charm chucked in, usually sent them scurrying away.'

The kids then presented us with a gift of their favourite snack - chocolate toasties - and Debs asked us if we needed anything. The one thing we really needed was furniture.

'KEITH!!!' bellowed Debs at the top of her voice.

Within seconds, he was standing in our kitchen.

'All right?' he murmured.

Debs reeled off eight different items she'd decided we needed and Keith, nodding obediently, trotted off to his workshop.

Back at the campsite, we started the generator for one last time, packed the few belongings that weren't covered in mould, and loaded them in the boot of the car. As a father-to-be, I had a new goal: to become a dad whose worldly possessions would one day amount to more than the meagre contents of a blue hold-all. Then we went to say goodbye to Agnes and Hamish. Hamish, as ever, was absent.

'I'll pass on the message to him,' Agnes told me, 'and you're welcome back any time. Have you enjoyed your holiday?'

We agreed that we had. Nicola quietly pointed out to me that there couldn't be many people who brought their own dishwasher on holiday. And then it was down to business, emptying the vending machines that I'd installed around the area. As I went from venue to venue, my heart sank. I discovered that of the original ten machines, the first seven had all met with different but equally hopeless ends. Some were broken, some had been stolen or mysteriously gone missing, and one was still there but locked up inside the premises of a business that had gone bust. And the comments I received ranged from unhelpful to bizarre:

'What machine?'

'We put it away 'cos the missus wanted to know if you do any colour other than red.'

'Been nicked, but you still owe me a pound.'

'Sorry, mate, as you can see, we haven't sold any tins. What are they anyway?'

And the weirdest one of all:

'It disintegrated on contact - blood everywhere.'

After all this, I took my time getting to the next venue, machine number eight, stopping for a cup of tea and feeling sorry for myself. But when I finally got there, the machine was still on the bar. And still intact. I couldn't believe it and felt like giving it a hug. Then, when I got closer, I realised it was still full. The manageress explained that it was jammed with a couple of twenty pence pieces. I shook it and tipped it upside down, determined either to get it working or at least get the 40p out. But it refused to budge. It was at this point that a softly spoken guardian angel appeared holding a screwdriver. A quick rummage later, he handed me the coins.

'You're new to this, aren't you?' he said.

'Yeah.'

'Thought so. How many machines have you lost?'

'This is the only one I've managed to get my hands on.'

'Got any more?'

'Two.'

'Right; they must be the ones I clocked yesterday. If you're quick, you might get a few quid from them.'

'How come you knew how to fix them?' I asked.

He pointed to the cigarette vending machine in the bar.

'That's my business,' he said, as the manageress handed him a drink. Then he dropped a cloth sack onto the table with the solid, metallic thud that only a large amount of coins can make. His name was Nigel and he reckoned there was no money in cigarette vending because of all the illegal packets coming in from abroad.

'But you must have more money in that sack than me and my wife can earn in a week,' I said.

'Aah, that's just turnover. Once you've paid the venue commission, the VAT and a few machine repairs, there's nothing left. I sometimes wonder if I'm just working for Her Majesty's Government as a glorified tax collector.'

'See,' he went on, 'what you're doing, that's an earner.'

'Is it?'

'Of course. You just need to anchor your machines down and don't forget the golden rule - only site where they sell. They saw you coming at the other places. My machines are fully bolted to the wall and they've got steel wrap-around bars.'

I wish I could have said the same about mine.

Nigel offered to give me a lift to my last two venues. He drove a brand new Range Rover and stopped off at his large, gated house on the way. If this was his idea of 'no money,' then I wanted to be just as unsuccessful as him.

We arrived at my next venue. Nearly empty. My shoulders dropped, forgetting for a moment that people might actually have paid for the tins. But on closer inspection, I found ninety pounds. Result! The coins gleamed like treasure as I counted them. Nigel came over, his bag thudding on the bar. His takings dwarfed mine, but that didn't stop him describing them as 'abysmal,' 'a bit of turnover' and, 'a service to my customers, I suppose.' He then helped secure my machine to the wall and we left, heading for the final venue. This wasn't quite as good as number nine, but it was still intact and there was money in the back.

While Nigel drove me back to my car, I probed him further about his supposedly not-for-profit business. He then handed me his card.

'Listen,' he said, 'if you see any venues needing my services, let me know. There'll be a couple of hundred in it for you. And nightclubs? You can double that figure.'

I watched his Range Rover purr off into the distance thinking I'd had a successful day all round. Even losing eighty percent of my business didn't bother me. I was far more intrigued by who I'd just met.

It took us all of five minutes to move into our new home. After that, we stood in the kitchen and I told Nicola about my day. To her concise summary, 'So you've lost eight of your ten machines?' I gave my optimistic reply. 'Yes, but you need to hook a sprat to catch a mackerel.' She then opened my cloth sack and started counting the money from Knutz About Vending's first trading week. Factoring in her wages and the money I'd earned from the mobile shop, we had managed to save nearly £600. Of course, it was nowhere near what we needed to equip and furnish our new house, but we were both just happy to be there. That night, we talked for hours about our future and our child and all the possibilities that lay ahead. Eventually, Nicola curled up on a blanket on the bare floor in the kitchen, with the two dogs either side and her head resting on my knee. All I could hear was the gentle crashing of waves up against the sea wall. I closed my eyes. It felt like I had arrived in paradise.

The next few days were spent turning our house into a home. My first priority was getting Bill over to install the dishwasher and with that done, we then collected our bed and various pieces of furniture we'd sourced from second-hand shops in the area. Keith was a regular visitor, delivering his latest creations: blanket boxes, large chests, small chests, a TV chest, bedside cabinets, a bathroom cabinet, magazine stand, post rack and coat hooks. Our wooden warrior even made us a kitchen table to go with the second-hand one we'd already got. As Debs said, 'You never know when you'll need a facking spare.' We were totally overwhelmed by their kindness - they wouldn't even take a penny for the wood. Keith's final creation was a bench-type seat which stretched through the living room and into the kitchen. I hadn't seen anything like it since visiting church when I was at school. We could now sit in the living room and just shuffle into the kitchen without getting up.

I had now received my European grant, and as I was still unsure what it was actually for, I decided that vending was the way forward. So I quit the mobile shop job to concentrate on my new venture. I only had two sites and enough stock to last me a couple months. The tins of nuts I had came from Spain, so I knew I'd have to try and find a new supplier closer to home sooner or later. I also knew that I wanted to meet up with Nigel again, so I arranged a meet.

I was very keen to make a good impression on him but the workshop that came with the house was bare, so I asked Debs for some help.

'KEITH!!!' she bellowed, nearly perforating my eardrum.

Keith promptly appeared from the under-stairs cupboard. I'd been next door on several occasions and Keith would always come out of this cupboard, like it was his domain. I explained that I wanted him to turn part of the workshop into an office. And I made it clear I'd be paying him this time. He made the furniture in two days and insisted on installing it all himself. I left him to it and went to bed with the distant whine of an electric screwdriver coming from the workshops.

The next morning when I opened the workshop door, my reaction was blunt: 'Oh, no, bloody hell, what's he done?'

He'd begun by partitioning the space, leaving one half with no natural light. At one end, there was some sort of counter and the other creations included an enormous table with bench seating for at least sixteen people, with some kind of turntable as its centre piece. He'd also covered one wall with at least a hundred wooden pigeon holes of varying sizes. I stood there, slack-jawed and not knowing what to think. Fortunately, Debs turned up and told me what to think.

'He's facking done well, hasn't he?'

'Er, yeah.'

'Right, let me explain.'

'Please do.'

'That gap at the end of the partitioning, that's your trade counter, right? I mean, everyone has a trade counter. Looks more professional.'

Debs went over to the table.

'You can work off it and have meetings at the same time,' she said.

'Brilliant, Debs, but what's with the turntable?'

'Ooh, you're not going to believe this.'

'Try me.'

'My Keith is a genius.'

'Genius,' I managed to reply.

'Yeah, you put your milk and sugar and your sandwiches on it, and spin it round so all your guests can reach what they need.'

I could feel myself going into shock, but Debs hadn't finished.

'And,' she bellowed, 'not forgetting your pigeon holes to keep your stock and spare parts, which is positioned perfectly for you to reach when people arrive at your trade counter.'

I managed to find what seemed the right thing to say.

'Debs, you're a star. And thanks so much to Keith. I'll let you know how we get on with the turntable.'

The day of the meeting with Nigel arrived, as did Bill, looking all dapper in his suit.

'I've left my van out of sight round the corner,' he said, equally determined to impress Nigel. 'I'd do the same with your car, if I was you.'

'Bill, it doesn't matter. When you see what Keith has done to our business premises, our two old bangers might actually benefit our cause.'

Bill was gobsmacked by the workshop, but once he was over the shock he pulled out a phone from a plastic carrier bag and positioned it carefully on the desk.

'Bill, please, no. What if he wants to use it? It's not connected. He'll think we're all round the twist.'

Too late. There was a knock at the big double doors. As Keith's trade counter blocked the main exit, I had to go out of the workshop's other door to welcome Nigel.

Bill was 'on the phone.'

'Richard,' he said into the lifeless handset, 'I can't do anything at the moment. I'm about to tie up most of my capital helping Duncan with his new venture. Anyway, we'll talk later.'

He replaced the receiver and got up to shake Nigel's hand. Pleasantries over, we all sat down at the end of the giant table and I came right out with my plan - I wanted to get into the cigarette vending business. Nigel smiled at that, like he'd already guessed, and began scanning the surroundings as if weighing up if it was worth giving away any of the precious information it had obviously taken him half a lifetime to pick up.

First up, we got a history lesson. We learned that the cigarette vending industry revolves around two companies, Mayfair and Sinclair Collis. Mayfair is owned by Gallagher's, one of the biggest cigarette manufactures in Europe. Sinclair Collis is owned by Imperial Tobacco, one of the largest cigarette manufacturers in the world. They both started cigarette vending when pubs and working men's clubs stopped selling cigarettes behind the bar due to large increases in tax and duty, and the resulting small profit margin. Vending machines, in themselves, were not the answer as the profit margins were tiny. The business only took off when the manufacturers started making special vending packs with only sixteen cigarettes, but selling at a slightly higher price than a full pack of twenty. Of course, it wasn't long before the manufacturers saw that this little side line was a serious cash generator, so they went after every outlet that would accept a vending machine. It wasn't long before they were generating millions in revenue.

However, once they had saturated the market, the problems began. As both companies grew increasingly eager for more plunder, they started poaching each other's sites, offering the managers or landlords larger and larger commission payments, and running outlets at a loss if need be. It was all-out war. And when major companies stand there and beat the business crap out of each other, the one thing that always suffers is customer service. But then independent operators come in and take over from the big boys for a while, and everyone's happy. Everyone, that is, except the big boys who wait a few weeks and then waltz back in with offers of big commissions to landlords and take back the business. An independent could lose half their sites in a fortnight and, eventually, they'll be bought out with an offer just generous enough to make it worth their while.

Against this background, it was all the more interesting that Nigel seemed to have done OK. He'd built up his sites slowly by buying out other independent operators when they wanted to sell, and soon he was looking after two hundred and fifty sites, and making a gross profit of between ten and twenty percent. 'So, if I was to try to enter the cigarette vending business, what would happen?' I asked. The answer was precisely nothing. First up, I'd need machines, and the distributors of these also happened to be the largest vending operators in the city, or even the county. They simply didn't supply to people who they thought might steal their sites. Secondly, I'd need stock. It had taken Nigel years to get an account with a large distributor. Otherwise, it was cash on collection, usually from the same company who supplied you with the machines. And if instead you purchased direct from the manufacturers and then went out stealing their sites, you'd find them 'accidentally' forgetting to deliver to you.

Nigel's pitch was deliberately negative, but he did offer one silver lining. The Holy Grail of cigarette vending, I learned, was the nightclub. A medium-sized club opening three nights a week could clear upwards of three hundred packets, and you could easily add an extra £1 per packet onto the vend price as the whole thing was a closed market. You could clear £500 a week per site, and the owner or manager didn't even bother to look at what they were getting in commission when they were taking twenty or thirty grand a night behind the bar.

Bill and I sat bolt upright in unison.

'You only need one,' he said to me.

I sighed and told him to try and set his targets slightly higher.

'No,' Nigel interrupted. 'Bill's target is high already.'

At this, Bill was ready to give up on our grand plan, but I still wanted to give it a crack. I asked Nigel who was the vending and cigarette distributor for the area. He gave me the raised eyebrow 'we're doomed' kind of look. Apparently, I needed to speak to a man called Big Al. He was the main man, operating out of a purpose-built depot in Glasgow and with about a thousand sites under his wing. Nigel gave me Big Al's number and wished me luck. By the tone of his voice, it was clear that luck wasn't going to get me anywhere with Big Al.

'He has a reputation,' explained Nigel.

'What kind of reputation?' I asked.

'Put it this way, he never has any problems with vandalism. If a premises gets broken into, the only item left untouched is Big Al's cigarette machine. You could leave one of his machines on a Glasgow pavement and not only would it be untouched, you'd probably find a vase of flowers sitting neatly on a doily. Rumour has it, if your venue is on fire, his machines will get rescued before you.'

After the meeting, Bill and Nicola were not shy in providing plenty of constructive criticism of my plans:

1. My first week in vending had resulted in me losing eight out of my ten machines.
2. I wanted to take on two of the biggest companies in the UK with no money.
3. I had a one litre Mini Metro.
4. And no telephone.
5. Big Al.

But I wasn't to be dissuaded. To me, it was the perfect fit - a cash only business that required me to deal with landlords and managers, with the promise of a bit of intrigue and good, healthy, dishonest competition. My conviction was just about enough to sway Bill and Nicola.

'Maybe it is the business for you,' Nicola told me.

'Thanks love,' I replied.

'Don't thank me. I just can't think of anything else you could do.'

It took a few days and many searching questions for Big Al to agree to see me. Glasgow reminded me of the Midlands, only colder. It was a real working city and everything, including the sky, was tinged with grey. I could sense the hardness of the place, not entirely in a dangerous way; more a 'if you cross us, beware, as it will be the one and only time' kind of way. I pressed an intercom and was buzzed into a holding room. Eventually, I was taken into reception and told to have a seat. It was all very palatial. A door opened and out came a guy who definitely wasn't big. He introduced himself as Neil, the managing director. I was shown into his office, a magnificent mix of leather and fish tanks. I took a seat as another door opened and in walked the two biggest guys I have ever seen in my life. Their names, fittingly enough, were Big Al and Big Jim, and they ran the business. Neil, by his own admission, only turned up now and again to sign cheques, spending most of his time playing golf on the Costa del Sol.

We exchanged pleasantries then got down to business. All three of them gave me the hard stare and a stream of questions: where, when, why, how much, who had sent me, who was I connected to? It became clear nobody had approached them for years and years looking to start up in cigarette vending. It really was a closed shop and they just repeated what Nigel had said - that there was no money in this business, it was all duty and tax, and they were just scraping up what few crumbs were left.

I knew all doors would be closed if I couldn't get their help. I was straight with them and didn't expect any pity. But I also knew I needed to show I was as tough as them, so I explained how life's events had led me to where I was now, sitting in front of them. My story seemed to have some kind of impact. The Bigs just shrugged their shoulders, but Neil opened his desk and showed me a vending machine brochure.

'Trade price six hundred and ninety-nine pounds,' he told me. 'To you, eleven hundred.'

I was then told how much a vending pack of cigarettes cost, which would mean slightly more than a few crumbs with those margins. But when he wrote down the price he was going to supply me at, I wasn't sure if he was going to help me or was trying to put me off. I went along with it anyway and asked if he would supply me if I found the sites.

'Duncan, I admire your bottle. You've come over here without being able to show you can actually afford even one packet of cigarettes, and expect us to supply you with machines and stock on credit. This could potentially take sites off people we already supply, people who we have dealt with for years.'

I nodded.

'And you're English.'

I nodded again.

'So, what do you think the answer is?' Neil said.

Ah. I got up to shake their hands and thank them for their time.

'Sit down!' he bellowed.

I sat down again.

'We will help you. It may look like a closed shop but all businesses need young, entrepreneurial blood flowing through them.'

I felt overwhelmed and started thanking them profusely.

'Let's not get ahead of ourselves,' came the terse reply. 'These are the rules. You never canvass an independent site - that means any site operated by people like us and Nigel. Sinclair Collis and Mayfair sites, you can do what you like with them, but you know the risks.'

'OK,' I said.

'And you don't damage our reputation either.'

I looked at him, not sure what he meant. He explained.

'Any new venue that you get to first, it's polite to ask the other operator in the area permission. He will probably turn you down, unless you've done him a favour.'

'Right.'

'Any venue phoning you up saying they have problems with their current operator, you always phone them and warn them. Are those guidelines clear?'

'Very clear.'

'Good. Cigarettes are on seven days' credit; machines you get ninety days' credit. As you trade, we will negotiate downwards. You stay within those guidelines and we will all get along just fine.'

When I got back to the safety of my own home, the reality of all those guidelines began to sink in. The only places Bill and I could target would be run by Sinclair Collis and Mayfair. And they would outmanoeuvre us at every turn. Everywhere else was out of bounds.

When I explained this to Bill, he was exasperated.

'Duncan, where does he expect us to go? The Highlands and Islands?'

I started grinning.

'Bill, I think you may have just found us a way in.'

'No, no, I wasn't being serious. Please, no, it involves the sea and it's miles away. It just wouldn't be cost effective.'

'Maybe, but it's definitely worth exploring,' I replied. 'Which is the nearest, most populated island to us?'

'The Isle of Mull?'

'Well, that's where we'll start.'

I phoned a few hotels at random without properly explaining who I was. Everyone gave me a bollocking about empty machines and coin jams, and asked when I was coming over. I still didn't let on that I wasn't their actual vending contact and, instead, I phoned Big Al to ask who would be the operator on Mull. He just burst out laughing, told me he admired my ingenuity and wished me luck.

Bill packed the car. With everything but the kitchen sink.

'What are you taking all this stuff for?' I asked as sleeping bags, coats, blankets, flasks and bags of food were squeezed into the boot.

'Three reasons: one, it's winter; two, this car; three, we're going to Mull. You do know how far it is? We could die, you know.'

Manhattan takes your breath away, but driving through Loch Lomond on a clear winter's morning just leaves you lost for words. I had to keep stopping to get out of the car and take in the scenery. It was truly magnificent. Bill had seen it all many times, so I just left him snoring under a heap of blankets. We crossed from Oban on the west coast. The ferry trip wasn't rough, according to the lady cooking fried eggs, but as I kept losing half a mug of tea whenever I walked back to the table, I begged to differ. However, we survived the crossing and drove out into even more stunning scenery. Once we were clear of the ferry port, there was no sign of people anywhere, just lots of hills and lots of sheep, and Bill muttering, 'Now do you see why I brought all these supplies?'

Finally, I saw a sign for a hotel, braked heavily and turned down a secluded lane. We drove until we came to a car park. The manager agreed to see us and I was about to launch into my sales patter when he interrupted me.

'Have you got a vending machine on you?'

'No.'

'Have you got any cigarettes on you?'

'No.'

The manager looked understandably confused, so I explained that I was there on a fact-finding trip. He then supplied us with key facts. The machine in the hotel was owned by Mayfair. It was filled every three weeks or so, but ran out within the first seven days. During peak times, it was empty within four days.

'If you're telling me you can give me a better service than Mayfair, then you're in,' the manager said.

That's exactly what I told him.

'And when you come over,' he added, 'can you get me a few other things?'

He wrote me out a list. He wanted boxes of crisps, matches and cigars. I agreed and got him to take some tins of nuts.

'Put twenty-five percent on for your trouble,' said the manager.

I agreed to that as well. Deal done, but the manager wasn't finished. He went into his office and came back with a selection of business cards for some of the other hotels on the island.

'Tell them I've passed their names on to you. If you can deliver on your promises, you should have the island sewn up.'

By the end of the day, I'd done just that. I hand-picked the largest hotels, did the deals and made it back in time to catch the last ferry. I sat at another table, also covered in tea, on a serious high. I had gained ten sites and a host of subsidiary orders for boxes of crisps and other assorted items. I was going to make a killing, and that was before I factored in the profit from the vending machines.

'I can make a killing here, Bill,' I said excitedly.

'Just one thing you've missed,' he replied, trying to dampen my mood. 'How the hell are you going to transport ninety-six boxes of crisps in a Mini Metro?'

But I had already thought of that.

'I need to speak to Keith.'

Debs just pointed to the downstairs cupboard. I opened the door and looking in, at last realised that escaping from Debs wasn't the only reason Keith chose to live like a troglodyte. He was sitting at a desk playing games on his computer, barely visible through the fog of cigarette smoke.

'Know anyone with a trailer?' I asked him.

'Nope,' he replied.

'Oh.'

'But I could build you one.'

'And we'll come and help you install your machines,' added Debs.

And so with my new team and sufficient transport, I made the return day-trip back to Mull. Keith's trailer was an unholy mix of Meccano and loft board. It resembled a shed on wheels and looked anything but legal. Keith and I were on point in the Metro, the trailer bumping along in the rear piled high with machines. Bill drove behind us in the pick-up loaded with crisps. He had Charles and Di, Keith and Debs's two greyhounds to keep him company. And Debs and her kids brought up the rear in their Volvo Estate. For security reasons, she was looking after the cigarettes. Bill was his usual cheery self, muttering about how all his money was now tied up in crisps. I was less gloomy but twice as nervous. I had just taken on about fifteen thousand pounds worth of debt. Eleven grand didn't need paying back for three months, but the stock was on a week's credit from Big Al. If these sites didn't perform then I'd be finished almost before I'd started. What worried me most was my hastily put-together team.

It took us hours to reach the ferry terminal. We never really got above thirty miles per hour, and had to keep pulling over to let the long train of traffic past. There'd also be unscheduled toilet breaks, but at least we didn't need to stop for food; everyone just waded into the crisps. I even noticed Bill emptying packets on the dash for the dogs to eat.

After an eternity and a half, we arrived on Mull and set to work. Any worries I might have had about my team soon evaporated. I couldn't have done it without them. I hadn't realised how complicated the machines were. They needed assembling and programming. Debs just ripped the instruction manual out of my hands and told me to go and collect the money we were owed for all the sweets and crisps.

The rest of the day was a blur of unloading crisps, hauling machines into venues, setting them up and apologising constantly to the management and customers on behalf of Debs. She had taken to her self-appointed role as head of security like a duck to water. One young bloke tried to swipe a packet of cigarettes as the machines were being loaded up. She grabbed him and twisted his hand behind his back.

'That'll be four pounds please,' she announced, taking a £5 note off him.

'Sorry, no change,' she added, with all her Cockney charm.

Bill spent most of the journey fast asleep in his cab, covered in crisp packets. His job was to mind the children and the dogs. Amazingly, neither the animals nor the dogs played up at all. Everything went to plan. Everyone was exhausted. Except the well-rested Bill, that is. So he headed up the convoy as we drove back home. Very slowly.

I had no intention of just sitting and waiting for the next week to pass until I could empty the island machines. A phone line was installed, and business cards and leaflets printed. I also placed adverts in the magazines and papers directed at the mainland pub and club sector. And I went out canvassing. Everybody I visited was willing to change there and then, to go with me rather than the big boys. I selected a few of the best sites, negotiating a better commission for the owner, and arranged to install in the following week. All of this was subject to the island division of my business going to plan.

Back at my office, the answering machine was beeping away merrily. Everyone I had visited had changed their minds. What I had offered them in commission had been doubled by my competitors. I knew this would wipe out any margin but returned their calls and matched their new offers. I knew full well they would go higher, but I was intrigued to see how well they would guard their sites. The following day they had gone higher. If I was to match it, I would be running at a loss. I again agreed to equal what they were offering. Within minutes, they were back on to me. The competition had gone even higher and offered some of them six months' commission up front. One landlord even told me they'd also agreed to throw in a washing machine. Others were getting a TV - they really wanted to hang to their sites.

Eventually I got a call from the general manager of Mayfair. He was quite abrupt, wanting to know who I was. He declared that they would never lose a site, especially to a company called Knutz About Vending.

'Well, if that's the case,' I told him, 'why have I just taken ten sites off you on the Isle of Mull?'

I made the next trip to Mull on my own, the boot full of cigarettes. Bill had taken over the crisp and nut operation and would be doing a fortnightly run in his pick-up. I did ask if anyone wanted to come with me, but nobody had truly recovered from the last journey. Truthfully, I felt the same and the doubts about the wisdom of this venture began to surface. But I cheered myself up by thinking that if I was driving myself to financial ruin again, at least the scenery was stunning. By the time I arrived at the first site, my nerves were jangling. I slowly turned the key in the door of the machine, barely able to squint in case the view was going to be a disastrous one. What if the machine was still full of cigarettes instead of money? I risked a peek. Just a few packets left. That was good. But was there any money? Yep, there it was. A mound of £1 coins. I pulled the box out and let out a loud 'Yes!!!' I re-filled the machine double quick after that. I just wanted to get to the next site. All but one of the sites performed even better than I could have hoped for. Although no machine had run out of stock, each had only a few packets left, which meant no one had gone without.

I floated back home and opened the door to the unit. Everybody rushed in and listened to the crash of the bags hitting Keith's enormous table. We'd cleared nearly a thousand pounds profit. And it was only winter. Come summertime, that figure would go a lot higher.

❦

At last, my entrepreneurial ambition was burning strongly again, and I wanted more. I felt I could take on the world. But I also knew I still had to deal with my past failures. The majority of people I was now meeting in business opened up when they learned some of what I had been through. This made me realise that perhaps it wasn't just me who had failed at some point in my life. However, I now knew first-hand how one business mistake had the potential to break a person. And since moving to our new home my name had gone back on the electoral role, meaning my creditors could find me again and re-start their attempts to get blood out of a stone.

The letters began arriving thick and fast. Everyone still wanted their money, especially from the bar venture which included the landlord, the council and various suppliers. Our old house had now been repossessed. I spoke to all my creditors on the phone, explaining my situation, but mostly to no avail. I was threatened again with court action and bailiffs. 'Bring it on,' was my reply. I wasn't going to spend the rest of my life worrying. If I could make enough money then I'd pay them back. If I couldn't, I wouldn't.

Summer arrived, which meant the sky occasionally changed colour. It didn't stop the wind and the rain, though. But the business was performing better than I could have hoped. And I was going to be a father soon. They were heady times.

I'd managed to relieve the likes of Mayfair of quite a few sites, even if I had to resort to a touch of sabotage to do it. This was what being self-employed was all about - making money but not having restraints, not having to conform, making your own rules up as you went along. I loved that feeling. Unfortunately, for legal reasons, I can't divulge what we actually did. Also, there was one person who didn't agree with my definition of self-employed - the Tax Inspector - and it wasn't long before I received a visit from representatives of the Inland Revenue. Now, I have no problem paying taxes. I believe in social justice, in the better off helping those who are less fortunate. What I object to is the huge amount of red tape involved, particularly when you're just starting off. If you can't be left alone to start up a business, then how can you make the money that will eventually be taxed?

The main man (known as The Rottweiler as once he'd got his teeth into something, he never let go) explained that they wanted to do a full record inspection, from before Ridler's Bar in Worcester right up to the present day. Every question was asked in a long, drawn-out manner intended, I reckon, to wear you down. But I was keen to co-operate until we hit the thorny issue of business records.

'Ah, I haven't actually got round to those yet. But I will,' I said.

'I take it you are registered self-employed for tax purposes?'

'No.'

'Can I have...?' and the Rottweiler reeled off a list of requirements.

'I think we might be struggling on those requests,' I replied cheerily.

He was starting to get angry now and bellowed a question about how long I'd been self-employed.

'Give or take, a year after leaving school.'

'Well, you will have registered something somewhere and it's your legal duty to keep proper accounts for seven years after the business closes, or gets sold.'

'The answer,' I replied, 'is still no.'

This did not improve his mood so I persevered as politely as I could.

'Look, I'm terribly sorry but I think you have had a wasted journey.'

The Rottweiler started to go red round the neck and launched into another long-winded tirade about tax evasion, fines, penalties and bankruptcy. But by now I had had enough and just got up, headed to the door and, without a word, gently guided him out of it.

∽

With the baby due soon, we let life settle into quite a tranquil routine. Nicola had given up her job and was now helping me run the vending business. Financially, we were better off than any time previously. I had found a niche market where I would take sites off established operators, run them for a while until they had stopped spitting feathers, and then package them up into batches of four or five and sell them to Big Al or other independents. I was clearing £5,000 a time, which was used to pay off our debts. We got decent furniture in our house and changed our car. In the evenings, we would walk the dogs up the beach and occasionally I would catch up with various people I had met for a night out.

But I much preferred it back at home, especially if it wasn't raining. Debs would get out the barbecue and we'd all sit and look out at the calm sea, knowing full well we needed nothing more out of life.

Summer turned to autumn and Nicola was now just days away from giving birth. Early one evening, I was driving through Loch Lomond on my way back from Mull, taking it easy, admiring the scenery. I stopped and wandered down to the loch to eat my sandwiches. It was a spot I often used, sited strategically next to a phone box, useful for business calls. I phoned Nicola to make sure she was okay, but Debs answered.

'Get your fackin' arse back here. Her waters have broke.'

It was a long night for her, but eventually nature took its course and at twenty-five, I became father to our beautiful daughter, Amy. I just stared at her for hours in total amazement. I told her I couldn't promise what the future might hold. But what I could promise was that all of us would be together on a journey, and that it was going to be as much fun as I could possibly make it.

CHAPTER THIRTEEN

'You want to start a savings plan for Amy.'

'Dad,' I replied, 'we've only just got back from the hospital.'

I had been told, lectured and warned about what it's like having children, but none of it had really registered. Before her arrival, our future was just about today, and maybe tomorrow if we were lucky. And suddenly here she was, lying in her crib. Of course, nothing had changed. Not really. As a person I still needed to achieve the goals I had set myself, otherwise what could I tell her in years to come? Sorry, Amy, I did try to succeed in business but life got a bit tough so I gave up? No, things were different now but the important things were just the same.

Bill, his brother-in-law, Colin, Colin's business partner, Dave and I sat in a semi-derelict office attached to the Metro car centre, working out our latest venture. Discussions had been going on for a month. Like all business ideas, this one had begun as a theory based on hypothetical earnings from providing a particular service. We'd then worked backwards trying to make the pieces fit: capital investment, marketplace, outgoings, etc. The plan was to set up a car hire business. The logic was simple enough - there was a garage with a disused office, and plenty of spare cars. I could work from the office, sorting out my vending business admin, while also handling car hire customers. And if I wasn't around, Bill would be. All they really needed was me as a third partner to put in some capital to pay for the insurance and the general launch expenses.

None of us knew anything about the car hire business, but on paper it didn't look too difficult. And for once, if it all went wrong, I wouldn't have to pack my blue holdall. I was investing a lot of my time, but only some of my money, and that was just the cash flow from my vending venture. We agreed on a name - Anchor Self-Drive; Anchor because it starts with the letter A and therefore goes higher up in the Yellow Pages, and Anchor because we would be based opposite an old harbour. Genius. We also agreed to get Keith to refurbish the office.

'But please,' I added, remembering the job he'd done on my workshop, 'make sure one of us is on site at all times when he's here.'

Colin nodded towards Bill.

'That'll be your job,' he said.

My job was to tell Keith. I tapped gently on his downstairs cupboard door and he emerged in a gush of cigarette smoke, like he was walking onto the stage of Stars In Their Eyes. When I explained what we wanted, his eyes lit up.

'Keith, it's just a straightforward job - a few floorboards need repairing and the walls need some tongue and groove. And a purpose-built desk. Nothing fancy and remember: less is more.'

Debs, who'd obviously been listening, came through from the living room and squeezed his cheeks.

'My Keithy's gone all commercial!'

Keith, in his usual gruff voice, refused to get so carried away.

'What's the budget?' he asked.

'Two hundred pounds.'

'No bother. You'll have change.'

With that sorted, I then worked on the advertising, hire documents, and terms and conditions for hire. I registered the business with the tourist board and anyone else who could help direct custom our way. Leaflets were printed, and I visited the hotels and bed and breakfasts in the city centre and near to our office. Our unique selling point was price - we were the cheapest in the area by miles. OK, so our cars weren't going to be the best, but I was assured they would be clean and reliable.

The cigarette vending business, meanwhile, was ticking over quite nicely, although the competition was fed up with me and had joined forces, instructing their lawyers to sue. Apparently I had sabotaged their business and they were looking for damages running into several hundreds of thousands. And they were serious, judging by the amount of post it was generating, all written on high grade paper from offices in the best part of Edinburgh. Most of it I didn't understand, so I would just reply using the same jargon, but this didn't stop the letterbox rattling. To them, it was about corporate pride; they couldn't seem to get their heads round the idea that some one-man operation was causing a multi-billion pound company so much aggravation. The Inland Revenue had also upped the stakes by teaming up with Customs and Excise and joining the queue of financial institutions that were out to get me. However, to me it was all about providing food and warmth for my wife and child. And it was going to take more than a strongly-worded letter from some corporate suit to put a halt to my activities.

I went to collect the advertising signs to stick on the car roofs, displaying our name and the words 'hire this car' next to the hire price. As we were on the main road, the idea was to strap these to the roofs of the cars and, hey presto, free advertising. I had very positive thoughts about this venture. I was sure we would make money. Not a lot at the beginning maybe, but who knows? Tiny acorns and all that. But first, it was time to survey Keith's refurb job. Not in a million years could I have predicted how it turned out. I was joined by the others.

'Ship ahoy, what do you think captain?' said Dave. 'Your neighbour is brilliant - a themed office for less than two hundred quid.'

'What theme?' I asked.

'Nautical. Can't you see?'

'Nope.'

'But the desk fronts are broadly shaped like a ship, and behind us there's a ship's wheel with hooks to hang the keys on. And it spins round!'

'OK,' I said, still far from convinced.

'Look at the wall. It's been painted to look like the outside of a ship!'

'Yes.'

'And the other wall has been painted blue with large white blobs. It's like the sea and clouds!'

'Is it?'

'And check out the strips of wood attached to the wall. They're railings! So, when you walk in, you feel like you're strolling down the ship's deck towards the desk.'

'That's not the feeling I get,' I said.

But I was clearly in the minority. At least we all agreed that the advertising signs were a winner, displayed for effect on the customers' cars waiting to be repaired. The actual hire cars were parked in the far corner of the yard. We had three Mini Metros (our economy range), a Ford Fiesta (mid-range) and one Ford Mondeo Ghia, which was really an LX model but the badges had been changed. That was our executive vehicle. Colin reckoned we'd have all of them rented out Monday, no bother.

He wasn't wrong. Come Monday, we had a flurry of phone calls. All the cars would be hired out by the afternoon. Or so I thought. The problem turned out to be with the guidelines for our customers. When they came in to book, we required two forms of ID, a valid driving licence and a £100 deposit left by credit card. Bring all that and you got the keys. Simple, right?

The first person through the door had brought his mum and brother as ID, and then accused me of calling him a liar because he didn't have a driving licence. The next one in thought he'd pay for the rental on return. The third guy, however, seemed to provide everything he was asked for. And he was renting the Mondeo for a whole month. The car was parked outside the office window and we walked round the vehicle, checking for damage, so he could sign the sheet. All good so far. I went back to my desk and sat down. I then watched him sticking his magnetic taxi signs all over it.

But at least we were getting plenty of enquiries, and we were soon running out of cars. So Colin and Dave decided to expand the fleet with another five Metros. They were just coming up for sale and weren't exactly in tip top condition. Colin and Dave's view was, 'What do they expect for seventy-five pounds a week?' My view was, 'I suppose, but lads - people will want the doors and maybe the bonnet to be the same colour.' In the end, we decided to hire out the mismatched Metros to people who couldn't pay the deposit. And if that failed, Colin and Dave instructed me to park the cars with the offending doors facing away from prying eyes.

The pair then gave me a 'you can do it' slap on the shoulder and left me to it.

Over the next two days, all the vehicles went out on hire. One was even snapped up by an American couple staying at the five-star Balmoral Hotel where a night's stay would cost more than our entire fleet. And with none due back until next week, I was able to concentrate on my own work. While Bill manned the office and dealt with future bookings, I dealt with the post, which was always bad news. Then, out of the blue came a phone call that was to change everything. It was a lady named Sue, PA to the managing director of a nightclub in Wolverhampton. Her boss, who'd seen my vending machines while visiting a pub-owning friend in Edinburgh, had been impressed by how modern they were. She was wondering if we were a nationwide operation. I sat bolt upright.

'Erm… yes… nearly… We cover the main cities and the outer areas.'

Sue explained that they were having a terrible time with their current supplier and were looking for another company to deal with. I asked her the usual questions about packets sold, vend price and commission. She didn't know the answers and my enthusiasm dipped. I half-heartedly agreed to visit her in a fortnight and made a mental note to cancel a few days prior. I then gave Bill a quick ring to see what was going on. Everything was OK and more bookings had been taken.

'Before you go,' he added, 'I've got a couple of questions.'

'Fire away.'

'What happens if someone mislays the keys?'

'Ask the lads to sort out a new set and charge them out of their deposit,' I replied.

Bill then gave me a registration number and asked what colour that vehicle was.

'How I am supposed to know that? I've only seen the cars once. And anyway, it's on the hire sheet.'

I put the phone down and wondered whether Bill was going mad. I arrived bright and early at the Anchor office the next day to see for myself. I had plenty to think about - prices needed to go up as we were too cheap, and I needed a plan for valeting and servicing the cars when they came back in. But first, there was the answering machine flashing at me.

There were four messages.

Beep: the concierge desk from the Balmoral Hotel had rung to tell us our American friends had returned, but without the car. It was sitting in the car park of a hotel in the Highlands and they wanted reimbursing for the taxi fare in exchange for the keys.

Beep: the lady who had mislaid the car keys - the one Bill had mentioned the day before - was informing us the car and her were at her mother's, but didn't leave the address or phone number.

Beep: a man's voice: 'Just to tell you that as no one came back to me with the colour, I was unable to locate the car in the car park and made my way back by bus.'

Beep: 'Duncan, it's Bill. Forgot to mention some toe rag has painted the letter W in front of Anchor on our sign above the office. Would you mind painting over it as it looks bad for business?'

Colin and Dave were hopping mad that customers would do such things. They kept muttering between themselves about how good the cars were and how dare they just dump them. I told them we needed some kind of recovery vehicle, which only seemed to outrage them more.

'We haven't got time to leave here and collect our own vehicles,' they shouted at me.

I told them to calm down.

'Look, just get me a recovery truck and I'll sort it.'

That shut them up. I could almost see the cogs whirring.

'You're on. Give us an hour,' they said.

I got on the phone.

'Debs, do us a favour? Get up to the Balmoral Hotel, go to the concierge desk and recover the keys,' I told her, before explaining the whole story.

'He said what?' she replied. 'The cheeky bastard. Leave him to your Auntie Debs.'

'And could you put Keith on the bus? Tell him I need him here urgently. I'm making him head of our recovery division.'

Even as I was replacing the receiver, I could hear her shouting, 'Keith!!!' I then told Bill to go round to the house of the woman who had lost her car keys.

'Find out from the neighbours where her mother lives,' I said. 'And if that fails, just wait outside till someone arrives.'

'But I'm meant to be going off to Mull,' he protested. 'My van's loaded eight feet high with crisps. I'll be robbed.'

'Well, at least you won't starve.'

It had been a busy morning, but I hadn't been beaten. Then, when I saw the recovery truck arriving, my first thought was 'that can't be legal.'

'See this? It's a genuine work horse,' Colin and Dave told me.

'I think I'd prefer a horse,' I replied, observing the five different shades of brown paintwork.

Keith turned up and the lads handed him large bottles of water and oil.

'Remember,' they told him, 'if you see the oil and water lights come on, pull over and just top her up. Also, keep an eye on the back tyres. Oh, and the winch is not as quick as it used to be.'

I scribbled down the colour of the vehicle that one of our customers had failed to find in the car park and handed it to Keith as he climbed into the cab.

'On the way back,' I said, 'pick the keys up off Debs for your next job.'

He got as far as the gate before he suddenly stopped and jumped out of the cab.

'Both warning lights have just come on!' he shouted.

Meanwhile, Bill had tracked down the keyless lady. Her mother lived a few doors down and that's where the car was. He hot-wired it and listened to the woman demanding compensation for losing the keys, and forgetting where she'd parked the car. So, two down, and just a trip to the Highlands to go. Keith and I set off north in the recovery truck, stopping every half an hour to top it up with oil and water. Dawn was breaking by the time we reached the hotel. We were half asleep as we reversed up to the vehicle and lowered the ramps. It was then we realised that the winch 'wasn't as quick as it used to be' because it wasn't there at all.

At that point, I just lay down on the gravel car park and surrendered. Keith put a cigarette in my mouth and lit it, as if I was a dying soldier. I just lay there motionless, while Keith sat in the cab with his head on the wheel. Eventually, I realised that no one was going to magically come to my aid, so I sat up and scanned the area. The road leading into the car park was on a slight incline. I woke Keith and told him the plan. We manoeuvred the car into position and left the truck with the ramps down. Then we pushed the Metro down the slope and onto the truck. Finally, Keith leapt into the moving car at the last moment and slammed on the brakes. This didn't stop the front of the car crunching into the back of the truck, but the damage didn't seem too serious - until we got into the cab. The seats had taken a bit of a battering and we ended up having to drive back with the wheel in my stomach and both of our faces just a few centimetres from the windscreen.

The car hire business was now putting me to the test mentally, physically and financially. What was supposed to be a part-time enterprise had become a 24/7 military operation. Every morning it was out with the ladders to paint over a freshly-applied letter 'W' on the Anchor sign above the office. The mystery artist had also started doctoring the signs on top of our cars, often while we were all in the office. Cars that didn't break down came back with the insides wrecked. I lost count of the times I opened the doors to take the mileage and thought, 'How many packets of crisps and McDonalds can someone eat?' It was also a revelation how many cigarette ends people could fit in an ashtray. And then there were the never-ending excuses why customers were late back, the sudden amnesia when you noticed a dent or scrape ('You're sure we left here with a front bumper?'), people driving off with a 'Hire this car - Wanchor Self Drive' sign still strapped to the roof, and the constant stream of speeding and parking tickets that needed to be sorted out.

I finally lost my temper - a serious rarity - with a French family who were insisting they had booked a one-way hire in the Ford Mondeo and wanted to know where our Heathrow office was so they could drop off the car. Their English was limited and their flight fast approaching, so I told them, no begged them, to not park at the airport but to find a nearby side street without yellow lines. They were to leave the keys up the exhaust and phone me with the street name. The phone went dead and I could only pray that they had understood. About half an hour later they called back. Everyone at the yard was waiting with bated breath. It was as if the car was the hostage and we were waiting to hear if the ransom had been paid. It hadn't. They'd left the car in the short stay car park at the airport. This news was received in the usual Anchor way - spanners clattering to the floor and lots of shouting, swearing and heads banging together. I closed the office door to shut out the din and made two phone calls - one to Keith and the other to the PA of the Wolverhampton nightclub boss. I re-arranged our meeting for the next morning and legged it. With airport parking charges, time was definitely money.

Keith and I raced down to Heathrow, arriving in the early hours and recovering the car which Keith took straight back to Edinburgh for an afternoon booking. Meanwhile, I headed to Wolverhampton. The PA looked shocked at my appearance. I hadn't slept in a day and my eyes had overdosed on motorway driving. But I blamed my ashen look on having just become a dad, which felt like a walk in the park compared to trying to earn a living. The PA quickly recovered from her shock and we got down to business. The nightclub's current vending supplier never turned up when the machine broke down, and they'd end up opening for the weekend with no cigarettes. She showed me their latest statement from their supplier. The club was selling fewer cigarettes than a high street pub in Edinburgh. I smiled when I saw the name of the company - Mayfair, one of the companies trying to sue me out of existence. We agreed a deal. I would supply new machines and get Mayfair to collect the ones they'd installed. Fatigue had overtaken me by then, but she asked me to wait while she printed something out for me. I was so tired I didn't have a clue what it might be. She then handed me four sheets of paper.

'What are these?' I heard myself asking.

'They're the addresses of the other nine nightclubs in our group.'

Nine.

Nine nightclubs.

Driving back up to Edinburgh, I kept glancing at those four sheets of paper on the passenger seat. I knew what it meant and what it entailed. Business is strange really, like attempting a puzzle. If you get it right, the prize is a better life financially. Up until then, I had always got it wrong but enjoyed doing it anyway. But now it was like I was being handed the puzzle and the solution all at the same time. I was exhausted and needed to phone home as well as speak to Bill, who was taking care of my empire. Bill answered straight away.

'Where are you?' he asked.

'M6, about an hour's drive north of Wolverhampton.'

I could hear him passing on what I had just said to someone else.

'What's up Bill?'

'Hold on.'

I could sense doom.

'Are you still there?' he said eventually.

'Only in body.'

'It's Keith. He's on the A1 just north of you.'

'Broken down?' I replied.

'How did you know?'

'Bill, are you asking me to give Keith a tow?'

'Yep.'

'I've got blurred vision and I'm in a Mini Metro. We need the recovery truck.'

But that was on the ramp being repaired. So, I ended up cutting across to the A1 and found Keith, who seemed quite chirpy and not at all annoyed that he had been on the road for eighteen hours. Perhaps he just associated helping me with long drawn-out journeys round the UK. It took us another fourteen hours to get back home.

I crept upstairs but Nicola was still up feeding Amy.

'Where have you been? When you phoned yesterday from the office, you were just having a cup of tea. Then last night you said you'd be home for dinner.'

'And here I am,' I replied, not entirely sure when 'last night' was.

'That was a day and half ago,' said Nicola.

I tried to tell her the good news about the nightclubs, but my head was swaying with exhaustion.

'Do you want ham or cheese?'

'Bed.'

'What about Mull?'

'Eh?'

'The stock's in the workshop and I've booked the ferry. One car, two passengers, like you asked at the beginning of the week. You should have left by now.'

Next door's light was still on. I could see Keith about to enter his cupboard under the stairs. I prized opened the window.

'All right, Keith, today's Mull and we're late.'

Once I'd managed to catch up on my sleep, I went back down south for a few days visiting the nine nightclubs, both to check out their machines and to confirm that the venues were actually real. The venues were all bigger than I'd been led to believe and I realised I would need to sell all my Scottish sites if I was going to do this opportunity justice. I'd also need to use up all my cash to buy enough stock. And then there were the machines to buy, which were going to cost well over forty thousand pounds. It wasn't going to be easy and although I'd come up with a plan, I couldn't do it without Nicola wanting it as well.

For the first time since we'd married we had some sort of stability, even if it was only on the surface. In fact, our debts were actually growing. I'd taken steps to reduce them, but it was still running into a near six-figure sum. Taking on these nightclubs would be the ultimate gamble. There wasn't a single guarantee attached to the venture, but I knew that if I could pull it off I'd be able to stand on tiptoes and just about look over the fence into the future. I'd always had vision, and after all these years of trying I couldn't stop now. To do so would definitely be failure.

So I talked to Nicola. She didn't even flinch and was as steadfast in her love and support as ever.

'Just a few questions,' she said.

'Go on.'

'Any chance you can make it before we end up with clicking teeth and smelling of wee? And I take it we'll be moving to an area of the Midlands that you haven't yet been ostracised from?'

With Nicola on board, I set off to slay one of the big boys of cigarette vending. Walking into the reception of their large offices, I was told by the young lady behind the desk that visits were by appointment only. When I introduced myself, she didn't know where to look and, picking up the phone and covering the mouthpiece carefully with her hand, she launched into a covert conversation. I was then informed that I should leave the building immediately and write a letter to arrange an appointment. I shook my head, got on my high horse and told her I was an empire builder, not a pen-pushing desk jockey. I demanded that someone see me immediately. More whispering into the phone and then a 'someone' eventually agreed, intrigued to see why I was here. So I told him. I offered him a deal - I'd sell them all my sites for an agreed fee and in return, they would abandon all legal proceedings against me. He seemed to soften at that, telling me this wasn't a business 'for people like you.' He said that a deal might just happen and added, 'I take it you're going expand your car hire business?'

'How do you know about that?' I asked.

He tapped his nose and said, 'Nothing gets past us.'

We shook hands and I said, 'I'll give you five days, otherwise I'll have to start looking to sell my car hire business.'

And then I tapped my nose.

My car hire partners, Colin and Dave, and I had all now become firm friends. They were brilliant, understanding my reasons for wanting out. We all agreed the business should keep going and when they asked me what, in my opinion, could be done to improve things, I gave them a three-point plan:

1. Cars that work.
2. An office that doesn't resemble a fair ride.
3. Catch the little bastards who keep adding the letter W to Anchor.

Timing and hard work was now everything. I needed to sell my sites, find a house and move south, negotiate a deal for approximately forty new machines, despite having no money, find a cigarette supplier and install the machines single-handed. And all the while I also had to fend off my creditors. Calculations, based on worst-case scenario, were telling me that I had a five-year hard slog ahead just to clear my debts. But if the figures came in better by just ten percent, it would knock a whole year off.

The offer I eventually received was a third less than I'd asked for, but they did agree to halt all proceedings against me. All I had to do was sign the document, meet their man on Mull to swap stock, and they would hand me a cheque. I scanned the small print and breathed a sigh of relief - it didn't contain a clause stopping me from carrying on vending.

I then went over to Glasgow to see Big Al and explain about my expansion plans and my hurried move south. I think he found the whole thing amusing but he agreed to tell the machine importers to deal with me direct and, crucially, to confirm to them that my credit was good. And I would still get ninety days to pay because, as Big Al explained, I was entering the big league now. I was grateful and told him that I'd keep him informed of how things went.

'No need,' he replied, 'I'll hear.'

We shook hands. I couldn't thank him enough for giving me a chance.

'It's a pleasure,' he told me, 'and I'll spread the word that when you turn up in a town or city installing in these clubs, you're not some upstart trying to muscle in on someone's business, but part of a national chain.'

Nicola and I packed our belongings and prepared to head off back down south. I sensed that she, like me, was going to miss Scotland.

'Look,' I said to her, 'we're on the up. We're leaving with more furniture and belongings than when we arrived.'

In fact, we were leaving with all Keith's creations because I didn't want to hurt his feelings by leaving them behind. Nicola nodded and went off with Amy and Debs and her children for a walk. I sat on the step of our empty house looking out to sea and having a cigarette with Keith. He didn't say much, apart from discussing our trips of doom over the UK. I wanted to thank him for everything he'd done for me, but decided to leave that until we were driving off.

Nicola came back, got Amy settled and said her goodbyes. I nodded to her to leave and went to the cab. I turned round to find Keith standing there. I went to shake his hand and he gave me a hug. I was trying not to cry, as was he. He told me it had been the best time of his life and he'd loved every moment he'd spent helping me. And in turn, I told him that he and Debs would never know how much they'd helped us.

'If ever you need anything, just shout. I mean it,' I said.

He nodded and looked at the floor.

'Duncan,' he said quietly, 'I sort of understand why you have to go.'

He was a man of few words, but a true friend.

CHAPTER FOURTEEN

Three words kept recurring in my head when we reached Birmingham: greyness, stability and doubt. We were on our way to Solihull, south of Birmingham, where we'd decided to start afresh in England. It made sense because it was close to motorways that could take me to pretty much every corner of the country, and it was also close to various members of my family. But everything was so grey. Not the grey shades of a Scottish summer but an all-encompassing greyness, brooding and dull. And doubt was flooding over me, doubt about moving my family from a happy place in order to have a shot at stability. I sensed that we needed to be more like some of the people I'd met on my travels; people with plans for the future, plans involving their homes and their children, building friendships and becoming settled in their surroundings.

Nicola had gone on ahead to check out our new rented home. Winding my way through the concrete jungle, I eventually found it - a three bed semi-detached. My doubt now grew with a strong sense of being enclosed. Everywhere I looked it was someone else's side of their house or wall. They had large fences - not for security, but to keep out prying eyes. And the noise! Cars, trucks and buses; tyres on tarmac. We'd left our house, the sea, beach, Bill, Debs and Keith, Mull and even the car hire business for this. The sight of Nicola and Amy and the dogs helped to quell my rising fear that I'd made another terrible mistake. At least moving in was uncomplicated. None of the main furniture fitted through the door so we had to leave it on the front lawn. I introduced myself to the next door neighbour and explained the problem, saying we'd be having a bonfire in the next few days. He turned ashen and scurried back through his front door.

I had a few days spare while I waited for suppliers to process my orders and finalise the opening of trade accounts. I'd said nuts to Knutz and changed my company name to AVS so, needing a new batch of stationery, I went into Birmingham city centre to look for a printer. I decided to drive past the old office block where I had started in leasing. I then parked in the same spot I'd used all those years ago, but this time I was in a Mini Metro, not a BMW 7 Series. The garages where Billy and Spike had lived were gone. Everything had merged into yet another office block. At least the old café was still operating and I fancied a cup of tea. The décor had gone upmarket but I recognised the same old faces straight away. Ordering my tea, I could feel everyone's eyes fixed on me and finally a pile of pennies dropped.

'It's you! The leasing man!'

They were overjoyed. Lots of smiles and handshakes and a full English breakfast on the house. The warmth of the welcome finally banished the greyness and doubt from my mind. I was up to my neck in debt, driving a clapped-out Metro, with zero possessions and a young family to provide for. If I'd just stayed in bed, I would have been better off. But I hadn't and any self-doubt about why I had returned vanished in that café. I suddenly felt quietly confident that I had made the right decision.

My vending machines were on the way, but due to cash flow issues the suppliers had changed their minds on giving me credit. I now needed to pay an £8,000 deposit and the balance in ninety days. I couldn't complain - they were still backing me to the tune of £32,000 - but the deposit wasn't in my forecast as I only had about £10,000 and needed that for stock. However, I'd also been declined an account by a major distribution company - the only one in the area who could supply me with cigarette vending packs - and was told instead I should pay by cheque. It was going to be really tight. The only way round it was to install and fill all the machines on a Wednesday, let them trade and then rush round on the following Monday emptying them all. I would then re-fill them, count all the money and deposit it in the bank before the cheque cleared. And I couldn't buy any more stock until the cheque had gone through.

The machines arrived by articulated lorry and each one was bolted to a pallet and covered in cardboard packaging. They were enormous - seven foot high and three foot across - and with the garage filled up immediately, we started to stack the rest on the patio. Then a lady walked past with her dog, both sporting identical hairstyles. She stopped and asked what I was doing and, when I explained, she went on to complain about the amount of lorry traffic since our arrival. I told her things would soon quieten down and she went off with a final, unimpressed 'Oh,' leaving me to place the last few machines on the driveway and the front and back lawns.

The machines needed to be put together and programmed before being installed, and I only had two days. But first, I had to contact the cigarette company whose sites I was taking. It was my old friend Mayfair and there was no way could I tell them who I was, or word would soon spread back up north. So, doing an impression of a vague employee, I spoke to Mayfair's area manager and said I'd been instructed to pass on the name of the company (mine) that was taking over. The reaction wasn't promising.

'Remove our machines? Who the hell do you think you are? AVS? Never heard of you. Is this some sort of joke?'

'No,' I replied calmly, 'just a request.'

'Who owns your company?'

'Not sure, never see them. I'm just on the factory floor, mate,' I lied. 'But can I pass the message on that you'll remove your machines in the next forty-eight hours?'

'You'll do nothing of the sort until one of the owners phones me back. And I want to know his name.'

Totally thrown off guard by this demand, my eyes scanned the room and finally fixed on a row of files on the shelf.

'The name's probably Lever,' I said.

'Lever? What's his first name?'

'Erm… er… Arch, his name is Archie Lever.'

'Well, tell Mr Lever to call me straight back.'

And it was crucial that someone did phone back but I couldn't think of anyone who would be up to the task. Ah well, it was down to me then. Putting on a deep, stern voice with an impatient and abrupt tone, I got through to the area manager once more. I told him I had a signed contract with the company in question, a contract which included the days I would be installing.

'And,' I went on, warming to the task, 'if your machines are still on site after I have been polite enough to telephone you direct, then I will have no alternative but to request that my installation teams remove them for you.'

The Man From Mayfair went quite sheepish.

'Are you that crowd from Brighton?' he asked.

'No.'

'So who is AVS? I've never heard of you.'

'All I can say is we are based down south and are expanding north. And I suggest that, in future, you might want to keep an eye on the competition.'

Back on the home front, the neighbours were keeping a keen eye on me as Nicola and I set about unpacking the machines and wheeling them into the house to build. The only thing I stopped for was sleep - limited to less than four hours - and to accept delivery of the cigarettes. This came in another enormous lorry, prompting another neighbour to express concern about the area becoming an industrial estate.

'It's about these lorries...' he began.

I stopped him and explained the situation.

'After this lorry, you'll only see my hire van, which will be a Ford Transit.'

The look on his face suggested I hadn't convinced him. He then stared at the cardboard boxes which said Benson and Hedges on the side in massive letters.

'Are these smuggled?' he asked.

I let that one ride, having no time for a neighbourly scrap. I needed to move the machines as quickly as possible. Unfortunately, as the hire company didn't have any Transit vans, I ended up with a seven and half ton truck with tail lift and a noisy recording of 'Warning, this vehicle is reversing.' With the house in a state of chaos and the dogs using the front window to jump in and out, Nicola was getting fed up. And the neighbours finally snapped, making their feelings known as I attempted to load the machines onto the truck.

'All we can see outside our bedroom window is a garden full of rubbish. And when I look out the front all I can see is this lorry...'

'The hammering and banging over the last two days has been horrendous...'

'This is a quiet road with nice people, and since you moved in, you've upset the whole neighbourhood...'

I was like a stuck record, apologising over and over again. Promising that the rubbish would be gone in the next couple of days, I then headed off to my first nightclub.

I learned four things very quickly about going to nightclubs on a weekday:

- It'll be easier to wake the dead than find a member of staff.
- The manager, in particular, is never there.
- The cashier is in charge.
- The cashier is always a woman, always fierce, and always smoking a cigarette while surrounded by very high piles of cash.

At the first nightclub, a ghoulishly white person, some kind of handyman, dragged his way to the door after I'd banged the thing pretty much off its hinges. When he realised I wasn't delivering beer, his attention wandered and then buggered off completely when I asked for his help. So I struggled up and down various flights of stairs with the machines balanced on my trolley. After installing my own, I felt completely dead and realised that at this rate, they'd need refilling before I'd completed all the other installations. I also noticed Mayfair hadn't collected their machines, although they had got round to emptying them of money. The handyman was my only hope. I tried being polite. Not a hope. I reverted to begging. It didn't even touch the sides of his apathy. Bribery, it turned out, was the key to his door. A couple of packets of Benson's and he was mine. Fifteen minutes later and the Mayfair machines were off the walls and into the cellar, and my new helper was telephoning ahead to his mate at the next club.

The cashiers were also happy to help for a pack or two of cigarettes. By the second day of installing, word had spread. A handyman would be outside waiting and the cashier knew my name without introduction. It might have cost me a £150 in cigarettes, but the nightclub's head office was already receiving good reports about me and my business, even if it was just about my politeness. The morning after I'd finished installing all the machines, the phone rang. It was one of the club cashiers.

'When you're passing,' she told me, 'could you just check your machines? I think they're empty and we're open again tonight.'

'They can't be,' I replied, 'I was only there yesterday.'

My stock sheet was very basic. It just said IN/OUT. No mention of brands, dates, machine locations, etc. All I knew was that I'd put four hundred packets in this club's machines and here she was telling me they were empty. This club was a hundred miles away and, as far as I could see, their machines were broken down already. Bloody hell. This was not a good start.

I could have given up there and then, I was so tired and my morale so low. And I still had to clear up all the wreckage on the

lawn and in the house. I resorted to telling Amy all my problems. She just looked at me and laughed while kicking her legs.
Therapy session over, I told Nicola that I was off out.

'Couldn't you have arranged this a bit better?' she shouted
from upstairs.

'Why?'

'Because your mother and two aunties are coming at lunchtime, and your dad's due round later as well.'

'Are they?'

'Yes. I did tell you all this before.'

'Don't worry, I'll be back as quick as I can.'

By the time I got to the nightclub, I was in a cold sweat with
nerves. The handyman was waiting like the doorman at a decent
hotel. He'd put all the lights on for me and was offering a cup of
tea. I grabbed what bit of stock I had left and made my way to the
machines. There wasn't a packet left. I grabbed the money box. It
was jammed. I gave it a tug and the weight of it made it fall out of
my hands. I locked it and went to the other two. It was exactly the
same - all the stock had gone and had been replaced with money.
I couldn't believe it. I'd just made £500. In one night. From one
club. I half-filled the machines with what stock I had left and told
the cashier the painful truth - that I'd messed up on the stock and
could she explain that to the manager? Another pack of Benson's
and a promise that I'd be back ASAP, and she was on-side and
telling me that a couple of the other clubs had sold out too. She
wasn't lying.

So, I had just made two grand clear from one night's vending and should have been celebrating, but this was nearly as bad
as the machines breaking down. I was making money all right.
Serious money. But I had no stock left. I phoned the clubs' head
office and said, half-truthfully, that Mayfair's misleading stock
figures were to blame for the shortfall. It worked. I was told to
take my time and get things sorted. They even offered to contact the other clubs and warn them of the problem to save them
annoying me.

'And you say this problem with Mayfair is not unusual?'
asked the woman from head office.

'It's rife,' I replied.

'Interesting.'

When I finally made it home, I couldn't wait to show Nicola all the cash I'd just collected.

'Where have you been?' she demanded. 'I've had to entertain your family all day.'

'Were they asking after me?' I replied, my good mood refusing to budge.

'No,' said Nicola, handing me a letter, 'but the neighbours are.'

The letter had been sent from the dozen or so houses near us. The neighbours had decided that I was engaged in some sort of illegal activity. And then there were the trucks delivering and parking at a private address, the mess in the garden and the noise going on into the early hours. It had all been noted and reported to the council and the letting agent. I was not a happy man.

'Leave it for now, your dad's coming round in less than hour,' said Nicola.

But I wasn't going to leave it. All the stresses and strains of the last week, the non-stop grafting, the lack of sleep, the highs and lows, the tension and angst, it all boiled over. I went outside and was halfway down the drive when I noticed our nearest neighbours sitting in their front room. I walked casually back to our front door and then, commando-style, crouched down and crept across to their lounge window. And then I suddenly jumped up. I could see cups and saucers nearly touching the ceiling, followed by a wave of tea. Pinning the letter up against their window, ready to launch into a passionate defence, I saw them lying spread-eagled and shocked in their armchairs. It made me laugh so I just left them to it. I walked back into my house, still laughing. Nicola wasn't quite so amused.

'What have you done? You promised we'd start afresh.'

The look of dejection on her face sobered me up.

'I'm sorry. I'll make sure that the neighbours are my top priority.'

To prove the point, I went into the garden to make a start on the mess. I piled a couple of pallets and a few boxes into a small pile in the corner and lit a fire. Back inside, I wanted to lift the mood and decided to let the money do the talking. Nicola was stunned when I poured the first cloth sack full of change onto the table and utterly speechless by the time I'd emptied all four. In all, there was nearly £9,000 in coins.

'I'm waiting for the catch,' Nicola told me.

'There isn't one. Well, apart from the fact we have to count it.'

She smiled.

'Duncan?'

'Yes.'

'About the neighbours complaining.'

'Yes.'

'I'm right behind you.'

We'd only been counting for ten minutes when Nicola screamed, 'The fence! It's on fire!' And it was. The blaze had spread to the cardboard boxes nearby and had set fire to three fence panels. I jumped up.

'Don't move!' I shouted at Nicola. 'Guard the money!'

Dashing around, I looked for something to put water into. Nicola ignored my orders and came to the back door with the washing-up bowl full of water. I threw it on the fire and she handed me a jug, the kettle and the refilled washing-up bowl. I started kicking the fence panels, reasoning that if I could flatten them then the fire would go out. One panel went down, giving me a view of the back of a neighbour's house. I ran up to their patio doors and banged on them, apologising and in the same desperate breath asked if they had a hosepipe. The fire had now spread to a fourth panel and the rubbish on my lawn was an inferno. By the time the hosepipe came out, six panels were alight and I was trying to bash them down with a shovel. One fell against the neighbour's shed, setting it alight. Two more neighbours then appeared with hosepipes and we finally managed to bring the fire under control.

I thanked them profusely, and apologised even more before walking back into the house filthy and soaked through. Dad was there. And true to form, presented with a fire-fighting son and a table covered in cash, all he said was:

'You need to buy a house.'

'What?'

'It's dead money, renting.'

⤫

It took us hours to count the money. But that wasn't the problem; getting more stock for my machines was. If I managed to get just fifty packs into a machine then it lessened the odds of someone complaining. If I could get over the serious hurdle of supplying enough stock for the weekend rush, I'd be off and running.

I telephoned the supplier and was told it would take forty-eight hours to process an order. And they didn't accept cash. I thought about driving up to Glasgow to see Big Al, but they didn't have the brands. The big seller up north was Regal King Size and I needed Benson and Hedges and Marlboro Lights. It was Nicola who came up with a plan.

'Don't laugh,' she said, 'but have Mayfair collected their machines yet?'

'Probably not,' I replied.

'Plug them in and buy whatever packets are left inside. You won't make any money but at least you'll have some stock.'

'Sounds good.'

'And,' she went on, 'your nightclub machines vend at about a pound more than the pub ones, don't they?'

'Yeah.'

'So why don't you drive around and buy up all the pub stock? At least you'll make something on each packet.'

'Brilliant!'

And we were off, emptying nearly every machine in the area. Nicola would pull up and wait in the van with Amy strapped in the middle seat, while I ran in with my cloth sack and bought as many packets as possible before the landlord chased me out accusing me of using counterfeit money. I managed to get several hundred packets and after I'd plugged in my competitor's machines and bought all their stock, I had enough just about to make it through the weekend.

As I'd only placed one order with the wholesalers, I couldn't just treble my next order. But they did, at least, up it by a third and Big Al came good, ordering the balance on my behalf which meant a quick diversion to Glasgow for me. By the end of my first full week, I had made it. Just. I'd sold approximately three and half thousand packets and cleared nearly five grand. Celebrating was still a long way off, however. I was living on my nerves, trying to build up stock so I didn't have to keep visiting the venues more than once in a week. Trying to predict sales was a nightmare. I'd phone the clubs to find out how they'd think a week night might go. The standard reply would be, 'We're not expecting much, a few hundred people tops.' The next morning, the cashier would be back on the phone telling me, 'Machine empty - we were rammed.' So I actually needed the machines to sell less whilst my hands were tied with limited stock supplies.

I was clocking up thousands of miles a week trying to keep everyone happy, but at least Nicola was home and beefing up the infrastructure. We'd hired two small vans, bought two mobile phones and installed a second landline. Nicola became chief cashier, which involved days of counting the change by hand and then bagging it up into £500 coin sacks. I would either recycle that cash through the clubs or dash to the bank to meet the cigarette supply cheque. As ever, improvisation saw us through. Even Amy wasn't exempt - her buggy could take £1,500 in change on the seat, the cash covered by a blanket with Amy, smiling, sitting on top of the pile.

After a few weeks' hard graft, I arrived home one evening and didn't think twice when I saw that the other van had gone. I had trouble getting my key in the front door and so didn't notice the note pinned to it. A few of the neighbours came out to see events unfold.

'You'll be lucky,' one shouted across the road.

I wondered what was rattling their cage. Everything had quietened down since I'd burned down six fence panels and gutted the neighbour's shed. I had, after all, offered to pay for all the damage, including new turf for all three of the scorched gardens. Then I finally saw the note written in Nicola's hand and pinned to the door.

I'm at the Travelodge, been evicted.

I tore it down and faced the angry suburban mob.

'I suppose you're all happy now, are you?' I shouted before getting back in the van.

I had to resist a strong urge to run them all over as I left to find Nicola.

❧

The motel room was as calm as any bedroom filled with two adults, one child and a couple of dogs all sharing. Nicola was OK and strangely apologetic, as if it was her fault that the neighbours had ganged up and fed our landlord a pack of lies. I was a smuggler and an arsonist and, what with all that money in the house, probably a racketeer to boot.

'I had ten minutes,' she said, 'so I got the cot and most of Amy's stuff. Oh, and I grabbed the money and stock.'

'Thank god.'

'I'm really sorry,' she went on. 'They were drilling the locks so I only had enough time to pack the one bag.'

She pointed at my trusty blue holdall, now filled with essentials for herself and Amy. Yet again, I'd ended up with nothing but the clothes I was wearing.

Business carried on as normal - I just told everyone we were relocating. At last, I was now beginning to get my stock levels right and I realised that the potential of the business was staggering. We were still very much in debt, but the profit we were making meant I would be able to settle my account for the machines within weeks, and I now had enough money in the bank to pay for my stock without running round the country emptying the machines to ensure the cheques cleared. So we decided to buy our own house - the deposit would only be two or three weeks' money - and I promised faithfully that I wouldn't do or say anything that would lead to us either being ostracised or evicted, or both. We agreed that Nicola would own the house and she would obtain the mortgage.

For the first time in my life, concrete plans for our future were being formed.

I'd been summoned to the nightclub firm's head office. I sat down and exchanged pleasantries, not having a clue why I was there. The door flew open and in walked a man big enough to block the light out.

'You're our vending man?' he barked.

I nodded. He handed me a couple of sheets of A4 paper.

'We've just bought these clubs. They all need your machines. That won't be a problem, will it?'

What could I say? I told him it wouldn't be a problem at all and I was dismissed.

Outside, I wanted to collapse into the nearest hedge. What I would need to do to honour this new commitment was logistically and financially mind-boggling. But on those sheets of A4 was the opportunity to turn my business into something vast, into the sort of operation I had always dreamed of running. My turnover was about to go over a million pounds a year, and yet there was just me and Nicola operating the whole thing from a room in a West Midlands Travelodge. I decided to splash out on a second room for the dogs to sleep in - you try getting a decent night's sleep with two hounds snoring and farting all the time, and then waking up on the floor with pound coins embedded in various parts of your anatomy.

I'd struck up a friendship with Tom, the night receptionist at the motel. He was in his mid-fifties and had been made redundant after working his way up from the shop floor to middle management at some car component company. At the motel, he was just punching his ticket until he could retire. I'd always stop for a chat. Over tea and cigarettes, we'd discuss how we'd both ended up at the motel. He had a wicked sense of humour and was more than happy to ignore the customers and the phone to talk to me. And when I mentioned my big new logistical problems, Tom was streets ahead of me with all manner of solutions. I knew there and then that I needed him on board, but I didn't want to embarrass him. After all, this guy was used to working for companies who operated out of more than a motel room. I needn't have worried. He approached me. And, to be honest, he probably saved my business.

Tom invited us all round, including the dogs, to his house to have dinner and to meet his wife. After the meal, Tom and I were left to chat about his ideas and plans. I could see the excitement on his face. After each of our conversations, he'd made notes that ran for pages and pages. My business problems, and Tom's solutions, dominated those pages. He was sharp, logical and experienced - everything I needed. My main problem was the need to buy another fifty machines and all the associated extra stock. Then I needed to store those machines before they were installed in clubs, not just in the Midlands, but further north and all over the south east of the country. But Tom had thought about all of that. To an impulsive guy like me, his attention to detail was mind-blowing. Things were going well, so it was time to throw in a little hand grenade.

'Tom, can I just drop into the mix that I still owe a hundred grand from previous exploits? And I know that as soon as I put the key in my new front door, the lovely people from the Inland Revenue and Customs and Excise will be waiting in the hedge.'

That didn't faze Tom.

'Have you registered with the Revenue?'

'No.'

'And what about National Insurance?'

'No.'

He was still cool as a cucumber. Even Nicola's mentioning that I tended to leave a venture with little more than the clothes I was wearing couldn't stop Tom. He offered the use of his garage as temporary storage for the machines. He then suggested systems to deal with stock issues, how to fill the machines and make sure we were at the right clubs on the right day in the right part of the country. I was worn out by it all. It was time to end the conversation right then and there.

'Do you want a job?' I asked him.

'Are you serious?' he stuttered.

'Anyone who goes into detail like you have deserves a chance to put his ideas to the test.'

'But you don't think I'm too old?'

'Certainly not. You know more about my business than I do.'

We shook hands on it, and within days Tom had set to work managing cash flow, helping Nicola to introduce some sort of accounts system and finding out when I would be debt-free.

The next month was one of organised chaos. I had to install machines at all the new sites, a task big enough for me to recruit a friend of Tom's as helper. Tom, meanwhile, sorted out all the stock issues straight away. We were still visiting the clubs two, or even three times a week to up the stock levels, but now every packet of cigarettes in those machines was bought and paid for.

Meanwhile, Nicola had found a three bedroomed detached house and had managed to obtain a mortgage through the Bank of Dick Turpin, one of those outfits that specialise in giving people a second chance. By the time we had to hand over the deposit on the house, all my machines were paid for so I could afford the atrocious repayment terms. It was a great day when I got a call from Nicola telling me she had checked out of the motel. That night, I would be coming home to a new house. But I wasn't expecting what happened next.

Walking into the kitchen and seeing Nicola carrying Amy round the garden should have been a wonderful sight. But I felt sad and removed from what I was seeing. That supposedly normal existence, the everyday occurrence of walking into your own home and seeing your wife and daughter in your own garden, left me wondering about what I had done. I knew then that I had traded in a lot for this new-found stability and normality. I had always considered myself a risk-taker, but here I was being drawn into the suburban lifestyle of a three bedroomed detached, with well-appointed, south facing garden and ample off street parking. It was the very least that Nicola and Amy deserved, but it left me feeling like I had gained a lot of money but had lost something along the way.

⌘

Business was booming. Word had spread around the night-clubs and large, late night venues and we were riding the wave of a new fashion for large venues. A two thousand capacity was the norm, but clubs were starting to open up with double that. And they were all trading four, five and sometimes six nights a week. One of the big cigarette vending companies would always be the initial supplier, but selling my own services took minutes. I would turn up at the owner or manager's office, which always had a big desk and leather sofa, a half-dead plant in the corner and the latest techno gadget, a symbol of the ridiculous amount of money they'd turned over during the previous week.

I'd take a seat and be informed that so and so up the road said I gave a better service and the latest machines. I'd agree and tell them I could install my machines within a week. And then they'd sign me up. They weren't interested in sales or commission. With their cashier usually up to her armpits in money, that was just chicken feed to them. My one golden rule was that if they smoked, I'd find out what brand and make sure they never bought a cigarette again. And if they didn't smoke, their deputy got the bounty instead. After a while, my nose for business was so well-trained that I could walk round venues and know how many packets they'd sell without having to ask. And Tom had pages of statistics to back me up on who smoked what brands, how many and on what nights.

We were raking in the cash, but it was always the chase that did it for me, not the reward. I would go after bigger groups of clubs just for the challenge. By now, the big national companies had found out who AVS was and they would try everything to squeeze me out. They'd say I was just a one-man band and, 'Don't believe him when he says he is national.' They'd offer my customers thousands of pounds upfront. But this just helped me to obtain the site as the owners had only good feedback about my company. Halfway through any negotiations, I'd get a phone call saying, 'Get your machines in now. I've just told that other crowd to fuck off.' What the national companies always forgot was that even though clubs were normally part of a chain, they were still run by charismatic individuals. And I made sure that they felt like the most important person on the planet.

Coming to the end of our first year, I had expanded to a hundred nightclubs, all with as many as eight machines in. This meant that over the Christmas period alone, I made £50,000 profit, which was stored in a metal cupboard in the garage. We had five staff, and various other people helping out from time to time. And we had upgraded to a top of the range counting machine - you poured in two grand in mixed change and it would spit it all out into plastic bags in minutes. The days of working the counting shift at the dining room table were over, but security was still zero. Our only defence was that we never attracted attention - even the vans we used were just normal, unmarked vehicles with the rear windows blanked out with newspaper.

Because security companies refused to collect from private addresses, we still banked the money by taking it in Amy's buggy. Only now our average turnover was up to £60,000 a week, and you could add another £30,000 to that on Bank Holiday weekends.

We'd all go to the bank with three grand in each hand, and repeat the journey two or three times, usually bringing the branch to a standstill in the process. Every now and then, Nicola would tell me about how well we were doing. Although all my debts had gone, I still hadn't come to terms with what was really happening. And the house was being refurbished from top to bottom but as much as I tried, it just didn't interest me. Nicola would show me our bank balance and all I would say was, 'Have what you want.'

At least I kept to my promise to not upset the neighbours, mainly because I was hardly ever at home. When I was, I did my best to integrate. I was always polite and tried to have a laugh and a joke, but I found it very hard to fit in with the suburban social circle. Nicola was making a lot of friends, especially through Amy attending nursery, and we would be invited to some dinner or other on a regular basis. Nicola had to brief me before each event, saying, 'Now remember: don't be sarcastic; don't insult their hobbies; no, you can't smoke and please, please refrain from speaking about your past. You know it just frightens them'.

With the cigarette business going great guns, I started to look for other ways to make money. I didn't want to stray too far from what I was doing, especially when I had access to venues that held four thousand people, all with large disposable incomes. It seemed daft not to exploit what was there on a plate for me. So the best option was to see what else I could sell to them. The answer came when I walked into the toilets of a nightclub while a lady was removing the front panel from a condom machine. It was déjà vu time - the clubs sold out and the suppliers took an age to restock or service the machines. The same lady also sorted out the toilet's air fresheners, and that turned out to be the key to everything. I left with one thought in my head - three condoms selling at £2 a packet - and made a few enquiries. A three-pack of condoms cost 20p, it turned out. That was the only research I needed to do to realise this would be my next venture.

The club managers barely knew where their toilets were, let alone cared about what machines were sited there or who supplied them. So I got in touch with the people who did the purchasing at head office, if there was one, or if it was an independent venue, I spoke to the accounts lady. However, instead of asking about the condom machines, I got them to check how much they were paying for the rental of the air fresheners. Roughly speaking, each venue was paying £1 to £2 a week per air freshener. Some toilets had six units in each and there could be up to ten sets of toilets. Over a dozen clubs, that was £50,000 a year in air fresheners. And my pitch to the managers was simple - I would supply air fresheners to them free of charge, saving them a pile of cash. All I asked in return was that I could install my vending machines in their toilets. Telling them that I'd save them £50,000 a year tended to stop them in their tracks. Within a month, I had orders to install five hundred condom machines.

To help me with this new venture, I head-hunted a quiet chap called Alan. He was hard-working, technically-minded and, having been employed by the vending machine distributors, ideal for what I needed. Within weeks, he had pretty much moved into my garage. He'd take delivery of fifty machines at a time and set them up ready for us to install. He never said a word or asked for anything, and didn't really offer any conversation, until we'd nearly completed the installations and I was tidying up for the evening. Opening the garage door, he dragged in a large cardboard box. Inside was a metal contraption. Alan gave me a conspiratorial look.

'Don't say a word to anyone,' he said.

'I won't, but can you hurry up? My dinner's nearly ready,' I replied, wondering about Alan's sanity.

He balanced the machine on its side and asked me to insert a £1 coin in the slot, wait a few seconds and then place my hands or wrist in the opening at the bottom. I did as I was asked and suddenly felt a fine spray of something wet and fragrant.

'Was that aftershave?' I asked.

'Yep,' he replied, quickly replacing the machine in its box as if I was going to steal it.

'Been working on it for years,' he told me. 'That's just a simple prototype. Imagine the possibilities - a pound for a couple of sprays of perfume or aftershave. Every nightclub in the country will want one.'

Alan had worked out that it would cost £20,000 to start the patent process and get a proper prototype built by an outside company. Then £50,000 would be needed just to bring it to market. And that was before you started mass producing it, getting distributors on board, hiring a team of people nationwide to install and service them, and maybe even franchising the whole thing. It was mind boggling. The next morning, I couldn't shut him up. All he wanted to do was talk about his invention. Eventually, however, money talked when I agreed to give him £20,000 to develop his idea. After that, I said, we'll talk again. It made his day when I handed him the cheque. But what he didn't know was that he had made my day as well. To be honest, I had no idea if the machine would ever work. But it was a brilliant idea, and the potential was what excited me more than anything.

Business had settled into a routine, and so had my life. I was making more money than I needed, Nicola was happy and Amy had started junior school. During calmer moments, I would reflect on the past. The memories of all the losses, hardships and failures were still very clear in my mind, but none of them made me sad. If anything, I actually missed those days. And most of all, I missed the people. I'd sit in my accountant's office, listening to him drone on about how my attitude to the Inland Revenue and the VAT man was costing me a fortune. I'd tell him it was the only fun I was having these days, which didn't impress him much. All I really wanted to know from him was how much money I could get my hands on if everything went tits up. He'd look through reams of paper and tap away on his keyboard, and never give me a straight answer. Instead, he'd lecture me on how this wasn't the way to conduct business but then confirm that I was on a stable financial footing. So I knew I was OK financially, but old habits died hard.

And hidden in the loft was my blue holdall. Inside was a change of clothes, some waterproofs, a few tins of corned beef and bottles of water, cigarettes and a few grand in cash. Just in case.

❧

It was soon time to move that holdall. Even if money doesn't change you deep down, it does bring about superficial changes. Although we had a perfectly adequate house, we could now afford to buy a much bigger one. So that's what we did. We found a new-build, part of four houses in a walled-off community. It was a five bedroomed detached house and it had everything we could have wished for. As a mark of success, it positively shouted that we had arrived. But I didn't feel any of it. In fact, I was starting to question the whole situation - my life, what direction it was taking, everything. I realised that it was probably best to keep such thoughts to myself.

CHAPTER FIFTEEN

I was still very much in contact with Nicola's dad, Bill. We'd been helping him financially, and one day he asked if I'd help him buy some cigarette machines and stock for various new venues he'd found in Edinburgh. While I was in Scotland, he added, would I mind popping in to see Colin and Dave, my former partners in the car hire business? I was more than happy to help with both requests. It was great to see Colin and Dave again. Repairing Mini Metros was a thing of the past - car hire was their sole concern these days. But even that had changed, with a fleet of sixty mainly new vehicles now. The only thing that hadn't changed was how much of a nightmare it was to run the business. However, they had also moved into property as house prices in Edinburgh were going through the roof. And they were sitting on a small empire worth millions of pounds, and with very little debt.

Sitting in their fancy new office, it was clear we had all come a long way. But I soon realised we weren't meeting up to congratulate each other. I was shown a set of plans that spread across the desk.

'Duncan, we've got this idea,' Colin told me.

'Go on.'

'Do you know anything about golf?'

'Only played it once.'

'Do you know anything about golf courses?'

'Nope, but I can see you two might.'

I then took a wild guess at their plans.

'You're going to develop houses round a golf course, aren't you?'

'Close,' replied Colin. 'We've bought into some land. Quite a lot of land. And we want to develop that land round our own golf course.'

I congratulated them. Dave took a deep breath.

'We'd like you to join us on this project,' he said.

'I really appreciate the thought,' I replied, 'but I'm flat out work-wise, and I haven't got that type of money. I mean, you're talking millions.'

'We don't want your money, we just want you on board to help us.'

Sighing, I admitted that I could probably manage it but I'd only be able to give them one day a month. And, of course, it would mean trekking up to Scotland.

'By the way,' I added, 'where is this land?'

'The Algarve.'

'People think we're mad,' added Dave, 'that's why we're asking you.'

I didn't quite follow the logic, so decided to take it as a compliment.

'Will you at least think about it? Bill's already said he's in.'

I said I would. As I walked out to my car, a van came flying into the yard. I did a double take. It was Keith. I ran over to the van, full of the joys. Keith gave me an 'All right?' in his usual gruff tone. I wanted to know how he was getting on. Better than ever, it transpired. He was doing all the refurbishment of the houses for Colin and Dave.

'You and the family coming to the Algarve, then?' he asked.

'I doubt it. Hang on a minute, are you going?'

'What do you think? And with all that work, I thought you'd jump at the chance to be the gaffer.'

I shrugged my shoulders.

'Well, it's a golden opportunity for me,' Keith said, 'and Debs loves the sun.'

We chatted for a while, catching up on what we'd both been up to. Before I left, I promised to visit them all in the sunshine.

'Oh, Duncan, just before you go,' Keith said.

'Yeah?'

'Where is the Algarve?'

As I drove over to Glasgow to catch up with Big Al, I thought more about the Algarve venture. It sounded fantastic, but I just couldn't see myself anywhere but in Britain, building up my vending business. And golf? I had good memories of the camaraderie I'd enjoyed with the golfers at the hotel, but still knew nothing about golf and even less about golf courses. On the other hand, I'd love to have teamed up with them all again. It was just that the whole thing seemed too far removed from my day-to-day reality. I was too busy, and too successful, to need anything new on my plate. At least, that's what I told myself. But who was I kidding? My stomach was churning at the thought of working with the gang again, of creating something new from scratch. I didn't want to miss out on that opportunity but I had responsibilities now - family, home, business, employees. I couldn't just chuck everything in.

Big Al wasn't his usual self. After a few gentle enquiries, I eventually learned that the company was being sold out to one of the nationals. We chatted for a few more minutes and then I thanked him for giving me my break and stood up to leave. As I opened the door, I stopped and asked him what he was going to do next.

'Have a holiday, go to Spain maybe and play few rounds of golf, then see which way the wind blows.'

'So, is golf a big deal on the continent?' I asked.

'Bet your arse it is. Have you seen what they charge to play? Anything up to a hundred Euros a round, and that's if you can get a tee time. Why?'

'Just asking,' I replied, and we wished each other luck in the future.

My business was now completely nationwide, vending cigarettes, condoms and even the miniature Smint mints from my machines. Alan, the inventor, continued to come down and show me the latest component for his aftershave machine. The £20,000 I'd loaned him had risen to nearer £40,000 by then, but I considered it a long-term investment.

And our new house was now almost ready. For years I'd had dreams and plans, and now I couldn't think of anything else that I could wish for. I certainly didn't lack for a social life. Now that I was a success, I'd been integrated back into my own family. It wasn't easy at first for them as they hadn't planned on me ever making a success of anything. Now that I had, they didn't really have a choice but to accept that I was someone who had done things his way. But soon, invites for all occasions came in thick and fast from people I barely remembered, beyond some sarcastic comment they'd made years earlier about me and my business skills. Most weekends, we'd be at a wedding or landmark birthday. I was there out of politeness, and as I listened to relatives going on about either their health or wealth, I realised that this could be me in years to come if I wasn't careful.

And if it wasn't a family gathering, there'd be the gala opening of a new club. I always got an invite and I always made sure I attended, if only to thank the owner or manager for their business. A new place was opening in Kent, so I volunteered to service some sites round the M25 and then take a drive down to the club. Arriving with hours to spare, I bought some lunch and parked up by a grass embankment opposite the club. I laid down on my jacket and was minding my own business enjoying the view, when a clapped-out van pulled up. The back doors flew open and out fell four lads who I could tell straight away were musicians. They wandered off into the new club and within minutes were ushered out again. I could overhear them moaning about how badly the tour was progressing, so I went over and introduced myself. I learned they were booked to lead the launch event but had arrived too early. We quickly got chatting about music and I mentioned that I'd done some band management in the past. It was a different decade, but nothing else had changed - still the same dreams backed by guts and determination, and let down by bad organisation and chaos.

I spent the rest of the day and night with them, helping them set up and pack up, wishing them well and turning them down when they asked me to manage them. But I did take a CD of a singer produced by a friend in his studio. It had been a brilliant night - the best I'd had for years. Driving home, I felt such a huge sense of anti-climax that I had to put it into perspective. After all, it had just been helping a bunch of badly organised musicians play to an audience who didn't really care if they were there or not. But even so, for one day I'd stepped out of my bubble of long days grafting and weekends spent tending to my suburban social life. It was a feeling that would return before long.

One Sunday afternoon, we were invited to a barbecue. For these social events, Nicola always primed me a couple of days in advance so that I'd behave. And I always did. But they were usually just an excuse to show off the latest domestic triumph. We'd been treated to a pond christening before now, and even a Gala Opening of a new patio. And I dreaded the small talk - if I said anything out of the ordinary, they'd be paralysed by confusion and maybe a little fear.

Now, with me, it has always been the smallest things that have led to the big decisions. Today was no different. When we arrived at the barbecue, I noticed a large, pink ribbon round the shed. So that was it, we'd been invited to the grand opening of a garden shed. This type of banality made me question what exactly I wanted out of life, and seeing the shed now brought all those thoughts about the Algarve racing to the front of my mind again. I tried to work it out. It's all so easy when you are protected from financial worries. You can live in a nice house, drive a nice car, provide for your family. But in exchange for what? I lived in an area I didn't like, surrounded by people who I had strived hard not to *be* like. And I had to pretend to be nice to them while they banged on about who they hated this week, house prices, a hint of DIY and where they were going on holiday. Meanwhile, I would drift on, never letting my thoughts interfere with my business or home life. I had too much respect for the people I relied on, and even more for the people who relied on me, to do otherwise. But it was wearing me down. Seriously wearing me down.

The crunch, however, came not with the shed but when we went round to visit our new house. It felt so soulless going from room to room thinking about how we could fill it with as much furniture as we wanted. We just didn't need it - we lived in a three bedroom house from which I was also running a business, and we still didn't use all the rooms we had. Going round this enormous house, I asked Nicola who was going to clean it and who was going to cut the lawn. I told her we'd need a day just to clean the windows. She thought about what I'd just said.

'We work hard all week,' she said, 'so we can pay people to keep the house nice.'

'Yes, but to be honest,' I replied, 'I'm either in the garage or sitting in the kitchen. I don't need all this.'

We spent the evening back home discussing our future. I was grateful for everything we had achieved. What more could a man want? I had a wife who loved me and had a steadfast belief in me. I had a beautiful daughter and a successful business. But I didn't know what I wanted, and that was the point - I just wanted to live for today, not with everything planned out weeks and months ahead,

'I can't take another social outing to another bloody shed,' I told her.

'So, what do you want to do?'

'Anything but this.'

'What about the new house?'

I apologised and told her it wasn't for me.

Nicola let out a deep sigh.

'I'm glad you said that,' she said. 'I wasn't looking forward to living there, either.'

I laughed more than I had for years.

'What about our current house?' she asked, when I finally stopped.

'Well, it's a roof over our heads but the excitement ends there.'

'So you want to sell up?'

I looked at her.

'Yes, I do. I want to change direction.'

'OK,' Nicola told me. 'Let's do it.'

Nicola knew how much I missed my friends since moving down south; and because she knew me so well, she understood that even though I'd spent years striving to achieve everything I'd got, what I really needed was another project - just for the hell of doing it, just because I could.

'But on one condition,' she added.

'Name it.'

'Can we please go on our honeymoon now?'

It took me just six days to walk away from everything I had created. All the invoices and stock sheets; the meaningless correspondence and endless, pointless phone calls; the business brunches and meetings; the machines that counted the money; the vehicles and timesheets; the wage demands and the balancing of the books. I just washed my hands of everything. Even my mobile phone. And every day since making the decision, I'd tried to come up with a better and better reason not to go ahead with it. But in the end, none of them could match the simple truth I knew deep inside myself - I wanted change. No, I needed change.

And now I understood why. I had spent all those years experiencing anguish, sacrifice, debt and, worst of all, loneliness to cross some kind of imaginary finishing line, only to realise that the prize at the end wasn't the happy-ever-after ending at all. The money wasn't the end that justified the means; it was just something that created bigger problems and new complications. Wealth didn't satisfy me because it had never driven me. I had never loved money for its own sake, I'd just enjoyed making it because it was the proof that I was doing the right thing; that I could succeed on my own, playing my own game, by my own rules.

Stockbrokers always say that it's better to travel than arrive. They live for the whisper about a bid for a company, a takeover or merger, and as soon as it's confirmed, as soon as the whisper becomes just another set of facts and figures, then the game is over and you move on. That was me, my life, in a nutshell. Winning was never as important as striving to succeed. It wasn't that I didn't want to compete in the business world anymore; I just needed to be creative, not bogged down by the day-to-day drudgery of it all. Success meant new parameters that you had to abide to. It meant lawyers and accountants. And success meant money, and money created its own little tyranny where your life was swallowed up dealing with people who wanted to manage that money, to spend it for you, to make sure you kept making it so they could have a piece of it.

So, I picked up the phone and made the call that any sane and successful businessman would have begged me not to make. I dialled the number of the national cigarette vending company - the one I had had so much fun relieving of their prime sites. I should have had an independent valuation undertaken. I should have sold my business on the open market. But to who? All my business had been done on a handshake. I'd always worked on the fly, improvising, scrapping and fire-fighting. If that was how I built up a business, then that's how I was going to sell it. But it wasn't exactly easy.

My rivals had stopped taking my calls months ago. They'd even stopped replying to my letters. I suppose my habit of sending them condolence cards (or one of their publicity shots cut out and stuck onto a picture of the Titanic) every time I took a site off them didn't really help matters. But to be fair, they gave as good as they got. The only way they would remove a machine from a site was once they'd received a request in writing from the owner. They were so pissed off with me that they'd happily leave a machine on site and let it get damaged to cause the owner aggravation knowing, in turn, it would reflect on me.

Eventually, the only way I got through to them was by telling them my call was on compassionate grounds. Although I could sense the disappointment when they realised I wasn't dead, they weren't particularly enthusiastic when I did tell them I was retiring from vending and wanted to sell out. Their response was short and sweet - the line went dead - and it took an age for anyone to finally take my return calls. Even then, my news was greeted with serious scepticism and offers to meet them at their office or at my house were turned down. Finally, they reluctantly agreed to meet me at a motorway service station on the M1.

It was like a scene from a bad kidnap movie. I had to sit at a pre-arranged table and wait. Then an area manager appeared. He had clear instructions on how the sale would work and what price they were offering. And it was nowhere near the true value of the business, but it was my choice, take it or leave it. I was offered twenty-four hours to make a decision. If I agreed, the deal would have to be completed in three days and all my customers informed that the two companies had merged. And there was an additional clause - I was not to have any involvement in cigarette vending for the next five years.

I knew there and then that I would agree, so the next day, back at the same table in the same service station, I met up with four crumpled men in equally crumpled suits, all of them trying to be corporate and correct. There were a few bundles of paper that needed my signature and then, as I was preparing to hand over the paperwork in return for the cheque, we were back in the kidnap movie. We both hesitated, as if half expecting the hero to burst in and blow the bad guys away. But who was the hero? I was David to their Goliath, so I suppose it was probably me. It just didn't feel like that. What I did feel as I walked outside with that cheque in my hand was a sense of pride. I had started the business not exactly from nothing, but certainly during a dark and difficult moment in my life, and I'd come through in one piece. The cheque I'd just been given meant that I could go on and achieve so much more. The money itself was just a figure, but what it represented was priceless. And the confidence that it gave me was the real prize.

The following morning it was time to shut down operations, which meant informing my loyal workforce. I couldn't have made it without them, so I gave them the toiletry vending business. In return, they bought the vehicles off me. By lunchtime, I was shut. Six days, from start to finish.

I still had a few loose ends to tie up, starting with a trip to my accountant to announce my retirement from the vending business. He didn't seem as pleased with my decision as I did, and tried to convince me I couldn't afford to sell up for a variety of tax reasons. I resisted, so that just left Alan, my other port of call. I hadn't seen him for a few months and was looking forward to telling him that I'd be devoting more of my time to his idea.

The door was answered by a little old lady who invited me in. It turned out to be her house, not Alan's, but fair play to the man - he'd clearly been looking after her well as the place was beautifully decorated and furnished. She knew who I was - Duncan from Birmingham - and as I sat down she presented me with a tray of tea and biscuits.

'I have high hopes for your son and his engineering skills,' I told her, 'and the future could be bright for him - and, of course, for you.'

'Ooh, I couldn't ask for any more,' she replied, 'what with you helping Alan and me. I am so grateful and, of course, Alan will never forget what you have done.'

I was glad to be of service.

'Will you be going to visit him?' she asked.

'Of course.'

'At my age,' she went on, 'I struggle to get to the shops, let alone fly halfway round the world.'

I nodded sympathetically, and then the words 'halfway round the world' kicked in.

'You mean he's gone on holiday?' I asked, with a growing sense of unease.

She smiled at my question, which didn't exactly reassure me. Neither did her reply.

'No, he's gone to live there.'

'Where?'

'Well, he met this girl and...'

'Where has Alan gone?'

'Oh, it looks wonderful, the sun shining, all the people have wonderful skin; would you like some more tea?'

I didn't.

'Where is Alan?'

'It's an island... begins with a T... near America, it will come to me.'

I changed tack.

'Do you know I helped Alan out with some money to pay for him to develop a machine?'

'No, but Alan said he had such a good job working for you.'

I sighed. Alan's mother didn't seem to understand and she still couldn't remember where her son had upped and gone to. I gave up and, saying my goodbyes, noticed a letter rack with my name on it in the hallway.

'Are those envelopes for me?' I asked.

'Alan always said, 'Any bills, Mum, put them in the Duncan rack.' He was over the moon working for you, you know.'

They were household bills. Alan, it transpired, had told his mother that I would settle them all. I left my address and telephone number and went back home to find Nicola waiting with some news for me. A woman called Beryl had rung. She'd looked on a globe after I'd left and remembered the name of the place where Alan was living. It was Tahiti. I slapped all the unopened letters on the table. Nicola started opening them as I explained what had happened.

'It's quite romantic really,' she commented.

'Not for me.'

'Maybe not.'

'You don't think we should pay these, do you?' I asked her.

'It will be on your conscience if you don't.'

So, I paid them. It wasn't like I couldn't afford it. We'd done an audit, working out everything we owned and had earned in the four years since I'd started the vending business. The result was quite revealing - our cash and assets totalled £990,000. Typical, I thought, I'd hit thirty and just missed out on becoming a millionaire. Being so close to millionaire status made Nicola and I laugh as it didn't really seem to matter. But having that much money was mind boggling. I phoned my accountant to double check that our calculations were correct.

'All the stuff you send me, statements and the like…' I asked.

'Yes?'

'Does it equate to a million pounds?'

'Oh, yes. But can I remind you…?'

'Not now,' I said, hanging up. He'd told me what I'd wanted to hear.

So, once I'd paid Alan's bills and written off the purchase of the new house by waiving the £50,000 deposit, off we went to Barbados for our long-awaited honeymoon.

୨ᦔ

The post-flight drive back up the motorway was cold, wet and depressing. Nicola picked a CD at random and slipped it into the car stereo and we soon got lost in the music. By track three, we had it turned up loud and as soon as it ended, I needed to know who had been singing. But the CD was blank, apart from a name and a phone number. Then I remembered, it was the CD given to me by one of the band members who I'd helped at the nightclub opening in Kent. There weren't any song titles but I had never heard anything so beautifully written. We played it again and again until we arrived home.

'Why don't you find out more about who that is?' Nicola said when we were putting our cases down in the hall at home. Her words were about an hour behind my thoughts. Because by then, I'd already realised what my next venture was going to be.

CHAPTER SIXTEEN

At last, I had time *and* money - the Holy Grail to most people - but neither of these could create something as beautiful as the song I'd heard in the car. They could, however, help make that song as successful as possible. So, I'd phoned the number on the CD, arranged a meeting, and was now driving into the grounds of a place called Trentham Gardens, just off the M6 near Stoke-on-Trent. It was a place that time had forgotten - a crumbling jumble of run-down and disused buildings, and massive glasshouses left to ruin, all surrounded by acres of once-flourishing gardens. I sensed that in its heyday it would have been teeming with visitors. But today it was just me.

A man called Ade, who had produced these songs, ran a small recording studio based in one of the near-derelict buildings. I eventually found an entrance and was guided in the rest of the way by phone. I walked up a dark passageway and climbed some old, rickety stairs. The whole gloomy area was heavy with the smell of damp and rotten wood. And then I pushed open a door to be greeted by a mannequin sitting at a desk. I shouted hello and decided that if no one answered within five seconds, then I'd be off. But a door in the corner of the room opened and out walked a guy in a shabby leather jacket and full-on mop top haircut.

'Welcome to my studio, The Sound of Silence,' he announced with a flourish. 'The name's Ade, record producer and visual poet.'

I followed him into his studio, the walls of which were decorated with an array of 'visual poetry.' Ade offered me a seat, pushing a stuffed badger smoking a pipe off a chair to make room.

'You're here about Jason Lockett, aren't you?'

Guessing that was the singer's name, I said yes. Ade leaned back on his chair, put his fingers on his temples and let the words explode from him.

'You'll be unlocking the mad, creative genius that I am, you know, and you'll need strength and passion to control my wild spirit, to tap into my talent. Have you that passion? Have you that passion? HAVE YOU THAT PASSION?'

Keeping my eyes on the badger, I said that I did. Ade then calmed down enough to inform me the song that had brought me here was called 'Be Who You Want To Be.'

'Ade,' I replied, 'I love the song - especially the lyrics - and I'd love to meet him.'

'Lyrics?' he shouted. 'They were written by Drew.'

'Who's Drew?' I asked.

Drew, it turned out, was Jason's song writing partner, a former double glazing salesman from Crewe. I asked him for a contact number.

'They just appear.'

'Well, where do they live?'

'As I said, they just appear.'

'OK. So, can you phone me when they appear?'

'Difficult,' Ade said.

'What if I pay you?'

'Will the day after tomorrow do you?'

The day after tomorrow arrived and I was back in Ade's domain. He sat opposite me, stroking a stuffed fox with a harmonica in its mouth, while the silence grew. And grew, until eventually I had to say something, anything, just to break it.

'Does he play that harmonica?'

'Yes.'

The silence resumed. Finally, Ade walked to the window and whistled. I half expected a large crow carrying a banjo to fly in, but instead the door burst open and a whirlwind blew in. It was Jason, complete with big beaming smile and the look of a man who had just fallen out of a skip. Behind him was Drew, a dead ringer for a young Terry Thomas. I went out for a walk with the two of them and it soon became clear they didn't have any real idea of what they wanted to do. They were just happy that someone was showing an interest. We soon agreed two things: 'Be Who You Want To Be' needed to be re-recorded, and Jason needed to get out there and perform live. Drew handed me a CD and we agreed to meet up with the rest of the band in a few days for a rehearsal. I said I'd organise the venue and contact the other musicians.

Back at home, Nicola showed me another batch of bills that had come through from Alan's mother. I agreed to keep paying them - my mind was elsewhere. I'd listened to Drew's CD. There were another six or so songs, all equally as good, but I realised straight away that they needed re-recording, ideally at a studio without pipe-smoking, harmonica-playing road kill. The first rehearsal was organised and the musicians turned up in their own sweet time. I soon realised that Drew and Jason were the main creative forces in the band; the rest were just along for the ride. They reminded me of the band I'd managed in my early twenties - naïve, broke and unprofessional. But I'd moved on since those days and this was a serious money-making venture for me. I didn't have the time or patience to carry anyone. So I told the lot of them that it was over, they had to go, even Ade, the producer who, it turned out, was also in the band. He told me he was the second best drummer in the world, but I didn't budge. He didn't take news well, ranting about how we were selling out, compromising the music and giving in to a faceless corporation.

'You're selling your souls to the devil,' he warned and then, coming right up to my face, addressed me; 'Go on, be honest, just be honest. Look, lads, he can't! I knew when I first saw you that you were the son of Satan! They're not going to go with you, so pack up your plans and leave my studio.'

I leaned over so I could see Jason and Drew.

'Are you in agreement with me?' I asked them.

'Bet your arse we are,' they replied, 'the guy is insane.'

And we left Ade to his badger.

From now on, it was just going to be me, Jason and Drew. I wanted to re-record three songs at a studio with a producer who had a track record with this type of music. The musicians would all be professional session players, guided by Drew. I told them that Jason would have to perform acoustically for now, perhaps with Drew in a supporting role.

Before I could start on getting Jason into a recording studio, I got a call from Nicola's father, Bill.

'I'm off to Portugal to see the lads,' he told me. 'The physical work starts in a month and they're just finishing off with all the officials.'

'Right,' I replied.

'Do you and Nicola fancy coming over with me?'

Although I'd turned them down before, the whole Algarve project was starting to interest me as much as the music. And I now had the time, money and self-belief to do both. 'Why not?' I replied.

We flew out and checked in to a five-star hotel. Nicola and Amy went off to find various wives and partners, while I tracked down Bill and the others. I'd been asked to attend a meeting between Colin, Dave and a few of the other members of the consortium. The only evidence I'd seen so far was some rolled-out plans on a desk, so I was keen to go. The meeting was held in an impressive boardroom with wall to ceiling windows overlooking the Atlantic Ocean. A magnificent display of food was laid out across an oval table, which had seating for at least twenty people.

Colin and Dave were the first to enter, along with Bill. They were as pleased to see me as I was to see them. Other people started to arrive, shaking Colin and Dave's hands as if they were a couple of foreign dignitaries. I was introduced as an old business partner who had gone on to more successful things. The table soon filled up with bankers, architects, engineers, golf course designers, representatives from the town council and speculators. I grabbed a chair from the corner and placed it at the head of the table.

It was slow going. There were clearly millions of pounds at stake but nobody seemed eager to do anything but ask questions. No answers, just questions. This puzzled me, but then again, I had no experience in big-time business. A few hours passed and the intensity didn't drop. When a few people got up, I thought, 'Thank God for that, it's over.' But no, it was just a coffee break. I grabbed Colin and Dave.

'Bit over the top, isn't it?' I asked.

'It's etiquette, Duncan, how things are done at this level. The days of snap decisions are over.'

'But why doesn't anyone answer any questions?'

'They will. Everyone goes away and then we'll meet up with the answers.'

'Right.'

'Look, there may be time at the end for you to tell everyone your thoughts. If you've got anything to say, please do. We'd welcome any comments.'

Coffee break over, I pulled my chair up and we carried on. We had now moved onto financial questions about budgets, overspend and problems concerning the villas and other facilities. Finally, it was my turn.

'As an independent observer and friend of the main investors, I have a couple of questions. Building work is about to start?'

Various heads nodded.

'So, when was the last time anyone here visited the site? And I don't mean just to have another meeting, but actually went round and saw the work for themselves?'

They explained that there were people on the ground reporting back to them about all that.

'If I can make a suggestion?' I said. 'Instead of being stuck in a room nowhere near the site, all meetings should be held on site with the people who have the answers.'

This was greeted with silence. My next suggestion fared even less well.

'You talk of overspend,' I said. 'Well, it strikes me that everyone here is the biggest culprit.' Grim faces around the grand room stared up from behind the huge mountains of extravagant food. I'd said my piece. Everyone filed out. No one shook my hand or said goodbye. Colin and Dave stayed behind and I apologised for any offence I might have given, but insisted that everything I'd said was true.

'We know, Duncan, and we did ask you if you wanted to join us.'

But I knew that I wouldn't have lasted two minutes with that lot if I was on board.

The following day, Nicola, Amy and I went for a drive out. I wanted to see the development for myself. I stood on a mound of earth, surrounded by bits of pipe, surveying a massive area of total inactivity.

'I told you there were more people at that meeting last night than there are here on site,' I ranted.

Nicola just rolled her eyes and asked if we could just go to the beach.

When the time came to head back to England, I met up with Colin and Dave in the hotel reception. They settled my account and thanked me for coming over. I promised I'd stay in touch and told them my door was always open - just not for dealing with suits round big tables, in five-star hotels.

We planned to be in the studio for about a fortnight, leaving the producer another five days to finish mixing it. But by the time we finished recording, we'd spent another ten days deciding to write in a full string section and hiring the musicians to play it. While all this was going on, I'd arranged several meetings with lawyers and promoters. I wanted these songs tied down contractually to Jason and Drew. We were planning to try the traditional route of getting backing from a major label, but I planned on launching my own label as well. If we got it right, I could always sell it or piggy back my label onto a larger one. Whatever happened, we were all legally tied in.

There are times when you get far more in return for the money you put in. When I'd first heard those songs, I loved them. Hearing them recorded professionally with full strings sent shivers through me. I knew what my net worth was, and that day I was willing to risk it all on those two guys. But it did mean the challenge of finding a gap in the market to launch a product that no one knew they actually wanted. Fortunately, you can hire exactly the same promoters that the big record labels use, and the same music pluggers, public and media relations, even the companies making the video promos. They're not proud - they will gladly take your money. The problem is all down to timing and finding a gap for your artist in the market. The numbers were daunting. A professional campaign over a three-month period, involving a couple of promos and the recording of an album, could cost me a quarter of a million pounds. People wanted money every which way I turned. And if I got the timing wrong or missed the play lists on the radio, that's the money gone. Literally. There was no going back saying, 'Any chance of another go?' It was Red or Black on the roulette wheel. Get it right and it could be telephone number earnings. Get it wrong and you'd walk out shirtless.

That risk didn't frighten me. In fact, it appealed to me. And the money was only a very small part of why I was doing it. I believed passionately in what I was trying to promote. Most of all, I'd got the buzz back. This was what I was. This was what I did.

Slap bang in the middle of it all, my dad visited to offer me his latest, long-term security plan.

'I wouldn't have sold up,' he told me, 'but now that you have, this is my idea: a convenience store, bright lights, selling food and drink seven days a week. You can't go wrong.'

'Not for me, Dad.'

'Wait for it, I haven't finished.'

'Go on.'

'Buy the freehold. That will be your pension.'

He meant well. He always did. But he never had got what I was about. And I guessed he never would.

I started making trips to London on a near daily basis, formulating a plan and getting everybody to come round to my way of thinking. I eventually managed to convince enough people that not only did I have the money, but I had the right artist as well. Everything was in place - all the deals were set up and the paperwork drafted. I'd spent over £50,000 to reach this stage. But they'd all heard the songs and agreed I had a product to market, so the plan now was to play a few showcase gigs to introduce Jason to this small army of people eagerly waiting, with their Mont Blanc pens poised over lucrative contracts. But before that could happen, I received a surprise caller to my house. Nicola answered the door and walked into the living room looking ashen-faced.

'Who is it?' I asked, jumping up.

She couldn't answer.

'Who's died?'

She just shook her head.

'Oh, Christ, it's not... not the VAT man?'

She just pointed to the door. I opened it, expecting God knows what, and let out an enormous sigh of relief. It was Alan, all the way from Tahiti and looking very dishevelled.

'I've come to apologise,' he said.

I let him in. I was caught right off guard. I should have felt angry, but the only feeling I had was relief that now he was back he could look after his mother again. I brought him a cup of tea and told him I was all ears. He explained that his idea for vending aftershave and perfume had been a genuine one, and still was. The problem was that as soon as I'd loaned him the money, he'd allowed it to go to his head. At one point, he'd ordered a specialist part costing £1,000. But the company making it had accidentally billed him £10,000. Of course, I paid it, not knowing, but Alan never got round to mentioning the £9,000 he pocketed when the mistake came to light. All in, I spent about £50,000 on Alan, only £500 of which was actually used to develop his machine, the rest going on his mother and his Tahitian girlfriend. The one time Alan had come to show me the fruits of his labour, he'd forgotten to bring the right part. He now explained how he'd nipped to B&Q and bought a part for a shower, passing it off as some bespoke piece of precision engineering. Nicola greeted this news by disappearing into the kitchen. When I went to check on her, I expected her to be as mad as hell but instead, found her giggling into a tea towel. I left her to it and went back to Alan.

'Right,' I said. 'Have you got any of my money left?"
'About fifteen thousand.'
'Where is it?'
'In my ex-girlfriend's bank account in Tahiti.'
So that was the end of that. All the money I'd loaned him would have to be written off as a bad debt. Maybe I should have felt angry, but I didn't. At the time, I didn't worry about losing fifty grand. We could always resurrect the idea another time, and Alan's whole adventure appealed to the romantic in me. It reminded me of my time spent in America.

'So, are you going back to Tahiti?' I asked Alan.
'No.'
'Why not?'
'I got deported. I think she was behind it.'

♊

As soon as we had got rid of Alan, the doorbell rang again. This time it was Colin and Bill. They'd flown over from Portugal for some meetings in London, but actually it was me they wanted to see. They went into great detail about how the whole Portugal project was coming along. It became clear that they were really trying to sell it to me: the financial returns; the climate; golf being such a growing sport and how people really wanted to live by golf courses.

'Like anything you do in life, Duncan,' Bill said, 'and you know it better than most, there are minor blips and hurdles.'

'You're over budget, aren't you?' I replied.

'Well, technically, no. You see, we've borrowed money against the development and get more money released when we complete each phase. At the moment, we're clearing the site, laying drainage and are nearly ready to start laying all the foundations for the course and villas.'

'But you're over budget, aren't you?'

'Yes. This will tip the project further into the red later on. And that would mean when we're nearing completion there'd be cash flow problems - right when you start to really bring in the members and the people who want to purchase.'

Colin then unlocked his briefcase and brought out wads of paperwork.

'Put that away,' I told him. 'I've got tons of that upstairs. Just tell me what you need in black and white terms.'

'We're short by two million.'

'OK.'

'But it may climb to three.'

'But I haven't got that sort of money,' I said.

'We know. But what you lend us we can leverage. Say, you give us half a million, you can borrow a further million pounds against it.'

'OK. What's in it for me?'

'We could give you a percentage of the project, plus whatever you invest we'll repay you back double in property, but at cost. So, a half a million pound investment could make you back two million at least.'

Maybe it was having that chat with Alan, of being reminded of all the fun and adventures I'd had - all the stuff that had gone out of the window when I'd made such a success of the vending business. Whatever it was, Colin and Bill's pitch really struck a chord with me.

'If I sold everything,' I told them, 'I reckon I could raise a shade under a million. But where would we live?'

'In the Algarve. You said it was wonderful,' said Colin.

Nicola nodded at that.

'Yes, but that was three days spent in a five-star hotel,' I said.

But to be honest, I was arguing for the sake of it. The adrenaline was already rushing through my body just thinking about the offer. How could I not go ahead when there was a chance of turning £1m into £5m? Who knows, maybe even to £50m? Yes, I could lose the lot, but meantime, I'd be back with the people I trusted and had missed so much. As ever, I worked out my finances on the back of an envelope. If my company loaned £2m, secured on their share of the development, £600,000 of that would come from me personally. I could then spare £200,000 for the music project and the rest of my near-£1m fortune would be used to live off. I'd come a long way from the time on a canal-side bench when a fiver was a matter of life and death.

My mind was made up. We would go to Portugal. It was just a matter of tying up the loose ends. We sold our house without waiting to complete - instead, we just left our details with the lawyer, boxed up our belongings and left. I considered dumping my blue holdall, still full of corned beef tins, water and some cash, then. To do so would represent progress, a complete break from the past. But something stopped me and in it went with the rest of our stuff. Having sorted out the English end of things, my mind turned to our life ahead in Portugal. I enrolled Amy in the area's only English-speaking school, while Bill rented a villa for the four of us (plus two dogs) to stay in. Both he and I would be commuting back and forth - Bill to Scotland for his vending business, and me to England to oversee my music project.

We flew out and arrived at the villa. It was owned, we were told, by a man who had made a fortune from one of those 'where there's blame, there's a claim' compensation businesses. Judging by the size of the place, there had been a lot of blame knocking about. Not that we could get in. Bill was meant to be there with the keys. But he wasn't, so I phoned the letting agent. Her English wasn't the best, and my Portuguese was even worse. By the end of the conversation, all I knew for sure was that Bill was off somewhere else on a rescue mission and a large delivery of wood was expected at the villa in the morning.

Bill finally turned up at dawn.

'Where have you been?' I demanded.

'Spain.'

'Spain? Why?'

'Debs and Keith,' he replied. 'They'd planned to drive down here in their converted van weeks ago but broke down in Spain, and have been stuck there ever since.'

He then explained that on the continent, if you break down on the motorway, you immediately get towed away to the nearest garage. So, Keith and Debs had ended up living in a mechanic's yard while Keith tried to fix his van. A week later, with the van still not fixed, the police were called to evict them.

'Keith and Debs' villa has the same agent as ours,' said Bill, 'that's how I find out they were stuck.'

'So where are they now?' I asked.

'On some wasteland in Spain. Debs is determined that Keith will have the van running again. It's their bit of home away from home.'

Explanation over, Bill finally let us into our villa. It was huge. There was enough room in the hallway to fit a standard British house. A double staircase led up to a galleried landing and seven bedrooms, five of which were en-suite. Downstairs were a further eight rooms, including a lounge which had four settees round an enormous table, with a vase sitting on top that was large enough for me to climb into. There were so many rooms, we couldn't work out what they were all for. Even the balcony off our bedroom had enough space for a table and eight chairs from which to enjoy the stunning views of the town and the sea beyond. And there was a pool, a huge games room in the basement and an acre or so of landscaped gardens.

'What do you think?' Bill asked me.

I was lost for words.

'It certainly fits in with your status,' he added.

I was still lost for words. But his comment did ring true. At that moment, I felt like I was on the verge of doing great things, making millions from the golfing venture, and Jason and Drew's music. And the villa certainly tallied with the idealised vision of life on the Algarve that people had shared with me before we'd flown out - fresh fruit breakfasts on the patio, moped rides to our grand new golfing development, where I'd sign a document or two and then enjoy a long lunch of freshly caught fish before banging a couple of bin lids together to liven up the sleepy natives working on the site. And then it would be back home in time to greet Amy from school, all in the pool before meeting up with friends for a barbecue, or a trip to the marina for dinner.

The reality, however, was a bit more complicated than that. Our palatial villa became cluttered within an hour of us turning up. First came the lorry-load of wood, which the letting agent had mentioned. Once it was unloaded, I had half a forest's worth of wood in the basement. Then another lorry arrived, this one stacked with gas bottles. I had no idea what they, or the wood, were actually for. After the lorries came the people. Two little old people, a man and a woman, appeared at the kitchen with beaming smiles and half a dozen teeth between them. She was waving a broom handle with a few twigs stuck on the end, so I guessed that she was the cleaner and waved her in. She promptly vanished somewhere deep inside. The old man wasn't holding anything.

'I bet you a tenner he's the gardener,' I said to Bill.

'I'll raise you twenty,' he replied, '...he's not got any tools.'

So, my first day in paradise and I was awash in firewood, gas bottles, an old lady who had disappeared already, and a gardener without any tools. And just as I thought it couldn't get any more confusing, two more people turned up on a moped holding a broom connected to a piece of hose. They were there to clean the pool, despite the fact that it was winter in the Algarve and far too cold to be even thinking about taking a dip. Once I'd dealt with all the deliveries and all the people, I was 1,200 Euros worse off. And then Bill demanded another 800 Euros for bailing out Debs and Keith.

I had barely settled in Portugal before I was flying back to England. The Artist and Repertoire people, who scouted for talent for different record labels, had all given positive feedback on the initial recordings we'd done. We were on a roll and I wanted to see Jason and Drew to confirm that we were going all out to finish the album. The meeting was as much for my peace of mind as anything else. I wanted to double check that they were up for it before I signed any more cheques.

I walked into Drew's flat. He was as upbeat as usual, and so was I after he played me the demos of the songs that we were going to record to finish off the album. The only thing missing was Jason.

'Where is he?' I asked.

'Bit of a snag there,' Drew told me. 'He's gone off for a few days.'

'Is there a problem?' I asked.

'Not really. He just said he needed some time alone to find himself. He thinks you're moving things along a bit too quickly.'

'I can live with that,' I replied, 'but make sure he finds himself before he goes back in the studio.'

Even though Jason was nowhere to be seen, the songs were so strong that I went ahead and booked the studio time. It cost me £25,000, but to my mind that was money well spent.

❧

Back in the Algarve, I was knee-deep in meetings. And meetings about meetings. There were meetings with contractors and meetings with investors, bankers and people representing the EU - by that stage, the development had obtained grant money from Brussels. My role was purely as an observer, and what I observed was mainly a lot of back slapping and everyone telling each other how great they were. Finally, we got down to what we were really there for. About twenty of us sat down at a large table, the lights dimmed, and two people went over to this enormous sheet and grabbed a corner each.

An architect stood up.

'Gentlemen! Every wish, every want, every whim will be catered for! I give you...' and the sheet was pulled off, revealing an intricate scale model of the golfing development.

I looked at Colin.

'How much did that cost?' I mouthed to him.

The architect carried on in his grandiose style about how great we all were, and even how much greater we all would become within a year or two. I wasn't having any of this. The only thing to show for the six months since I'd first gone to a meeting about this development was a lovingly crafted model of it. I stood up, ignoring Colin's attempts to pull me back down by my shirtsleeves.

'Can I stop you all?' I began. 'This looks and sounds all very nice, but where's the bricks? Is anyone actually doing anything? I haven't seen a schedule of works, I haven't seen a single time-table, just this model.'

Everyone just sat there staring wide-eyed at me and my outburst. After a pregnant pause, an unofficial break was tactfully announced.

'Duncan, you agreed to come along as an observer,' Colin said to me once we'd found a quiet corner.

I nodded, but reminded him I was also an investor.

'We're all in this together,' I added.

'It doesn't work like that.'

'With all due respect,' I went on, 'the people in that meeting don't have a clue what it's like to fail. The majority of them can afford to drop a few million and it wouldn't hurt them one bit. You can't tell me that this project is too big to fail.'

'Trust me,' said Colin.

'I do, but remember, there's not too many people like me about.'

'I know. You're one in a million.'

'No, Colin, I'm one in about two and a half million Euros.'

I didn't go back into the meeting. I would only have started shouting again. I obviously needed to adapt to how big business operated and until I did, I was better off out of the way. Instead, I went back to the villa. The electric gates opened and I was greeted by the sight of a van, a trailer and all manner of belongings scattered across the driveway.

'It can't be Debs and Keith,' I muttered to myself. 'Bill went to rescue them weeks ago.'

I got out of my car and walked round to the kitchen.

'How the facking hell are you?' boomed a voice.

Yep, it definitely was Debs and Keith. And Debs was keen to tell me everything that had happened. The cleaner and gardener had joined us by then, so I leaned against a kitchen unit because all the seats were taken.

'Seven weeks it's taken! Seven facking weeks! One wrong turn my Keithy took! One facking wrong turn in Madrid and you end up stuck in Spain. That wouldn't have happened in England, I can tell you.'

'But why did it take you so long to get here?' I asked.

'You tell him, Keithy.'

Keith told me the whole story in his usual, concise way.

'Parts,' he said gruffly.

'Well, at least it's all fixed now?' I suggested.

Keith just shook his head.

'We got a tow,' said Debs, 'and the man needs paying. And our rent's due on the villa, which we haven't even facking seen yet. But don't worry, we'll pay you back as soon as Keith starts work on all them golf buildings that must have gone up by now.'

Oh shit, I thought; there was no work for Keith, not for a while yet anyway. So, their rent wasn't going to get paid any time soon. There was only one thing for it - Keith, Debs, their three kids and two dogs were going to have to move in.

Our spacious, luxury villa was filling up fast.

While things were getting complicated in Portugal, they weren't much better in England. I'd spoken to Drew, who was preparing for the latest recording session, but there was still no sign of Jason. It seemed like he still hadn't found himself, which meant I'd had to fly back and find him instead. The only lead I had was that he was staying in a caravan in a field in North Wales. I started my search by going to Jason's local in Stoke. The place was dead. The only customer was sitting on a bar stool, asleep, head first in an ashtray and the girl behind the bar just stood there, hypnotised by daytime TV.

'Excuse me, I'm looking for Jason Lockett.'

Nothing.

I waved my hands to get her attention and repeated my request. She just pointed at ashtray man.

'That's his mate,' she replied and then screamed, 'Tony!' at the top of her voice.

The barmaid's screeching didn't work so, I gently prodded him.

Nothing again.

So, I flicked his ear a few times and finally he stirred. I took several deep breaths. My future in the music business was riding on a bloke stinking of booze, who looked up at me with blood-shot eyes. He did know Jason and between drunken anecdotes about his ex-wife, he told me that he could take me to him.

'Brilliant,' I said.

'One for the road?' he replied.

'No problem.'

The barmaid pushed a pint glass up to the whiskey optic until it was about half full, I paid, Tony covered his drink with a beer mat and zigzagged out to the car.

With the windows down and the radio on full blast, Tony sang us all the way to North Wales, occasionally thumping the dashboard to indicate that we needed to turn left or right. We went up and down hills, and the hours rolled past. Darkness fell and I was starting to have enough of my drunken guide, who looked like he was minutes away from another ashtray moment. Just as I was contemplating my future in music coming to an abrupt end in the middle of nowhere, Tony shouted, 'Stop!' and pointed to a dark field. And then he passed out.

I could see a flicker of light in the distance and I had no choice but to check it out. The light was coming from a small caravan. I took a deep breath and knocked on the door. When Jason answered, I looked up to the dark sky and quietly said thank you. He nervously invited me in, looking dejected that he had failed in his attempt to disappear. But I was just as nervous myself. I had unearthed a genuine talent who didn't seem to want to exploit it, despite (or maybe because of) the six figure sum I had riding on him. He talked and I listened.

'My everyday life has been as a struggling musician, suffering - I mean really suffering - for my cause. I always had that glimmer of hope that one day someone would come along - someone like you - who'd tell me I was the one. It was the chance that my dream could become a reality that kept me going. But then, when you did come along, I suddenly realised if it does all come good, I won't have any dreams left. Just responsibility to a pyramid of people.'

This really hit home because I knew exactly what he meant. I felt the same way about success myself. So, I wasn't particularly surprised by what he told me next.

'I'm sorry, I can't go into the studio. It's over.'

Booking that studio had cost me hours of my time, and the small matter of twenty five grand.

'Look,' I told him. 'I can re-arrange the studio, don't worry about that. But what about the showcase gigs in London? Surely, as an artist, it would be nice just to confirm that you were right, that you could have been signed, even if you don't take it any further?'

'I'll think about it,' replied Jason, before suggesting I stayed the night.

We dragged my guide out of the car and pushed him through the door, head first. He collapsed on the floor, so we used him as a foot stool and carried on talking most of the night. We were alike in so many ways. Was I worried about Jason? Not really. I hadn't heard anything that could touch these two guys musically. If anything, I was frustrated by the fact that my financial timetable could be affected by the delay. So all I could do was wait and hope.

⁓

I swapped an empty Welsh hillside for the chaos of our Portuguese villa, now officially full to bursting with Keith and Debs' clan, and the various relations of mine who had started paying us visits. I'd never had so many people wanting to visit me before. Perhaps it was my sparkling personality. Or just the villa, the sunshine, the pool and the free use of the vehicles.

The golfing development was starting to gather pace. We could see a clear way ahead, costs were rising but still well within the contingency of the business plan, and Colin and Dave were happy and seemed to have everything under control. We'd spend our days in my office in the villa, Colin and Dave dealing with any Portuguese problems, while I frantically telephoned people in London to rearrange gig dates, playing for time while hoping Jason would change his mind. In real terms, this meant lying through my teeth, explaining to everyone that we were still going ahead, that there had been a mix-up on my part - anything to quash the rumours that Jason was getting cold feet. I knew, however, that if nothing changed, my days in the music business would be over.

Colin and Dave were committing everything to the Algarve project. All their UK property was up for sale - and selling well above the asking price. They then diverted all the proceeds into the golfing development. At a push of button, a figure with six noughts (and sometimes seven) went from one bank to another. Inside that room, money was only discussed in telephone numbers. None of it felt real, in my eyes. But it was enough for me to be swept along with the enthusiasm of it all, so I upped my equity in the project by a further £500,000 - money I'd been planning to use to set up my own record label. I'd already spent £30,000 just exploring the possibility, and the problems with Jason meant I had abandoned the idea. I figured that if he did actually come good, a major label would snap him up.

By then, being the only one at the villa with any actual cash, I was forking out left, right and centre, feeding twelve people plus guests and paying all the bills, which were eye-watering. The cleaning lady had recruited help, and her husband had started helping Keith full time with a complete re-build of his non-mobile, mobile home. Not that I minded much. It didn't matter what was happening in the outside world, the villa was full of non-stop action from dawn 'til dusk. The sound of the gong would summon us all to the table for dinner, served by the cleaning lady who had promoted herself to full time cook. We would all sit down to some of the best food any of us had ever tasted, occasionally discussing the future, but mainly just chatting about the day.

It was now just under a week until the first of the two showcases I'd arranged for Jason. People had been calling, asking for me to confirm that everything was going ahead. I hadn't heard from Jason at all. Neither had Drew. But I was going to leave cancelling the gigs right up until the last minute in the hope that Jason would come good. I would actually understand if he didn't want to go ahead and try for the big time. But for my own selfish reasons, I wanted to find out if I had been right about him. I just wanted to get the nod from someone who makes or breaks new talent that my instinct was correct. That confirmation would have been enough for me.

My mobile rang. It was Drew, as calm as anything. He announced that we were on for the gig, that Jason was up for it.

It was great news, but I couldn't settle. Not until he had walked onto that stage. We all agreed to meet a few hours before the gig. Walking into the venue, I noticed Drew but there was no sign of Jason. All my doubts resurfaced.

'Where the hell is he?' I demanded.

'Calm down,' Drew told me, 'he just needed some fresh air. He's gone for a stroll. Don't worry, he seems fine.'

But I did worry and twenty minutes before they were due on stage, there was still no sign of Jason. He hadn't even sound checked. People from various labels started arriving. I just nodded at them from across the room. I couldn't go and talk to them, not while Jason was still AWOL. The promoter came over and asked if there was a problem.

'No, no, not at all. Why?' I lied.

'So, where's Jason?'

'Oh, just gone for some fresh air.'

'What, for nearly three hours?'

I couldn't answer that. He knew there was a problem, and so did I.

'If I don't see him in ten minutes, it's off,' the promoter informed me, giving me and Drew that smirk that said we weren't just amateurs, but out-of-town amateurs.

The ten minutes came and went. I looked round the room, half expecting to see the promoter staring at me, doing a throat-cutting gesture with his hand. Instead, I saw Jason waltz in with that big, beaming smile on his face.

'Right,' he said. 'I'm ready.'

I just sat there open-mouthed, staring at him, speechless. He climbed on stage with Drew, adjusted his microphone, said a few words and then started singing 'Be Who You Want To Be.' All those years of pain and hardship, and all the tension and doubt of the past few weeks were worth it, just for those few minutes of magic on stage. I was fucking right, you know. He was as brilliant as I'd told everybody all along. The pats on the back from various movers and shakers in the music industry confirmed it. They were all telling me they'd see me at the next gig. It was all I needed to hear. He'd knocked them all dead.

Nothing could dent my enthusiasm, not Keith collecting me from the airport in his mobile home on its maiden voyage since being re-built. Not it breaking down at the car park ticket barrier and returning to the villa on the back of a tow truck. Not even Nicola telling me that we were spending four times more on the villa than we'd budgeted for. My music career was finally coming to the boil and the golfing development was steaming ahead.

I was greeted by pages and pages of paper in my office, figures and documents which the fax machine had spewed out while I was away. The table was overflowing with post, all of it for Colin and Dave. As far as I was concerned, it could all wait until the lads turned up the next morning. However, when they did appear at the villa, they weren't looking their usual selves. I suppose it was understandable, given that they'd liquidated their entire property portfolio and obtained various loans to bankroll the development. There was no going back for them. They were joined by a couple of suits - an accountant and a lawyer - so I left them to it for a couple of hours until I was summoned back in. I saw elbows on the table and hands on temples. That was not a good sign. It never was. The accountant and lawyer started to speak but I had to stop them after about five minutes.

'Whatever you have to say,' I told them, 'please say it in black and white.'

So they did.

'It looks like we are going into administration. A board meeting has been scheduled for tomorrow. We will, of course, vote against it but we won't have the final say.'

I couldn't believe what I was hearing and could barely get any words out.

'But what's happened? We haven't even laid a brick.'

'I'm afraid we will need more investment, a capital injection, before we can do any of that. The figures have been revised several times - that's why you're involved - but it's still not enough.'

'But what about all the money from Colin and Dave's properties back home?' I asked. 'And my loans. I mean, we're talking millions and millions here.'

'We know. But it's still not enough. Everyone's shareholding will be diluted.'

'But we will still have something, won't we? Please say we'll have something.'

They shrugged their shoulders. Colin and Dave had gone ashen.

'Lads, surely you've got more clout in this project? You can't just let this happen, can you?'

They just looked like two abandoned children, lost and confused. I kept asking whether the money had been spent yet.

'Yes and no,' came the reply.

'You mean it's been pissed up the wall, don't you?'

'Well, I think you overpaid for the land, and the fees for various corporate bodies to get you to the building stage were a bit on the high side.'

'High side? You mean fucking vertical,' I replied.

We talked for hours, trying to work out what we could do. As far as I could gather, we'd spent nearly all our money on buying the land and forking out for consultancy fees, and what little was left wouldn't cover the massive build costs needed to turn all the grand plans into reality. Because of all this, the banks had got twitchy and were refusing to release any further funds. So, unless we could find new investors to stump up the cash needed to buy the project from the administrators, it was more or less dead in the water. Even then, we'd need to find millions of Euros while giving away more equity, more of a stake in the whole project.

'No way can we let this happen,' I said. 'Three million Euros I've invested in this project and for what? A couple of sandwiches around a table.'

I asked the lawyer and accountant how much new capital we'd need to raise to be taken seriously.

'Ten million Euros for starters, and the balance to build. But you can borrow the balance.'

The whole project was going way above our heads. It was becoming a constant merry-go-round of refinancing without anything physically getting done.

'But, Duncan,' said the accountant, 'debt is how we all make money. That's how the lads became multi-millionaires - through debt. And that's how you got here, I presume. It's the new way of operating. If you don't ask you don't get.'

I realised at this moment that I was looking into a different business world. Mine was one where the gains only start to roll in when the hard work's all been done. Here, however, fellow investors - bankers, lawyers and accountants - were like dark shadows, collecting as much profit from the development of a project as from its successful operation. I had struck up good working relationships with a lot of people along my travels. The nightclub operators wouldn't have a problem raising a million in cash. And the scale of the project would appeal to their vanity. Other possible recruits included the likes of Big Al. But the rest of the people I'd done business with simply couldn't afford to lose a million on a project like the one I'd got involved in.

Before all that, I needed to call a meeting at the villa. We all congregated in the kitchen and I stood at the top of the table, like a captain explaining to his troops that we might have to retreat from the battlefield. Even the cleaner and her extended family had joined us. The look on my face soon quietened everyone down and I told them the news.

'I'm not going to beat around the bush. I think the golfing project has gone tits up.'

The long, drawn-out silence said it all. I tried to explain as best I could, but even I was unsure of what I was saying. Nicola just sat there with Amy, her eyes shut. Debs was speechless for the first time ever. Even I was lost for words by then, and it took Keith to break the ice.

'Bloody good job we bought that mobile home,' he said, and everyone burst out laughing.

The mood lifted.

'It's not quite as bad as it seems,' I went on. 'There is a glimmer of hope. We're not out of money, I still have cash and we have two throws of the dice left. Number one - if, and it's a big if, I can raise approximately ten million I might be able to salvage the project. Number two - I still have Jason. He's due to perform a major showcase. It's long term but the wheels could soon start rolling and, let's face it, he is one hell of a singer, we all agree on that.'

Everyone nodded, 'Let's do it,' chairs were pushed back and the meeting broke up. I asked Colin and Nicola to come down to the office.

'Right,' I told them, 'let's have it straight. Colin, if this all goes down the pan tomorrow, what do you have left?'

'A couple of run-down flats.'

'What about the car hire business?'

'It's worthless. It's in debt and all our time and energy has gone into this. Look, Duncan, if I'd known this was going to happen, there's no way I'd have asked you to invest.'

'I'd made my mind up,' I replied, 'as soon as I saw the plans back on your desk.'

As a gesture, Colin offered us one of his flats, but I declined. To me, this was far from over yet. Nicola pulled out a folder.

'Back in the kitchen,' she began, 'you said we have cash.'

I nodded.

'We have about a month's worth, six weeks at most. And that's if we ignore the utility bills that are now overdue. Ten thousand Euros a month we've been spending, and that's without trips back to the UK.'

'We could cut and run now, if you want,' I replied. 'Or we stay, I hit the phones and, fingers crossed, Jason works his magic.'

'Cut and run?' Nicola said. 'Why bother saying that when we both know it's not going to happen?'

When Colin got up to leave, he patted me on the shoulder as if to say, 'Good luck to you, mate, but I've given up.' His world had ended. But I wasn't going down without a fight. I had fifteen people I reckoned I could approach. My list had extended to independent operators in the vending industry, their net worth far greater than mine. I didn't have a plan, I wasn't even sure what return they would get or how much I actually needed from each person. I would just ask them direct for one million Euros each and take it from there.

My pitch went along the lines of:

'It's Duncan. I don't know if you remember me…'

I'd jog their memory and then launch into my sales patter, and end with the words 'about a million pounds.' At that point, I'd expect the phone to go dead but it usually didn't. I'd managed to attract some initial interest, so I'd then explain that our lawyer and accountant would speak to them and, if they wanted to take it further, they could fly out to see for themselves. Not even the immediate need for the money seemed to bother them. Meanwhile, the project went into administration. As far as I could see, this meant that any money left was going to be spent by men in suits sorting out the mess left by the previous men in suits. Like I said, it was just a merry-go-round.

Prior to flying off to London for Jason's second showcase, I had a meeting with our lawyer and accountant, together with Colin, Dave and Nicola. I was congratulated for my couple of hours' worth of phone calls. I was told that I had generated interest from eight individuals and, if the figures and security stacked up, we could raise over ten million Euros. But only Nicola and I seemed pleased at the news.

'The potential investors will be flying over in the next couple of weeks,' the lawyer went on. 'We have lodged an interest and will be forming a consortium with the other investors.'

Colin and Dave cut the meeting short as they had various other meetings to attend. They congratulated me and left. When the lawyer had me to himself, he explained the reality of the situation for Colin and Dave.

'You do know that's them finished? And you're not out of the woods either, what with your debt. But with this new investment, I'm sure something can be worked out because we will have a lot of collateral available to us now.'

I questioned their fees and what was in it for them.

'Don't worry about us. We will be looked after.'

The mood in the villa hadn't changed. Everyone was still upbeat, probably because none of them knew what the hell was happening. And that included me. As I prepared to fly back to England, Nicola told me that money was now seriously tight and, when I got back, we would need to implement some austerity measures.

❧

I wasn't going to take any risks with Jason. I travelled up to Stoke and made sure he and Drew were physically in the car as we set off for London. Our destination was a private members' club near Notting Hill called The Cobden Club, a place where you could relax and drink in relative peace. We were ushered into the main room. Several acts were performing that night and Jason was third on the bill. I felt excited but calm enough - hearing Jason say he wanted this more than anything settled my nerves. The room was empty and the first act wasn't due on for at least an hour so, I headed off to find a phone and catch up on events back in the Algarve.

By the time I returned, the room was full. All the tables were taken and the bar area was packed. When I recognised a few faces from the previous gig, I let out a sigh of relief. To my mind, these people were clearly taking Jason seriously. I got chatting to some A and R men from a label. They had heard of Jason but, however hard I pressed them, they wouldn't say if he was the reason they were there. I gave up hassling them and went backstage to check on Jason. He gave me a thumbs-up and even bought me a drink.

Halfway through the second act, I was growing in confidence. If that's the competition, I thought, we'll walk it. I was now standing at the bar in a semi-circle of about ten people when I saw Drew waving for me to come over.

'Everything OK?' I asked.

'Yes, should be.'

'What do mean, should be?'

'Well, you know, Jason's had a few pints.'

'Is he pissed?' I asked.

'No. Well, not really. Perhaps it's just me. I'm nervous.'

'You're nervous? What about me? At least you're going to be on stage. I've got no control over this.'

I wished Drew luck and re-joined my new best friends at the bar.

The way they walked on stage, I could see perfection unfolding. They just looked the part - confident and with just a hint of arrogance. I was sure they'd whip this lot into a cheque book feeding frenzy. I couldn't wait for them to start. They took to their stools and adjusted their microphones. Jason didn't say anything. Drew started playing his guitar. The song they'd chosen to start with had a thirty second intro, which only Drew played. And he was playing it well. No, he was playing it perfectly. Jason still didn't say anything. He just stared out at the crowd, looking every inch the pop star, the front man. And then it was time for him to join the song. This was it. His moment of glory. My moment of glory. The moment when all my hard work paid off.

I heard a loud twanging sound from Jason's guitar, like he was thumping it. It wasn't the best of noises and my immediate thought was, 'Shit, he is pissed.' Jason then put his hand on the mike. But he hadn't tightened it properly so it flopped down and banged into the stand. He got off his stool to re-adjust the mike and caught the stand with his guitar. The feedback had me running for the door. When I turned back, things were going from bad to worse. The guitar's impact with the stand had broken half its strings and Jason had the look of someone who had completely lost it. To his credit, he stayed up there and started the song. The only problem was, he was singing different lyrics to the song Drew was playing. It was all too much for me. I couldn't bear to witness Jason's total pissed-up meltdown so I stood outside the room, paralysed, peering through a crack in the door.

The first song ended. They were due to perform another two songs but Drew had already had enough. He walked off. Jason didn't notice and ca rried on singing for a while before going for the grand finale. He leapt off the stage with his guitar still plugged in. The leads were yanked out when he landed and the whole disastrous event finished with a loud bang from the PA system. I walked out onto the pavement, leaned up against the wall and lit a cigarette. People came bounding out through the door before suddenly stopping and realising they had come face to face with the person responsible for what had just happened. They glanced at me and quickly scurried off into the night.

Drew came out and stood next to me. He couldn't say any-thing and I didn't want him to. We were then joined by Jason. He looked at me and I just shook my head and handed the car keys to Drew.

'I'm off for a walk now and then I'm going back to Portugal.'

Jason came running up behind me.

'Look, I'm really sorry. I don't know what came over me. I swear my drinks were spiked. Is there any hope or have we blown it?'

'No, you haven't blown it, Jason. You can come back from this. Your music is a lot bigger than you and Drew. But for me, it's game over.'

I shook his hand and we parted.

I just wanted to get away that night. I walked aimlessly for hours, my mind just empty. I'd look up every now and then and see a change of postcode on the street signs. I felt totally dejected and sorry for myself. Only the thought of getting run over stopped me from sinking to my knees in the road. I was mentally and physically exhausted by the time I stopped in a side street and sat on a wall. I didn't have any feeling at all. I pressed my palms together, trying to feel my fingers. I wasn't cold, just numb with failure.

What had just crumbled in front of me contained all of my ambitions, all of my commitment to what I believed in. It was like the events, not just from the past months but my whole life, were now staring at me full-on.

The hours passed. I went right back from my school days all the way through to the Cobden Club disaster, shuddering at the thought of all those decisions I'd made. It had always seemed easy enough to justify to myself why certain events had panned out the way they did, but the bottom line was the blame was down to me and me alone. But even now, there was something to make me smile inside - the simple feeling of joy I shared each time we all sat around the table in the villa, with Colin, Dave, Debs and Keith all laughing out loud. Maybe the tiredness kicked in then but it was like a big weight had been lifted from my shoulders. Despite all the things that were going wrong, I still felt in control. I was still in a position where I could make a decision about the situation.

In fact, I had one final, and massive, decision to make.

By the time I boarded the plane, it was becoming clear that events were moving faster than I thought. When I'd tried to buy a ticket, three out of my four credit cards had been declined. As a result, Nicola wanted me to be picked up by Keith in his mobile home, which he said was up and running again. I wanted to pay for a taxi, but was persuaded otherwise. It was the first of our new austerity measures I suppose, but I ended up getting the taxi anyway - Keith broke down halfway to the airport - and I was greeted by Nicola and Amy, all beaming smiles as usual, telling me to sit down and tell them all about how Jason had got on.

While I'd been away, the cut-backs had started to kick in. The rent was due, we'd been served notice that the electric would be cut off in the next few days and there would be no more gas bottle deliveries. Keith and Bill were devising a way to run extension cables from the next door villa's patio area. A little room which concealed the pool pump had a couple of plug sockets and they wanted to tap into the power from there. I reckoned that would mean using at least two hundred feet of cable, which was bound to be noticed. But Bill had thought of that.

'We'll camouflage the lead by feeding it through the hedge and under the patio furniture. They'll never notice, not that they're ever in. And Keith will be on lookout while I'm doing it.'

Leaving them to it, I went to meet up with the lawyer and accountant outside a beautiful, and probably very expensive, restaurant with multi-million pound yachts moored in the nearby marina. They were slavering at the thought of all those juicy fees they'd be claiming for organising the restructuring of the golfing development, and they wanted to brief me on how we should work it.

'Forget Colin and Dave and get rid of all those other people who hang on to you,' they told me, 'they're just freeloaders and that's all in the past. You will be firmly seated at the top table from now on.'

They had it all worked out - the companies, loans and security. I couldn't help but admire their planning and foresight and nodded in agreement to all their plans. After the roller coaster ride from hell, the tracks were at last levelling out - and they were right, I was still on board. But thinking back to the success of the vending empire, and realising how much bigger this was, I then couldn't help but add up the human cost. I couldn't just forget my friends. And even if I could, how long would it be before the inevitable question arose, 'What next?'

Later that evening, I met up with Colin and Dave at a local bar. I knew this would be the last time I'd see them before they headed home but I didn't want to talk about the loss they were facing. The look on their faces was enough to tell me their dream was over. I also didn't want them to worry about me or how they could try to solve my situation. I just wanted to see if they had any future. In spite of us all putting on brave faces, the atmosphere was heavy. They had invested everything, only to see all their assets turn into horrendous debt. Bankruptcy was coming their way; that was a dead cert. And it was only because they kept insisting that I told them about the grand plan that had been devised in time to rescue me, but was too late for either of them. The sadness in their eyes told me what I needed to know.

I took a deep breath and told them that I had turned the plan down.

'Why?' they asked me immediately.

'I didn't come out to the Algarve to see you ruined. I didn't even come out here for the chance to make loads of money. I came out to help you, to be with my friends. I could stay on now and maybe turn this whole thing round, but it wouldn't mean a thing if you and the others weren't here with me. And besides, I'm shit at golf.'

It was soon time for us all to part. Debs and Keith were off to the Costa del Sol - a joiners' paradise, apparently. Debs came past me on the patio dragging two large suitcases, with her kids lumping various bags and bin liners to the mobile home.

'That's another thing about facking Spain.'

'What?'

'The food. It's facking British. None of this foreign muck you get here.'

Keith looked up at me from the driver's seat, ignition key in hand.

'Duncan, there's nothing on this vehicle that hasn't been changed.'

'Go on then, start it,' I replied.

He turned the key. Nothing. We left them to it.

By pulling out of the Algarve consortium I'd lost all my money, so we were off back to the UK. We loaded up the little old car that I'd bought a few days before. Our belongings didn't take up much room, leaving just enough space to squeeze in my blue holdall. The dogs jumped in and I closed the boot.

I took one last walk through the villa to check we hadn't left anything behind. The sound of my shoes on the marble floor echoed in the huge spaces. As I pushed open the doors to all the different rooms, I kept thinking that only a day earlier someone would have been in there, filling the place with the noise of a TV or music, or a conversation which always ended in laughter. That had been the norm. Now, the place was soulless.

Then I walked into my office and looked at my desk. It sat there, empty and taunting me with my failure as an entrepreneur, but it didn't stop me smiling to myself. What the hell would I have done if it had been a success? Really - what would I have done? You can't have adventures; you can't have fun when your life is spent with one eye on safeguarding your millions.

All those years thinking I needed something else, be it money or success or recognition - now, for the first time in my life, I understood what I actually wanted to take from life: nothing. What did I actually *need* apart from my family and friends? Nothing. My career as an entrepreneur may or may not be over, I thought; that's for the future. I'd certainly failed so far at sustaining any success, and maybe always would. But at least I'd succeeded at *trying* and, most importantly, I'd succeeded at being happy.

And that meant I had everything a man could possibly want.

POSTSCRIPT

So, am I a 'failed entrepreneur'? I made a mess of almost every venture I tried, but I did at least try. You see, if I'd followed the conventional routes I'd been pushed towards so many times, it would have been a life sentence for me. Instead, I've had the time of my life finding my own way and, to me, that is what being entrepreneurial is really all about. And it also means you can be an entrepreneur or a failure but not both; not at the same time. So, the next time you feel tempted to try something - anything, big or small - it may work out or it may not; but pat yourself on the back just for trying. It means you're alive.

Entrepreneur: someone who tries as often as it takes and, God willing, will keep trying, driven by a love of freedom, opportunity and other people – and, perhaps, because they simply can't do anything else.

DICTIONARY OF LIFE

WHERE ARE THEY NOW?

Father: West Midlands, retired, checking annuity rates daily.

Mother: West Midlands, retired, cake baking.

Bill: Scotland, retired (again), broke.

Bert: West Midlands, broke and then deceased.

Keith and Debs: Spain, contributing to the downfall of the Spanish economy.

Colin and Dave: Scotland, working but broke.

Alan: Manchester, inventor, broke.

Drew: Staffordshire, songwriter, broke.

Jason: Staffordshire, singer/songwriter, broke.

Big Al: South Africa, retired, not broke.

Jon: West Midlands, leasing, wealthy.

Nicola: West Midlands, accountant, solvent.

Duncan: West Midlands, entrepreneur/author, broke-ish.

Printed in Great Britain
by Amazon.co.uk, Ltd.,
Marston Gate.